Street Fight

Street
Fight

The Politics of Mobility
in San Francisco

JASON HENDERSON

University of Massachusetts Press
Amherst and Boston

Designed by Jack Harrison
Set in Adobe Minion Pro
Printed and bound by Thomson-Shore, Inc.

Library of Congress Cataloging-in-Publication Data

Henderson, Jason Mark.
Street fight : the politics of mobility in San Francisco / Jason Mark Henderson.
pages cm
Includes bibliographical references and index.
ISBN 978-1-55849-999-7 (pbk. : alk. paper) —
ISBN 978-1-55849-998-0 (hardcover : alk. paper)
1. Urban transportation—Political aspects—California—San Francisco.
2. Transportation planning—California—San Francisco.
3. City planning—California—San Francisco.   I. Title.
HE310.S36H45 2013
388.409794'61—dc23
2012050132

British Library Cataloguing-in-Publication Data
A catalogue record for this book is available from the British Library.

For my father, Russell Joseph Henderson (1948–2011)

CONTENTS

Preface & Acknowledgments   ix

List of Abbreviations   xiii

Introduction: *San Francisco's Politics of Mobility*   1

1. How We Get There Matters
Ideologies of Mobility   17

2. San Francisco's Mobility Stalemate
A Historical Geography   38

3. The Second Freeway Revolt
Removing the Central Freeway   54

4. Between Walkability and Freeways
The Politics of Parking in San Francisco   87

5. "We Are Not Blocking Traffic, We Are Traffic!"
The Politics of Bicycle Space in San Francisco   112

6. Transit First? *The Politics of Financing Muni*   139

7. Disciplining Muni
Revanchism and the Gentrification of Transit   160

Conclusion: *San Francisco as National Bellwether*   192

Notes   203

Index   231

PREFACE & ACKNOWLEDGMENTS

The research and writing of this book were interrupted three times in seven years. In 2005 I initiated a summer of archival research and was enthusiastic to be writing about San Francisco, when, on August 29, 2005, Hurricane Katrina wiped out most of my hometown of New Orleans. For two years I struggled to make sense of the catastrophe, which to my mind was not a natural disaster or even a levee failure but the consequence of a rise in the sea level and global warming, the dangerous expansion of sprawl into the backswamps that once protected the city, and the destruction of Louisiana's wetlands by oil companies and their eight thousand miles of canals. These three factors—global warming, sprawl, and oil—coupled with the rigid channelization of the Mississippi River, converged to make New Orleans vulnerable, and it cannot be ignored that the nexus of all three of these is automobility. The politics of mobility became more urgent to me, and San Francisco's experience became more relevant as inspiration and bellwether.

I redoubled my efforts to think through the politics of mobility in San Francisco and began this book with the help of a sabbatical from San Francisco State University. As I neared completion of the first draft, tragedy again befell Louisiana. In April 2010 the Deepwater Horizon blew out, and for eighty-four days millions of barrels of oil gushed into the Gulf of Mexico. The spill was yet another in a long litany of problems associated with oil dependency and driving, including the fact that as a nonrenewable resource, oil supplies are declining, and what oil remains is found in remote, harsh environments such as deep beneath oceans. Expressing what some call San Francisco values, local bicyclists protested at a local BP filling station whose customers routinely blocked a key bike lane. True to form, politicians promised to make the bike lane safer, resulting in a push to have the first fully separated cycle-track constructed in San Francisco. San Franciscans were making the connections that so many people in the rest of the United States refused to see, making it even more clear that this book was sorely needed.

While I was revising the manuscript in 2011, my father, Russell Joseph Henderson, suddenly fell ill from cancer. As much a comrade as a parent, my dad was a relentless community organizer, political operative, and lobbyist in New Orleans. He taught me to think critically, and he was eager to see me write this book. In fact, on the day I arrived at the hospital where he lay dying, he was angry that I was not home working on the book. He had read most of the draft and his question was always, How come we can't do here, in New Orleans, what they do in San Francisco? Finishing this book became even more imperative after he passed away. If cities like New Orleans are to survive, it will be because cities like San Francisco have helped show the world how to do so.

The origins of this book go back to 2002, when I completed my dissertation on the politics of mobility in Atlanta and the South. Atlanta was a city where reallocating street space for automobiles was and still is unimaginable, despite ample room to do so. Much of the foundation of this book draws from that project, and I want to especially thank Andy Herod for his advice and support and for exposing me to the critical geographical literature on political economy and the production of space. That literature was the means by which I began to see transportation largely as an ideological problem as much as a technical one.

I was fortunate to land my first tenure track job at San Francisco State University. Special thanks must go to Joel Kassiola, former dean of the College of Behavioral and Social Sciences at SFSU, for providing research stipends and course releases over the years. The SFSU Faculty Affairs division also provided summer research stipends and course release time that enabled me to focus on the book, and the President's Leave with Pay Award allowed me to complete a first draft. Andrew Oliphant, Jerry Davis, and Nancy Wilkinson were patient colleagues who encouraged me to write the book, and a former graduate student, Mary Brown, put together a wonderful thesis on parking history in the Mission, on which I was proud to help.

This book is informed by ten years of empirical research on San Francisco's politics of mobility, including archival study, participant observation, and interviews and discussions with stakeholders in debates about mobility in San Francisco. Many people helped in this endeavor and deserve recognition. Dave Snyder is one of the most influential transportation activists in the Bay Area, if not the nation. The former director of the

San Francisco Bicycle Coalition, founder of Livable City, and now director of the California Bicycle Coalition, Dave read early versions of the introduction and several chapters and gave me much encouragement. I spent hundreds of hours discussing San Francisco's politics and culture with Steven T. Jones, aka Scribe, the City Editor of the *San Francisco Bay Guardian*. Ever the publicist, Brian Smith winced at some of the earlier versions of the book and helped me think about making it more accessible to a wider audience. Cheryl Brinkman, Rich Coffin, Kearstin Dischinger, Bryan Goebal, Bert Hill, Will Rostov, and Lilia Scott are the core of a monthly happy hour at which I learned more about transportation in San Francisco than I could have in any academic setting.

In Hayes Valley, Robin Levitt, who tirelessly campaigned to remove the Central Freeway, generously read and reread the sections on the freeway. Patricia Walkup, former president of the Hayes Valley Neighborhood Association, mentored me on all things about the valley, and her brother, Lee Walkup, allowed me to possess all of her extensive archives and files after her passing. This was a treasure trove of material on the freeway campaigns, parking debates, and neighborhood politics. Adam-Millard Ball, who practically wrote the city's parking reform code, read early iterations of several chapters.

Among the hundreds of people I have spoken with over the years, the following individuals stand out for sharing more than a book's worth of insights about San Francisco's transportation and land use politics: John Billovits, Chris Carlsson, Gerald Cauthen, Peter Cohen, Lisa Feldstein, Sue Hestor, Aaron Peskin, Tom Radulovich, Peter Straus, Andy Thornley, and Calvin Welch. Special thanks to Aaron Golub, who collaborated with me on an earlier version of the bicycle chapter, and to Michael Webster, an excellent and patient cartographer who made the maps for the book.

Portions of chapter 4 appeared in *Antipode* 41.1: 70–91 as "The Spaces of Parking: Mapping the Politics of Mobility in San Francisco," and parts of chapter 5 appeared in the *Journal of Transport Geography* 19.6: 1138–44 as "Level of Service: The Politics of Reconfiguring Urban Streets in San Francisco, CA." I thank the editors of both journals for giving me permission to reprint.

At University of Massachusetts Press, Brian Halley reached out and asked me if I'd be interested in working with him and the press on this book. Brian has been a stellar editor and has patiently shepherded me through the publishing process and put up with my inane questions. My copyeditor Lawrence Kenney did a remarkable job of cleaning up my manuscript.

Important friendships also gave me confidence and encouragement as I wrote, and so I am blessed to have Richard Bates, Michael Crutcher, Michael Daum, Greig Guthey, Margot Higgins, Richard Kay, David McNally, Steve Quick, Stanley Steinberg, Glenda Sweatman, and Norma Wood in my life. My brother Jonathan Henderson gets extra credit for keeping up the fight in the Gulf of Mexico. Finally, my mother, Mary Louis Battalora, taught me to ride a bike, to appreciate streetcars, and, in my adult years, exposed me to Europe, where I realized the amazing possibilities of cities that are not dependent on cars.

ABBREVIATIONS

ABAG   Association of Bay Area Governments
ASTAC   Association to Simplify Traffic and Abate Congestion
BART   Bay Area Rapid Transit
BOMA   Building Owners and Management Association
Caltrans California Department of Transportation
CFCTF   Central Freeway Citizens' Advisory Task Force
DPT   Department of Parking and Traffic
DPW   Department of Public Works
FHWA   Federal Highway Administration
GHG   greenhouse gases
HVNA   Hayes Valley Neighborhood Association
LOS   level of service
MOBNP   Market and Octavia Better Neighborhoods Plan
MTC   Metropolitan Transportation Commission
Muni   Municipal Railway
SFBC   San Francisco Bicycle Coalition
SFCTA   San Francisco County Transportation Authority
SFMTA   San Francisco Municipal Transportation Agency
SFPD   San Francisco Planning Department
SPUR   San Francisco Planning and Urban Research Association
TAD   transit assessment district
TEP   Transit Effectiveness Project
TIDF   transit impact development fee
USDOE   United States Department of Energy
USDOT   United States Department of Transportation
USEPA   United States Environmental Protection Agency
VMT   vehicle miles traveled

INTRODUCTION

San Francisco's Politics of Mobility

THE POET LAWRENCE FERLINGHETTI is an icon of San Francisco's countercultural politics. During the 1950s and 1960s Ferlinghetti and the poet-activists who gathered at his North Beach bookstore, City Lights, invigorated political culture in San Francisco, establishing the city's reputation as a bastion of civil rights, environmentalism, and world peace. Ferlinghetti and the bohemian activists of the beat era were part of a wider challenge to the corporate and militarist agenda of the United States. Although they sometimes remained aloof from the local day-to-day politics of San Francisco, they cherished and defended the city's unique tolerance of dissident values. Like much of San Francisco's counterculture politics, their ideas and contrarian spirit inspired many people throughout America during the turbulent sixties and are legendary today.[1]

Most aficionados of the beat era know that these poets and artists often romanticized the highways and byways of postwar America, as epitomized by Jack Kerouac's *On the Road* and Marlon Brando in the film *The Wild One*. Few would associate poets like Ferlinghetti with a critical analysis of American urban transportation policy. Yet in 1998, more than forty years after the infamous "Howl" incident in which he and Allen Ginsberg challenged the censoring of free speech, Ferlinghetti was honored as poet laureate of San Francisco by then-mayor Willie Brown. The poet there-

1

upon offered a pointed countercultural critique of America's obsession with automobiles.

Speaking in front of City Hall at the ceremony honoring him, the new poet laureate lamented that the automobile, coupled with the materialism of the dot-com boom and gentrification, was killing San Francisco's poetry. That is, automobility was destroying the intimate, personal, and emotional experience of San Francisco as a place of inspiration and meaning. He meant that the city was becoming less welcoming to people with low incomes and was losing its tolerance for the bohemian life, its civility, and its public spaces to atomistic market forces centered on automobiles. He warned, "All over America, all over Europe in fact, cities and towns are under assault by the automobile, and are being literally destroyed by car culture."[2] He called on San Franciscans to give bicycles and pedestrians absolute priority over automobiles and to close much of the inner city to cars.

If San Francisco had been a leader in challenging the conservative mainstream social norms of the 1950s and 1960s, Ferlinghetti's radical critique of automobiles reflected the zeitgeist of San Francisco politics in the late twentieth century and the early twenty-first. Perhaps more than the residents of any other major city in the United States, a growing cadre of citizen activists, professional planners, and politicians in San Francisco are challenging the system of automobility, that is, the combined impact on the built environment of motor vehicles like cars and trucks, the automobile industry, the highway and street networks, and corollary services, in addition to the centering of society and everyday life around the car and all the spaces in which cars are found and used.[3] In the late 1990s, as Ferlinghetti urged San Franciscans to confront what he called *autogedden,* voters were deciding to tear down a segment of a 1950s-era freeway.[4] A few years earlier the city had replaced another freeway segment, the Embarcadero Freeway, with a new tree-lined surface boulevard that included bicycle lanes and a streetcar in the median. And since 1991 thousands of bicyclists have engaged in monthly Critical Mass rides that usurp the space of automobiles.

Today, in more mundane ways, San Francisco's planning and advocacy establishment is changing zoning laws to limit the amount of parking for cars, encouraging new high-density, car-free housing adjacent to transit stations, and pushing for street space to be reallocated for "transit-first" policies such as lanes restricted to buses and new signals that preempt car traffic in favor of transit. For some, this contestation of automobility is about reclaiming urban spaces from automobiles, limiting their use, and, more poignantly, changing cultures so that the whole concept of high-speed mobility and car ownership is deemphasized. For others it includes subtle critiques of the geography of modern capitalism and a critique of a way of life centered on unfettered hyperconsumption, the speeding up of everyday life, and competition rather than cooperation. And for most it is about preserving the poetry of the city that Ferlinghetti idealized.

The Politics and Ideology of Mobility

To be sure, the contestation of automobility in any American city is an extremely polarizing affair, and in San Francisco it is no different. The city's accomplishments should not be overromanticized. In San Francisco the effort to demolish freeways was met with opposing initiatives to have bigger, wider, faster rebuilt freeways, and the debate over how to accommodate cars continues to divide the city. While two freeway segments did eventually come down, they were relatively short in length, and freeways and automobiles today dominate much of San Francisco's urban space. Meanwhile the city's financially strained bus system moves at a snail-paced eight miles per hour on congested streets and, worse, five miles per hour in the downtown, about the same speeds transit moved in the 1920s.

In 2006 an anti-bicycle lawsuit, litigated by two persons calling themselves the Coalition for Adequate Review (CAR), successfully delayed the city's implementation of bicycle lanes for over four years. And in 2007 a ballot initiative sponsored by conservative businessmen sought to impose more off-street parking, not less, in all of the new housing built in the city. This Parking for Neighborhoods Initiative was defeated by 67 percent of the voters in November 2007, but had it passed, one of the most progressive parking policies in the nation would have been overturned. Real estate developers continue to build more off-street parking targeted at luxury condominium buyers with cars, and many motorists oppose bike lanes that might interfere with on-street parking. In sum, San Francisco might have a local social movement that offers a pointed critique of automobility, but it also has a vociferous politics that defends the automobile and its spaces.

San Francisco has a contentious politics of mobility, a struggle over what type of transportation mode, whether automobiles, transit, bicycles, or walking, is developed in the city, and how urban space is configured to make various modes functional. The politics of mobility includes debates about how streets and urban space should be governed and regulated, and who determines this governance and regulation. While these debates are common throughout the United States and indeed the world, the degree to which this politics is accentuated in San Francisco makes it a compelling case study and bellwether.

The basic gestalt of this book is to take the examination of the politics of mobility a step further by deconstructing the ideologies that undergird and inform the debate about streets and urban space. I consider ideology to be a system of ideas and representations that dominate the minds of individuals and of groups participating in the politics of mobility. Ideology, as broadly construed here, includes ideas about what the scope of government should be vis-à-vis automobiles, transit, bicycles, and pedestrian spaces, how decisions should be made and what values should be pursued with respect to each mode. I elucidate how three competing ideologies—progressive, neoliberal, and conservative—have come to dominate the contemporary political discourse about urban mobility in San Francisco and arguably throughout the United States.

Briefly, progressives, invoking concerns about the environment and social justice, seek to use government to limit the overall amount of automobility in the city. They seek to achieve this through the reallocating of street space to public transit, bicycles, and pedestrians. Progressives in San Francisco want to use government as a tool for regulating private development's interaction with the mobility system by limiting parking for automobiles and by requiring fees and taxes that support public transit and affordable housing that are proximate to good mobility. There are fissures, nuances, and sometimes contradictions in the relationship between progressives and mobility, but a fundamental tenet is that urban space should be dictated by a collective public good, environmental stewardship, and social equity. Moreover, the progressive spirit questions the need for excessive, unfettered movement.

Progressive ideology, as it is manifested in San Francisco today, contrasts with the ideological belief of neoliberals, who, while sometimes pursuing the use of state power to maximize private profit, fundamentally believe that the allocation of urban space, as a scarce resource, should be determined by market forces. Neoliberals, consistent with the broader agenda of privatization of space and market-based pricing of public access to space, envision a mobility system shaped by pricing and markets rather than by regulation and collective action. Unlike progressives, neoliberals have no necessarily predetermined vision of urban space, but do feel the built environment must be allowed to develop with the efficacy of the market. Movement, paid for by the individual user, should be unrestrained. Yet such efficacy can include a commodification of nonmove-

ment or slower movement or the package of quality-of-life goods surrounding the "walkability" and "livability" of the city, a package reserved
for those who can afford to enter. To that end, neoliberal mobility includes
the aggressive use of government to both enhance mobility and rein it in,
but only inasmuch as government policy helps realize the goals of profit
and facilitating economic growth and development.

Rounding out San Francisco's politics of mobility is a conservative
ideology of mobility. If progressives believe government should actively
discourage automobility and neoliberals theoretically believe the market
should decide, the conservative politics of mobility posits that unfettered
movement is a prerequisite of individual liberty and freedom and that
government should proactively accommodate uninhibited movement,
mainly by car, even when that requires generous subsidy or undermines
broader, collective environmental and social goals. The conservative politics conjures rigid cultural arguments such as "automobility is American"
or "Californian," considers automobile usage a natural right, and insists
that government mandate abundant space for automobility throughout
the city to accommodate people's love affair with automobiles and their
absolute need for them.

San Francisco is far from a bastion of the conservative ideologies associated with broader American politics, especially regarding social issues
such as gay rights or religion. A mere 9 percent of registered voters are
Republican, often, but not always, a proxy identifying the presence of conservative politics.[5] Thus I use the term *conservative* with reservation and
contingency. Yet there is a pronounced conservative element in San Francisco politics of mobility, particularly in the hill districts and the west side,
where automobility is central to many people's everyday life. Conservative
discourse has mounted challenges to the progressive mobility vision of
restricting automobility.

This book is an exploration and elaboration of how each of these ideologies contains normative visions of mobility and space that are enunciated in the political landscape of San Francisco. I examine the evolution
and shifting of these ideologies and how they have interacted, overlapped,
and sparred in the political arena to produce the spatial and mobility outcomes manifested on city streets today. The narrative does not focus on
personalities. I purposefully limit emphasis on key activists, politicians,
developers, and other central actors, not because they do not matter but
because emphasis on individual agency can divert attention from the attempt to understand the ideological context within which such personalities and characters operate.

My central argument is that in considering transportation, just as in the consideration of other aspects of cities, one cannot transcend ideology or hope it goes away. It is not enough to acknowledge that transportation is simply political and that politics is a process whereby individuals and groups define what is important and what is not important to society and everyday life. One must also comprehend the underlying ideology guiding the various political positions with respect to transportation and mobility. In examining the politics of mobility in this way, I hope to persuade readers to ask how and where they fit into these critical debates, and I also hope the book will help them frame their own experiences and understandings of mobility. Most important, however, the broad ambit of the book is that San Francisco offers a compelling opportunity to appraise the politics of possibilities of challenging and replacing automobility. There has never been a greater need to do so.

Urgency

The time for rethinking automobility is urgent. Globally, cities consume 75 percent of the world's energy and produce 78 percent of global greenhouse gas (GHG) emissions, and automobiles are a rapidly growing component of this state of affairs.[6] Transportation is the fastest growing sector of energy use and GHG emissions, and this fact is in great measure owing to the expansion of automobility. A global scientific consensus posits the need to stabilize atmospheric CO_2 at least to 350 parts per million by 2050 (current levels are at 395 parts per million and fast approaching 400). That goal will not be achieved if the number of motor vehicles in the United States increases, as forecasted, from the present 250 million to 325 million in 2050. Nor will it be achieved if the world sees the number of motorized vehicles—cars, motorcycles, trucks, scooters, electric bikes—continue to increase at the current rate of 3 percent annually between now and 2030, which means there will be a total of 2 billion vehicles, 1 billion of them passenger cars.[7] "Sustainable motorization" or an "enlightened car policy" might contribute to reducing some emissions but will not lead to climate stabilization.[8]

There is no realistically viable substitute for petroleum that can provide the levels of automobility Americans and, increasingly, the global middle class expect while also meeting existing U.S. industrial and residential energy consumption patterns. Yet the world is moving closer to peak oil, that is, the maximum rate of production followed by decline, if it hasn't happened already, and tremendous global instability will accompany peak oil if the mobility system is not retooled.[9] If the world's fleet of gasoline-powered automobiles shifts to electric, hydrogen fuel cells, or biofuels, the change will draw resources away from industrial, residential, and food systems, or it will have to be an entirely new layer of energy production. Untenable amounts of GHGs will continue to be emitted, and the world will still hit atmospheric carbon levels of 450 and 500 parts per million (and maybe even higher) within this century. The reality is that for the foreseeable future an electric car is a coal-fired car.

Tremendous amounts of energy are required to produce substitutes for petroleum, and the nuclear, solar, wind, and geothermal capabilities to produce that energy are unreliable or unrealistic at the levels at which global automobility is forecasted. Massive quantities of petroleum will be needed to manufacture wind turbines, solar panels, and other cleaner energy sources. If the world is to replace what is used in the equivalent of oil energy consumed by automobility today, thousands of five-hundred-megawatt power plants will be needed to bridge the gap between demand and supply that will occur by 2030.[10] That would basically be six thousand power plants built to sustain the system of automobility. In view of the nuclear disaster in Japan in 2011, the world is not likely to build thousands of nuclear power plants to supply power for electric cars, no matter how hard the nuclear lobby works to get plants built, and the consensus on climate has already suggested that more coal-fired power plants are not a good idea. Moreover, future emissions from automobiles do not include the full life cycle of automobiles, which itself contributes to massive emissions and fossil fuel consumption.[11]

The United States has 4 percent of the world's population but 21 percent of the world's cars, produces 45 percent of the global carbon emissions that come from cars, and overall produces 25 percent of the total global GHG emissions while consuming 23 percent of the world's oil annually.[12] If China had the same per capita car ownership rate as the United States, there would be more than one billion cars in China today—double the current worldwide rate.[13] If Americans expect China, India, and other developing nations to realistically address global warming and peak oil, America will need not only to provide leadership, but also to decrease its appetite for excessive, on-demand, high-speed automobility. An incremental adaptation of allegedly clean automobility is not enough. Rather, Americans must undertake a considerable restructuring of how they organize cities, and that must include the rethinking of mobility and of the allocation of street space.

Reflecting this urgency, people and organizations throughout the world are rethinking the connection between mobility and cities. In the United States a social movement loosely known as the livability movement seeks to reduce car use by reconfiguring urban space into denser, transit-oriented, walkable built forms, a development pattern also associated with smart growth or new urbanism.[14] Made up of a broad array of environmental organizations, housing advocates, scholars, real estate interests, and many local, state, and federal officials, the livability movement does not propose to eliminate the automobile but does desire to reduce the need for car use. The movement is primarily focused on land use and transportation policies that counter sprawl, a discontiguous pattern of low-density development centered on widespread automobile dependency and characterized by excessive congestion, consumption of open space, smog, and global warming; furthermore, sprawl is responsible for the nation's insatiable appetite for oil.

Livability advocates call for reductions in annual vehicle miles traveled (VMT), that is, less driving, in order to reduce GHG emissions and oil consumption as well as to address a plethora of other social and environmental problems stemming from high VMT and sprawl. Some suggest a need to redesign American cities to reduce driving by 25–50 percent of present levels by 2050, an enterprise that will require freeway removal, reduced parking, and replacement of road space with other uses.[15]

The concept of livability and the idea of rethinking how future cities are built were given new urgency when, in the financial crises of 2008–12, some of the hardest-hit areas were the sprawling edges of metropolitan areas with high levels of average daily VMT.[16] Nationwide, gasoline prices edged above four dollars per gallon, causing more duress for financially strapped but automobile-dependent households. Responding to this crisis, President Barack Obama made livability part of his agenda by establishing the Partnership for Sustainable Communities.[17] For the first time in U.S. official discourse the president's cabinet secretaries spoke with remarkable candor about how their transportation policy would emphatically encourage people to drive less. While it has been met with substantial resistance from skeptical members of Congress, the partnership nevertheless set a precedent in that it has elevated the dialogue about the need to reduce automobile dependency in ways that may be transformative in the near future.

In California, where 23 million cars ply the roads and where household driving, the fastest growing source of statewide emissions, produces 30 percent of GHG emissions, lawmakers formulated a policy to reduce VMT by reconfiguring land use toward compact development.[18] Known as

Senate Bill (SB) 375, or California's Sustainable Communities and Climate Protection Act, it is one of the most comprehensive efforts in the nation to reduce driving. In the Bay Area, regional transportation and land use agencies, which coordinate planning but do not have authority to mandate specific actions by localities, have responded to SB 375 by proposing to reduce per capita driving by 10–15 percent in 2035 while simultaneously absorbing an additional 2 million people and 900,000 housing units into the region.[19] What's more, 70 percent of that new growth, that is, 1.4 million people and 630,000 homes, is planned to be concentrated in relatively dense geographic areas within existing urban and suburban nodes known as priority development areas. Only 3 percent of future growth would be built on greenfields. The Bay Area is planning for compact cities, and, coupled with national advocacy for livability, planners are taking a hard look at the details of how this might look and what will be adequate to reduce VMT.

Why San Francisco?

It would behoove the national livability movement to look to the City of San Francisco. San Francisco's transportation metrics exceed even the most ambitious proposals of the livability movement, and its density, together with its emerging policies with regard to cars, establishes a standard that should probably be emulated by other cities in terms of addressing GHG emissions, energy policy, and social concerns related to mobility. It is also an exceptionally livable city by many indicators, is consistently ranked as one of the most livable in the United States, and has a very high, arguably insatiable demand for new housing (which brings some uncomfortable affordability issues).[20] In many ways San Francisco embodies both what the livability movement is trying to achieve and what can go wrong.

People in San Francisco drive less compared to the rest of the nation. Whereas the average annual household VMT is roughly 20,000 miles nationally, San Francisco's household VMT is less than 10,000 miles per year.[21] San Francisco's daily per capita VMT, roughly 10 miles per day, shows that via a denser urban fabric and a comprehensive transit system the livability movement can strive for significant reductions in VMT. Moreover, San Francisco's per capita vehicle ownership is at 580 automobiles per 1,000 persons, whereas in the United States as a whole per capita ownership stands at 828 per 1,000 persons.[22] Thirty percent of San Francisco households are car-free, substantially higher than the national rate of 8.7 percent.[23] The ratio of 0.58:1 per capita ownership and 30 percent car-free households remained steady through the decade of 2000–2010 despite the increasing wealth and population of the city overall.

San Francisco is also a benchmark for transit, bicycling, and pedestrian mode splits (that is, the share or percentage of travelers using a particular type of transportation). In 2010, 17 percent of all daily trips in San Francisco were taken on public transit, a contrast to the less than 2 percent nationwide.[24] The figures contrast even more starkly in regard to commuting trips, of which about 5 percent nationally are taken on public transit compared to 31 percent in San Francisco.[25] Some 50 percent of commuters traveling from anywhere in the Bay Area to downtown San Francisco use public transit compared to just 9.4 percent of commuters to other Bay Area employment nodes. Of all San Francisco commuters, regardless of their employment location, 33 percent take transit to work. The city's transit agency, the Municipal Railway, or Muni, is the seventh largest in the nation, with 700,000 daily boardings, and has the fifth largest bus fleet in the United States, following New York, Los Angeles, Chicago, and Philadelphia, cities with populations of well over one million. Muni also emits only 1 percent of the city's total GHG emissions, while cars and trucks emit 48 percent.[26]

Meanwhile, while less than 10 percent of all daily trips in the United States are by walking and bicycling, in San Francisco 20 percent of all daily trips are taken by these nonmotorized modes.[27] San Francisco has one of the highest rates of bicycle use of any large city in the United States, with only Portland having similar rates for all trips, and Portland, Seattle, and Minneapolis having comparable rates of commuting by bicycle. While federal estimates are that 1 percent of all trips are by bike, bicycling for daily travel increased in San Francisco from roughly 1 percent of trips in 2000 to 6 percent of all trips by 2009.[28] Between 2005 and 2009 bicycling increased 53 percent, amounting to 128,000 daily trips.[29] In some inner neighborhoods of San Francisco the mode share of bicycling approaches 10 percent for all trips. Sixteen percent of San Franciscans ride a bike at least once a week, and 75 percent of voters in San Francisco support new bike lanes.[30]

Furthermore, transportation planners in San Francisco have proposed that by 2035 a 30–30–40 mode split be reached as part of a sustainability goal for the city. The vision is to reduce driving in the city to 30 percent of all daily trips (down from 65 percent today) and to increase daily transit trips to 30 percent while increasing walking and bicycling to 40 percent of all daily trips.[31] Comparing urban mobility to the food pyramid, the

San Francisco Municipal Transportation Agency (SFMTA) advised that a bottom-heavy reliance on cars for mobility was unhealthy and needed to be replaced with transit and nonmotorized transport as the foundation of urban movement.

Population density has a major influence on San Francisco's relatively low VMT and low car ownership rates, coupled with relatively high non-automobile mode splits. The city's roughly 805,000 residents, or 16,445 persons per square mile, make its residential density high by American standards. San Francisco is the densest large city in the United States after New York City (Manhattan's overall density is more than 66,000 persons per square mile.)[32] In San Francisco's northeastern core, Chinatown and the Tenderloin have densities of around 100,000 persons per square mile, similar to many parts of Manhattan.

Surrounding the northeast core of San Francisco is the so-called Victorian Belt, a collection of historic neighborhoods ringing downtown San Francisco from Pacific Heights in the north to Hayes Valley, Alamo Square, and the Haight-Ashbury in the west, to Duboce Triangle, the Castro, the Mission, and Bernal Heights in the south (figure 1). Some of these neighborhoods have densities exceeding 45,000 persons per square mile and are comparable to Brooklyn, New York. Yet despite their high density they are considered comfortable, livable neighborhoods, and, with housing prices at roughly eight hundred thousand dollars for a two-bedroom flat, the housing market suggests there are not enough of these neighborhoods. Beyond the Victorian Belt are less dense neighborhoods like the Sunset and Richmond districts. The Sunset has a residential density ranging from 7,000 to 15,000 persons per square mile, low for San Francisco but not low compared to most of urban and suburban America. Because the Sunset and Richmond are in the infamous fog belt of western San Francisco, housing prices are not quite as high as those in the Victorian Belt, but they remain very high relative to prices in the Bay Area and nationally.

Despite the relatively high density, city planners, complementing the proposed 30–30–40 mode split, have approved an ambitious urban planning effort called Better Neighborhoods. The project re-zoned large swaths of former industrial areas for intensive residential and commercial infill development centered on transit and walkability and have new zoning rules that restrict the amount of parking made available to residents and visitors. Originally proposed in 2000 in response to the pressures on housing and transportation that arose from the software and Internet technology

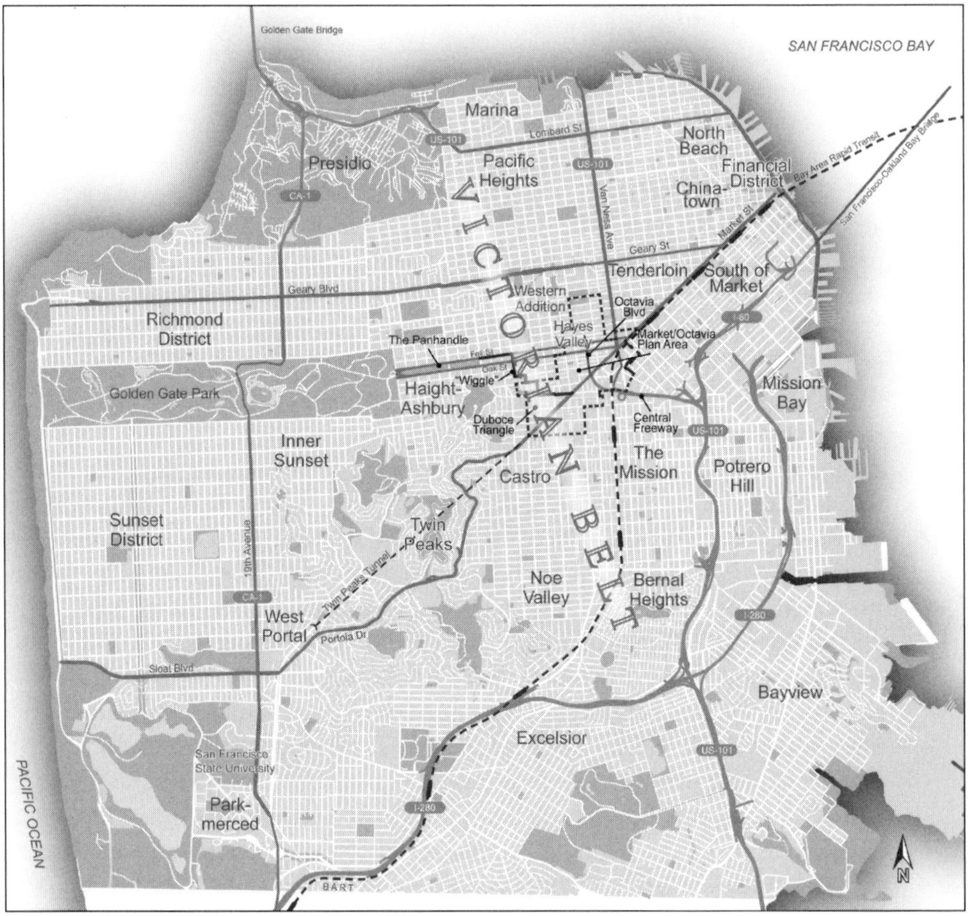

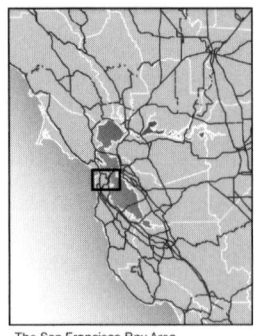

The San Francisco Bay Area

2 Miles

Figure 1. Geography of San Francisco, including neighborhoods and primary transportation routes discussed in this book. Cartography by Michael Webster.

boom, the scheme resulted in an extensive allowance for densification in strategic parts of the city, such as the postindustrial waterfront and older light industrial areas that industry has vacated. The re-zoning also encourages infill on scattered surface parking lots in parts of the city. As it is expanded, including adaptive reuse of several former military bases, the cumulative re-zoning could amount to 90,000 new housing units built in the city by 2035.[33] These re-zoning efforts are probably among the most ambitious examples in the nation of the implementation of the tenets of the livability agenda.

Understandably, physical geography affects these dense development patterns. San Francisco has a unique, complex topography that includes steep hills on a peninsula and water on three sides. In one sense San Francisco is a seven-by-seven-mile walled city with limited access and egress points. To the south of the city San Bruno Mountain provides a fourth physical barrier. Two southbound transportation corridors straddle the eastern and western flanks of the mountain, while the two transportation routes north and east must cross water. Los Angeles, on the other hand, sits on an expansive coastal plain with few geographic impediments and comparatively lower residential density, an average of 7,500 persons per square mile. Los Angeles and Sunbelt cities like Houston, Phoenix, San Jose, and Atlanta have room to sprawl in almost every direction and few physical barriers to transportation routes.

Yet physical geography does not fully explain San Francisco's mobility and density metrics. Just because the city is at the head of a peninsula does not mean it is therefore naturally dense or naturally susceptible to lower rates of car usage—that is overdeterministic. San Francisco's suburb to the south, San Mateo County, also has considerable geographical constraints on development. The suburbanized area of San Mateo County straddles a narrow flatland between a line of north–south hills and the bay. Yet, by contrast with San Francisco, the county's per capita VMT is upward of twenty-two miles per day, and the percentage of car-free households is less than 5 percent. In the entire Bay Area region, where development is physically constrained by mountain ranges and the bay, suburban counties have average annual VMTs of eighteen miles per day, only 8.5 percent of households are car-free, and transit ridership rates are below 10 percent for all trips. Something beyond physical geography and population density is influencing mobility. As I argue in this book, the impressive mobility statistics of San Francisco are the result not simply of unique geography and physical setting but also of politics and ideology.

Yet despite having 30 percent car-free households and the highest transit ridership west of the Mississippi River, San Francisco today ironically has one of the highest density of automobile registrations in the United States, at over nine thousand motor vehicles, including conventional automobiles, sport utility vehicles, and light trucks, per square mile.[34] This seems contradictory and is difficult to comprehend at first. How can a city with relatively high transit usage and low rates of automobile ownership and automobile usage be saturated with automobiles? The juxtaposition of high vehicle density and less driving in the city is another critical issue the livability movement should consider. Although San Francisco preserved its walkable Victorian and early modern neighborhoods, it injected automobiles, parking, and wider streets into the urban fabric.

This seeming contradiction makes it more challenging to usurp the spaces of automobiles in San Francisco than it would be in, say, Portland or New York City, both of which are the equal of San Francisco when it comes to investing in green transport. Portland may stand out as the nation's most green transport city, but it is a place where, owing in part to its far lower density of automobiles, it is arguably easy to stripe in bicycle lanes. Compared to San Francisco, Portland has relatively low suburban-style residential density, a low density of automobiles, and more capacity to reallocate road space. New York City, on the other hand, does have the lowest per capita car ownership in the United States, but it also has a lower density of vehicles per square mile than San Francisco. Additionally, a substantial amount of the daily public transit use in New York occurs underground or elevated, out of the mix of congestion that plagues Manhattan's streets. In San Francisco the bus system carries the bulk of passengers, and even the light rail lines are, for much of their routes, on surface streets in mixed traffic. It has an underground subway, but it is limited to a narrow corridor of the city. In San Francisco almost all political decisions about allocating street space to transit, pedestrians, and bicyclists come at the expense of the space and travel time of automobiles. This fact creates an emotionally charged, often vitriolic, and sometimes volatile situation as well as a lively local political discourse about bicycle lanes, parking, and public transit. Historically it has also resulted in a mobility stalemate, which means all travelers suffer frequent unpleasant delay, tension, stress, and conflict (see chapter 2).

San Francisco's built environment is the concept of livability overlaid by continued high rates of automobile ownership, and this makes San Francisco a trial run of how livability may or may not unfold in other places. If the nation does in fact implement widespread livability policies, will the increase in population density and mixed uses they create simply be overrun by a concomitant increase in the density of cars, as seems to be the case in San Francisco today? Will the livable communities and smart-growth movements really be just "lipstick on a pig," new urbanism with parking in the back? The fact that so many people still own and drive cars in San Francisco, despite the high density and excellent transit coverage, is probably the most profound issue to consider, and it suggests that auto-mobility is not simply contingent on the built environment. Automobility is also ideological. It is therefore useful to examine, as I do here, ideology and mobility in more detail.

The Plan of the Book

Chapter 1 expands on the idea that mobility is ideological and lays out the argument of why it is important to consider ideology in transportation debates. It provides an overview of the three ideologies dominating the politics of mobility in San Francisco, outlining progressive, neoliberal, and conservative mobility in detail. In addition, the chapter touches on how the three ideologies overlap and suggests that contingent, tentative ideo-logical détentes or alliances occur in specific instances.

Chapter 2 is a historical geography of how the contemporary politics of mobility in San Francisco came to be. It summarizes the freeway revolts of the 1960s but also discusses how rapid transit proposals were diluted and truncated. This resulted in a mobility stalemate, whereby everyone using streets has an unpleasant experience, but any improvement to one mode of transport comes at the expense of others. Rather than a freeway or rapid transit grid, streets carry the burden of mixed car and transit traffic, mak-ing it challenging to prioritize and allocate street space today.

The politically charged debate over removing a segment of freeway damaged in the Loma Prieta earthquake of 1989 is the subject of chapter 3. It introduces the nuanced progressive–neoliberal détente and rapproche-ment pivoting on reurbanization through freeway removal, a notion that conservatives lambasted. The chapter closes with a cautionary discussion of the gentrification that has accompanied freeway removal and compli-cated the progressive politics of mobility in the city.

I take up the politics of parking in San Francisco in chapter 4, which begins with an overview of the spatial consumption of parking and how this affects urban form. It discusses the ideological debate over reduc-ing parking and imposing new parking reform policies in the city. I sug-gest that parking policy, like freeway removal, is more than a debate over transportation planning: it is about whom the city is for and who decides, questions that are rife with clashes over gentrification and social equity.

In chapter 5 I explore the rise of bicycle politics in San Francisco, outline the spaces of bicycling, and consider how traditional traffic engineering techniques must be reformed if bicycling is to have a meaningful role in urban mobility. The chapter traces the ways in which progressive, neoliberal, and conservative ideologies interact in the debate over reconfiguring urban streets to accommodate bicycling, a process which includes the revamping of traffic engineering and environmental analysis techniques. Moreover, like the debates over parking and gentrification, San Francisco's bicycle politics is complicated by the fact that in tech-savvy, youthful cities bicycling is not just hip but also sells real estate, and this too has important implications for progressive visions for livability.

Chapters 6 and 7 explore the relationship between transit, ideology, and class politics. It begins with an introduction to how the Municipal Railway, or Muni, is primed to reduce the city's carbon footprint and energy consumption, but only if adequate funding and street space are made available. Yet San Francisco's street space is a zero sum competition, and, as with the politics of bicycling, there is considerable opposition from neoliberals, conservatives, and even some progressives when it comes to their street and their parking spaces. Moreover, the debate over how to finance Muni is suffused with class and racial undertones. San Francisco's transit politics is a reflection of broader revanchist trends to discipline public employees and recapture transit from lower classes, and this is a sobering reality that the livability movement must grapple with.

The book concludes with a hopeful Map of Progressive Mobility that provides a conceptual framework for expanding the politics of possibilities for reducing automobility. By way of this case study of San Francisco, my intention is to outline an inspiring, yet tempered and cautious account of the politics of possibilities for rethinking automobility in other cities. This book does not pretend to have a magic bullet for reducing automobility, but it does consider what can be learned from San Francisco, which in many ways is at the cutting edge in challenging automobility in the United States. Through this it is hoped that the reader will find inspiration but also context and a useful template of how the rest of America can begin rethinking automobility and thus preserve or reestablish the poetry of their cities, towns, and neighborhoods.

CHAPTER ONE

How We Get There Matters
Ideologies of Mobility

MY AIM IN THIS BOOK is to focus attention on ideology. An enduring legacy of transportation studies is that scholars, planning and engineering professionals, policymakers, and advocates suggest that movement can be decoupled from ideology. This tendency is especially evident in quantitative, data-driven methods in which there is often a claim of apolitical, dispassionate, objective, and unbiased professionalism in transportation analysis. For example, the planners and engineers who built the Interstate Highway System asserted their detachment from politics and presented an armor of objectivity.[1] Today many engineers, planners, politicians, and everyday people also profess to be nonideological when it comes to transportation, instead invoking common sense.[2] Ideology is thereby sometimes an "unconscious system of concepts" rather than explicit.[3]

Taken further, automobility is so ubiquitous and universal in the United States and even in San Francisco that it seems as if the act of driving has no meaningful ideological dimension. Ideological parameters may involve nuanced discussions about what type of fuel or propulsion device is more ethical, moral discourse over miles per gallon, or how one interacts with other road users, but not the act of driving in and of itself. To fight automobility as a form of movement can be akin to fighting human nature. Automobility seems to be inevitable, not historically contingent.

Such an outlook not only reinforces behavioral practices of driving and legitimizes policies accommodating cars but also contributes to a veil of consensus produced through education systems, child-rearing practices, the organization of work relations, and everyday life centered on cars.[4]

Yet how we get around does matter, does have ideological undertones, and can be what the geographer David Harvey described as an "unaware expression of the underlying ideas and beliefs which attach to a specific social situation."[5] In that vein, the urban theorist Mike Davis admonished that there is a need for more, not less, ideological politics in debates about cities, of which mobility is a central component.[6] For example, to get at the crux of what shaped Los Angeles, Davis examined the unyielding "programmatic tenacity" of ideological conservatives. The progressive counterweight in Los Angeles was ineffective, Davis contended, because it was vague, fragmented, and less ideologically tenacious. Davis insinuated that progressives needed to produce a more coherent and resolute ideological charter. Similarly, Harvey lamented that, at the national and global scale, there has been little or no coherent progressive opposition to the neoliberal agenda of the late twentieth century and the early twenty-first.[7]

Seizing on this dearth of cohesive ideological resistance, I want to sketch how mobility is conceptualized vis-à-vis three competing ideologies, progressive, neoliberal, and conservative. That mobility is ideological is not a novel observation. A "new mobilities" paradigm in the social sciences and humanities considers mobility to be culturally nuanced but also a fundamentally important factor underpinning material, social, political, and economic processes.[8] The new mobility paradigm compels one to look at the wider ideological assumptions about mobility to understand how and why decisions involving that phenomenon are made. Just as the social philosopher Henri Lefebvre theorized that the character and nature of urban space reflect dominant modes of production and social relations (and power) within a given society, so, too, mobility contains embedded social relations, and understanding this notion requires deconstructing the assumptions that lead to a particular ideology of mobility.[9]

Progressive Mobility

I begin with an overview of progressive ideology because many progressives are at the leading edge of the challenge to automobility and recognize the urgency inherent in this task. Progressive conceptualizations of mobility contest the status quo. Broadly speaking, progressives approach problems like environmental degradation and economic inequality systematically and understand the world through what George Lakoff calls empathy-based values.[10] That is, other people's misfortune might occur because of systematic inequity rather than because of individual responsibility. To progressives, personal responsibility toward oneself includes social responsibility toward others. Empathy-based values are opposed to the neoliberal framing of a laissez-faire, free market, which assumes that one's seeking of self-interest will maximize everyone's interests.

Progressives believe that a systematic approach requires that government work for the public good. Government can and should ensure environmental sustainability and social equity, and government must intervene in the production of the space of a city, for example, by creating affordable housing, securing jobs and fair wages for workers, and limiting the privatization of public services and public spaces. Progressives believe that urban planning should be used to achieve social equity and that it is necessary to the orderly guidance of development; development cannot be left to the whims of capitalist speculation or be exclusively controlled by elites. Rather, there must be democracy in planning, and the right to the city must be shaped by democratic access to decisions about the value of land and who gets to live there.

Sometimes labeled the Left Coast city, San Francisco has a tradition of politically progressive politics and a citizenry that is ready to confront and critique capitalism.[11] As leftists, progressives in San Francisco oppose the neoliberal agenda of real estate developers, thereby making land use and transportation policy central to progressive politics.[12] Historically, progressives battled developers over urban renewal in the Western Addition and South of Market neighborhoods and were assertive in political debates over growth control and high-rises office buildings in downtown San Francisco.[13] By and large, progressives were mostly concerned with the environmental and social impacts of growth and stressed that in the absence of growth control the displacement of blue-collar jobs and the working class would accelerate as housing prices escalated, the result of new professionals bidding up rents. San Francisco and the Bay Area also had a strong current of progressive environmentalism, an environmentalism that included a circumspect challenge to capitalism that is more present in the Bay Area than elsewhere in the United States.[14] The geographer Richard Walker argues that Bay Area environmentalism took a distinctive left turn and is more socially committed than anywhere else in the country, has behaved more militantly, and has articulated an opposition to both government and capital. The Bay Area's environmental movement has tended to be the area's most vocal opponent of the production system that makes capitalism work, such as automobility, sprawl, and freeways.

Despite progressives' robust engagement with land use politics in San Francisco, there is little scholarly work on how they explicitly address mobility, with the exception of their historical opposition to some freeway proposals in the 1960s (see chapter 2). The limited examination of San Francisco's progressive politics of mobility is unfortunate because livability advocates nationwide often highlight the city's freeway removal, walkability, parking policies, bicycle politics, and relatively high public transportation ridership as being inspirational, yet they overlook or underestimate the key role progressive ideology has played in producing those outcomes.

A progressive framework conceptualizes mobility as a systemic problem that requires deep social commitment and responsibility. How we get there matters. It posits that there can be too much mobility, as exemplified by high levels of VMT in the United States, and that excessive mobility results in both environmental degradation and major social inequality at a local, national, and global scale. The main problem, obviously, is that automobility is part of a wider, systemic moral and social problem of overconsumption and disproportionate materialism.

Automobility, as a system that dominates urban movement, ruins a city because it is noisy, unhealthy, dangerous, and isolating. It lends itself easily to competitive aggressiveness and selfishness. Automobility occupies scarce space in cities and marginalizes pedestrians, cyclists, transit users, and anyone without a car. It also represents an intensive commodification of movement. The middle class, in viewing automobility as freedom, must pay a high price to be a citizen-driver. They then sit in traffic and face higher and higher operating costs and entry fees in order to participate in society. Moreover, to provide the system of automobility, the U.S. government endorses or ignores violence and totalitarian regimes abroad in order to maintain a steady supply of cheap oil.[15] Even while many contemporary environmentalists may embrace green cars, like hybrid gasoline-electric cars and cars powered by electric battery, the ultimate contention of progressive ideology is that green cars are not a viable solution to the systemic nature of the problem. Hybrid and electric cars remain resource intensive and exhibit the antiurban, antisocial traits of conventional cars. The system itself must be transformed to achieve environmental and social stability.

The moral code of social responsibility compels advocacy and community organizing, and in San Francisco nonprofit organizations are influenced by a progressive framework. Among such groups are the twelve-thousand-member San Francisco Bicycle Coalition and its junior partners, Livable City, which focuses explicitly on reducing the spaces of automobility, and Walk San Francisco, which advocates for pedestrian-friendly environments and walkability. Taking a more regional perspective, Transform (formerly the Transportation and Land Use Coalition) exhibits a progressive ideology in advocating for public transit and a rethinking of urban form. These organizations have paid staff but rely heavily on dedicated grass-roots volunteers in carrying out almost all of their activities, including public speaking, letter writing, fundraising, and organizing of events. In the local media, the *San Francisco Bay Guardian* and the online *StreetsblogSF* are outlets for advocates of a progressive mobility vision.

The rank and file of these organizations include professionals in the arts, design, and media, software, social and healthcare workers, architects, teachers, and other urban workers who value urban authenticity and a bohemian landscape. Many make a lifestyle choice to live in the city and are often inclined to live in older, preexisting housing in the Victorian Belt rather than in new condos or high rises. They are more dependent on government jobs, tend to support social programs in voting and politics, and work in their chosen field less for personal gain than for attempting to realize their reformist ideologies. Their class structure is often shaped by occupation.[16] Many among them are not from the traditional white, ethnic, blue-collar working class, which had occupied much of the Victorian Belt in the mid-twentieth century, but are highly educated tech workers, managers, and consultants. They are less focused on workplace rules and wages (standard labor union issues) than on localized quality of life issues such as traffic and transportation, the environment, and the preservation of neighborhoods and historic resources. In sum, many livability concepts are localized in San Francisco by progressives.

However, progressive mobility is not simply environmental or urbane in outlook but also includes a populist concern for working-class and minority access. Improving mobility for the working class is crucial to accessing the greater societal goals of alleviating poverty, ending racial injustice, and providing greater equity. Yet improving mobility does not mean increasing mobility. Proximity to jobs, services, and amenities is more important than long-distance, high-speed automobile access or express bus rides. The emphasis is instead on the need to create more affordable housing close to jobs, and concomitantly creating jobs in proximity to where workers live, regardless of income. Thus a fully rounded, robust progressive mobility includes strong elements of class and racial struggle and of conflict over social relations in the production and consumption process.

In addition, progressives invoke environmental justice, or the right to live in an unpolluted environment. For example, air and water pollution from automobility is recognized as a major health problem in poor minority neighborhoods. From an equity perspective, the working poor have the lowest levels of access and the lowest quality mobility yet bear a disproportionate share of the externalities, or secondary consequences such as air pollution, in comparison to the mobility enjoyed by wealthier stratums.

A fully coherent, unified, and tenacious progressive mobility agenda has not been put into practice. While many livability advocates, particularly bicyclists, are well organized and well endowed economically, a broad progressive mobility movement is less organized and more ad hoc, often coalescing around immediate threats such as cuts to public transit service or fare increases or specific modes like advocating for bicycle lanes without considering transit impacts. Organizations focused on affordable housing, tenants' rights, youth advocacy, and immigrant rights often converge around an issue only to disappear as soon as the issue fades into the background. Many organizations oppose transit fare increases, among them the Mission Agenda and the Mission Anti-Displacement Organization, Single Resident Occupant (SRO) Families Unite, Senior Action Network, Chinatown Community Development Center, the local chapter of the Service Employees International Union (SEIU), UNITE HERE!, representing hospitality workers who are heavily dependent on transit, the Council of Community Housing Organizations (CCHO), and People Organizing to Win Environmental and Economic Rights (POWER).[17] These organizations rally when the city proposes to increase transit fares or to cut bus service, but they do not articulate a long-term comprehensive mobility vision. Their posture is decidedly reactive rather than proactive and often narrowly focused on public transportation as a social justice issue for specific ethnic or workers' groups. They neither exhibit a pronounced anti-automobile stance nor engage in the broader livability discourse with the same fervor as other progressives.

Within the broad progressive political tent in San Francisco, tensions and contradictions can frustrate progressive power, even when progressives held a majority on the San Francisco Board of Supervisors between 2000 and 2010. For example, many environmentally oriented progressives have embraced the concept of congestion pricing and increasing the cost of parking in the city as a way to underwrite public transit and reduce the attractiveness of driving. While in the long term many transit-dependent workers stand to benefit from an increase in the funding of public transportation, in the short-term low-income workers and households who depend on driving view congestion fees and the pricing of parking as a regressive form of taxation. When debates about the price of parking and about congestion pricing flare up, this class divide is pronounced and complicates development of a comprehensive progressive mobility vision.

Many populist-leaning progressives look upon the livability agenda as suspect because it is perceived to be a leading contributor to gentrification and displacement. As more affluent people seek out urban living near good transit, the areas that are primed for livability increase in market value. Evictions and rent escalation then push the working poor (and, in San Francisco, the middle class) out of the region's most transit-accessible, walkable, bikable neighborhoods. To overcome that tension progressives demand government intervention in the real estate market, such as rent control and inclusionary housing laws, but by all accounts these policies are not stemming the tide of displacement in San Francisco.

That livability is accompanied by gentrification is probably one of the most challenging dilemmas for progressives to overcome. On the whole, progressives identify displacement as a fundamental problem that must be resolved. In progressives' ideal world, they might have resolved it long ago. However, the reality in San Francisco, as elsewhere, is that other ideologies, namely, neoliberalism and conservatism, are also shaping the politics of mobility in the city and make it difficult for progressives to resolve some of the internal tensions and schisms noted above.

Neoliberal Mobility

San Francisco may be known as a progressive bastion, but it is also a neoliberal city.[18] It is a major global financial center, and, together with Silicon Valley to the south, was ground zero for the software and dot-com boom of the nineties. In 2012 San Francisco was undergoing a second Internet boom centered on social networking and Internet service companies. The city is an incubator of capitalist enterprise and has a culture that celebrates unfettered individuality as a main ingredient of entrepreneurial wealth generation. It has also seen its share of commercialization and privatization of the landscape, from corporate naming rights of ballparks to charter schools. Like most American cities, San Francisco has capitalist landholders who are cognizant of the role mobility plays in maintaining the "exchange value" of the city, or the financial value of land when bought, sold, or rented.[19] As a result, there is an intense struggle over the commodification of housing, quality of life, and public space, and mobility is at the center of this struggle.

Capitalism has an extraordinary need for mobility, as mobility is part of the critical infrastructure that enables the production and circulation of capital.[20] Roads and transit lines are the primary conduits of urban mobility, but they are also conduits of capital flows and arbiters of exchange value. The objectives of neoliberal mobility are to reduce circulation time, have quicker turnover of commodities, and thus quicker profit accumulation. As the scale of the capitalist economy grows, so does the demand for more mobility. Improving the speed and access of transportation systems becomes synonymous with economic growth and individual advancement. "Better" mobility is measured in terms of, and conflated with, higher speed and greater spatial range.

Capitalism's built-in drive is to create a spaceless world that facilitates the mobility of capital, labor, and information.[21] However, such a position is deeply contradictory because the networks necessary for mobility are fixed in space, and, as the demands of the market change, these fixed infrastructures must be modified or destroyed and replaced.[22] New territorial configurations and a reshuffling of space based on new technology mean that older infrastructure becomes a barrier to new configurations. Thus neoliberals, in the guise of real estate developers, landowners, bankers, financiers, and producers of new mobility, communications, and distribution technologies, are actively engaged in the politics of mobility in order to ensure that the spaces they need are built and then reshuffled or destroyed and replaced under their terms.

As the system of automobility reaches its limits in terms of environmental pollution, congestion, resource unavailability, and practicality for sustained profit, neoliberals have actively sought to steer new mobility investments to shape cities in ways that maintain the exchange value of their property and fixed-capital investments. This is a principal logic of smart growth, which as a development pattern is meant to counter sprawl while preserving capitalist dominance in the production of urban space. For example, the central argument of *Growing Cooler: The Evidence on Urban Development and Climate Change,* a publication of the Urban Land Institute, includes many of the tenets of livability and is presented in a somewhat progressive tone, but it is also a neoliberal response to the urgency of climate change in that the policies promoted are geared toward preserving neoliberal real estate power.[23] The book's main premise is that for-profit real estate, with the assistance of government policy, can be steered toward livability. This includes major investment in high-speed intercity rail, in urban public transit, in the retrofitting of urban space for walkability and bicycling, and in enabling of dense infill development in formerly low-density areas. But it also emphasizes the use of market-based pricing of roads and parking while reducing public subsidies to automobility, while simultaneously subsidizing new, "clean" engine and designer fuels to nudge automobility away from oil- and carbon-intensive emissions.

In 2008 the thrust of the argument made in *Growing Cooler* was incorporated into SB 375, which, as noted, is known as California's Sustainable Communities and Climate Protection Act. This act was not only the first law in the United States to explicitly link driving and sprawl to global warming but also one of the nation's most comprehensive efforts to promote reurbanization and infill.[24] SB 375 stemmed from two years of debate, was amended fourteen times, and shifted from a more progressive mandate to a largely voluntary, incentive-oriented approach, light on penalties and less robust than many environmentalists had hoped for. This particularly neoliberal slant was born out of compromise in an "impossible coalition" of homebuilders, local government officials concerned about loss of autonomy, and environmentalists willing to make concessions in order to see the legislation adopted.[25] Homebuilders and developers were especially warm to the compromise because it came with special waivers and exemptions from bureaucratically cumbersome environmental review of urban infill projects.

As exhibited by SB 375, neoliberals need government to implement the new mobility armature identified as necessary for the circulation of capital. Yet, contrary to those of progressives, neoliberal discourses argue that mobility should be allowed to develop with the efficacy of the market and not for collective goods and goals separate from the market (in the case of global warming legislation like SB 375, warming threatens economic activity). Government investment in transportation should be targeted at that which will be profitable, not necessarily socially beneficial. Neoliberals promote a mobility system shaped by pricing and markets rather than by regulation and collective action for the public good, consistent with the broader agenda of the privatization of space and market-based pricing of public access to space. This includes consideration of privatizing public transport and of privatizing the construction, operations, and maintenance of transportation infrastructure. Moreover, neoliberal mobility pivots on *increased* mobility for the capitalist class, not on limits to mobility.

The mobility regime of neoliberalism can be described as state-backed commodification of mobility for private gain with the imperative of competition over collective solutions. This is manifested in the separation of infrastructure into premium and basic mobility.[26] Premium mobility networks include exclusive urban spaces that are islands of wealth and power connected by electronic express toll lanes and congestion charging zones where one pays a fee to drive into certain parts of cities, new, premium high-speed rail and luxury motor coach bus service, skywalks, and private shopping malls; they encompass such accoutrements as express lanes for airport security and first- and business-class air travel, all connecting the most favored in society through airports, toll roads, high-speed rail, and telecommunications. Neoliberal planning features specific projects centered on these premium mobilities rather than on the city as a whole, including small, special-purpose districts and affluent enclaves or premium network infrastructures.

Progressive transportation and livability advocates, including many backers of bicycling, affordable housing, and transit justice, challenge neoliberal mobility by urging a slowing down of movement through mobility reform, specifically automobility, in a way that privileges other modes and by collectivizing mobility as a whole. These tactics threaten to bluntly devalue the fixed capital spaces of the existing transportation palimpsest in which neoliberalism is vested as well as to thwart future profits in new neoliberal configurations. For neoliberals, private property and private mobility are optimal ways of organizing the built environment, and neoliberals are generally uncomfortable with public ownership of infrastructure and services. Furthermore, some of the more pronounced characteristics of neoliberal mobility include the concept of possessive individualism, a so-called cornucopian discourse about technology and the transportation future, revanchist policies toward urban space and livability, and a strong antiunion stance on debates about financing transportation systems, particularly public transit.

Possessive individualism, favoring individual private ownership over collective ownership, is a core part of the neoliberal ethos and is shared by conservatives.[27] Private consumption within the home takes precedence over public consumption, including private yards, private clubs, and private malls instead of public parks and civic spaces, and, most important, private automobiles over public transport, unless separate, premium-class seating is available in public transport. It includes an intensive political withdrawal from collective forms of action like public transit in favor of personal mobility and secession from the public sphere. The geographer Don Mitchell calls this the "SUV model of citizenship," centered on privatized, unhindered, cocooned movement through public space, whereby people feel they have a right not to be burdened by interaction with anyone or anything they wish to avoid.[28] Possessive individualism stems from the dominant neoliberal frame that personal responsibility is more important than social responsibility toward others. This translates into rigid fiscal responsibility toward the types of government programs that progressives would like to implement and expand.

Neoliberal mobility also includes the celebration of unfettered mobility, and this exhibits a pronounced cornucopian strand.[29] The term *cornucopian* is borrowed from the literature on sustainability and development, wherein there has been an ongoing debate over what the role of technology and government should be in addressing environmental and social justice concerns. While progressives are generally pessimistic regarding the potential of technology to resolve the contradictions and problems of unrestricted mobility, neoliberals believe that technology is able to maintain high levels of mobility. Free markets and technological innovation, they assert, will allow ecological problems that stem from mobility to be resolved. Technological innovation, meanwhile, emanates from the unchaining of individuals from regulation and control by government. The key is to unshackle the restraint imposed by excessive regulation and to let innovation blossom.[30]

Neoliberals are not dismissive of the entire livability agenda promoted by progressives, and in fact, as described in *Growing Cooler* and in California's climate change legislation, have expressed enthusiasm for some of the main tenets of livability. The distinction between neoliberals and progressives is that neoliberal notions of livability are decidedly revanchist, that is, they seek to reclaim the city for business, for the middle and upper classes, and for the functioning of the private market and private property, rather than allow for notions of collective, public, egalitarian livability. To neoliberals, livability is a premium physical arrangement that is connected to a globalized, high-speed transport and communications network. Neoliberal livability includes a commodification of quality of life, including the walkability and high-speed transit accessibility of neighborhoods.[31] Livability is a boutique lifestyle to fulfill urban dreams, and the right to have a walkable environment is also a commodity. Neoliberal livability requires that the neighborhood be made safer and more marketable through the embourgeoisement of wide swaths of the city.[32] Unlike progressive visions of livability, the neoliberal version includes maintaining car ownership and therefore includes convenient, albeit market-priced parking. Despite the desire for a boutique, human-scale, walkable configuration, neoliberal mobility includes one's unfettered ability to cover vast distances very quickly, even if just to travel to another boutique configuration in another global city.

A revanchist livability involves discontinuing local government programs that support the urban underclasses, practicing a kind of benign neglect by defunding social programs, mandating tax cuts, and instituting supply-side economics, and using zoning to edge out the working class and unruly classes, such as the homeless and mentally ill, from the city center. Real estate developers, corporate capital, and entrepreneurially minded politicians desire to shape the city through "accumulation by dispossession," the process of displacement through gentrification.[33] Valuable urban land is captured from low-income people who have lived there for years through proliferation of market-rate housing, upgrading of the built environment, and increasing of adjacent land values and through the incremental raising of rents and fees and displacing of housing with luxury parking, all the while reducing local tax burdens and developers' impact fees that fund local community-serving programs for the underclasses. Moreover, in San Francisco revanchism is pronounced in the discourse over Muni. Neoliberals think the problem with Muni is unreasonable not just because of labor militancy from the transit operators' union but also because of unruly passengers who are mostly poor and should be discouraged from using the system through fare increases. The transit system needs to be cleaned up in order for it to be more livable and in order for transit-oriented development to maximize profit. Ultimately a two-tiered, that is, a premium and a standard class, transit system is desired.

A central tenet of neoliberalism posits that labor unions obstruct wealth and innovation and overburden taxpayers, especially property owners. This is manifested in debates over the pensions and healthcare costs of municipal workers such as unionized transit workers. Neoliberal strategy toward labor includes municipal fiscal discipline as well as policies that cut municipal social service budgets and push out the poor, raise local fees for specific services (user fees), and scale back urban public services that do not optimize efficiency and profit, for example, transit service like buses for the working poor that are not geared toward commuting or accessing nodes of capital accumulation. A principal objective of neoliberals is to downsize the public sector workforce, such as public school teachers, clerical workers, and unionized staff for city operations.

In San Francisco, Muni's transit operators' union is often vilified in neoliberal discourse as the fundamental problem with Muni's budget and finance (see chapter 7). Neoliberals argue that if Muni is to be an efficient and optimal transit system, then the labor union must be weakened. Meanwhile many neoliberals promote privately operated, lower-wage transit for the exclusive use of tech workers and outsourcing of transit planning, maintenance, and, ultimately, operations.

San Francisco and the wider Bay Area have a strong neoliberal contingent engaged in the politics of mobility. It is dominated by the real estate development class, which is socially liberal and tied to the national liberal Democrat network in U.S. politics, including such figures as former Speaker of the House Nancy Pelosi, Senator Diane Feinstein, former vice president Al Gore, and former president Bill Clinton. While they align with progressives on conventional liberal social issues, such as gay rights and relaxed immigration policies, they diverge on economic issues, on which they side with developers on land use, taxation, and deregulation of development. These "corporate liberals," as many progressives identify them, favor lower taxes and lower impact fees on development and want less regulation on real estate.[34] Among their organizational ranks are the San Francisco Convention and Visitors Bureau, the Golden Gate Restaurant Association, representing the city's major restaurants, the Building Owners and Managers Association, which represents commercial office building owners and managers, and the Committee on Jobs, a collection of forty corporate landowners in downtown San Francisco, including the Gap, Williams–Sonoma, AT&T, Bechtel Corporation, and Charles Schwab. These organizations have waxed and waned in strength but have maintained vocal positions on a variety of mobility issues, including transit funding and hostility toward the transit workers' union, parking policy, and traffic management.

The San Francisco Planning and Urban Research Association (SPUR), made up of architects, planners, real estate consultants, land use attorneys, and many affiliated professionals and academics, is, among neoliberal organizations, the most consistently engaged in the city's politics of mobility. SPUR shares many policy platforms with the national livability movement, including progressive ideas about mobility, and has made the urgency for addressing climate change a central platform, advocating reducing automobility through compact development.[35] Some San Francisco progressives, particularly in transit and bicycle advocacy, ally with SPUR on pricing automobiles and on some transit policies.

Yet, as suggested above, that alliance complicates more comprehensive progressive organizing, as it inadvertently pits populist, working-class progressives against parts of the livability agenda. Moreover, as a neoliberal organization with a progressive tint regarding automobility, SPUR sees San Francisco's identity politics, neighborhood resistance to development, and historic preservation ethos as barriers to providing housing and infill in the city that address regional sprawl and climate change.[36] SPUR also departs from progressive mobility on such issues as public employee unions and how to create affordable housing. Its stance is that union rules are a substantial cause of Muni's fiscal crisis and that some fares should be raised, while it resists progressive policies requiring deeper public subsidy of affordable housing and higher taxes on businesses to support public transit, housing, and social programs. To some extent, SPUR embodies a complex juggling act between progressives and conservatives in San Francisco's politics of mobility. To understand that kind of maneuvering it is necessary to understand San Francisco's conservative politics of mobility.

Conservative Mobility

As a progressive city with a neoliberal hue, San Francisco is far from a bastion of the conservative ideology found in American politics, especially regarding social issues such as gay rights, religion, and immigration policy. Yet there is a pronounced conservative discourse in San Francisco that protests efforts to reallocate street space toward other modes, opposes efforts to densify the city around public transit, and advocates that new development in the city should have abundant and inexpensive parking. Whereas progressives believe government should actively discourage automobility and neoliberals believe the market should dictate mobility patterns, the conservative politics of mobility in San Francisco are to use government to preserve automobile access throughout the city. The conservative discourse balks at neoliberal proposals to price automobility through congestion charging, increased tolls, and increased parking fees.

Fundamentally, in a vein similar to that of neoliberalism, conservative ideology emphasizes individual responsibility over broad social responsibility.[37] Unlike progressives, conservatives do not think about responsibility as relating to broader systems such as the economic structure of society. Instead, they think in terms of direct causation and of each individual being responsible for the consequences of his or her actions. For example, poverty is a result of individual shortcomings caused by personal and moral characteristics, not of structural themes like socioeconomic forces that are beyond an individual's control. Getting to work on time and providing for one's daily needs are not collective concerns but the responsibility of the individual.

Yet conservative discourses reason that economic self-interest is not sufficient to hold society together and thus depart from some aspects of neoliberal ideology. Individual responsibility includes responsibility toward family, religion, and patriotic duty toward country. Such responsibilities can include making sure families are safe from crime via gun laws that allow easy gun ownership, including religion as part of the public education system, passing government zoning laws that restrict certain uses and certain people that threaten conservative values, and advocating for a legal system that ensures conservative religious values are part of public policy. To conservatives, the free market can be very unstable and sometimes requires government intervention. The role of government is to stabilize and enable individual responsibility, not necessarily to be absent from everyday life. Intellectually, conservatives do not unequivocally condemn government programs because some do provide stability.[38]

In the context of these attitudes, conservative ideology and automobility work well together. The individualist character of automobiles is fused with the idea of direct control and personal responsibility. Government holds together the system of automobility through access to cheap fuel and free roads and low taxes on automobility, and it ensures both that taxes on automobility are used to build ample road space and that abundant parking is supplied through local zoning and transportation policies. Government should guarantee and accommodate automobility, not seek to discourage it and make it more expensive. Government-sponsored road building and other explicit policies that encourage motoring reflect an optimal use of government to stabilize conservative social relations centered on automobility. This contradicts contemporary neoliberal thought, which increasingly critiques government subsidy of automobility, in fact, of all modes, and demands that pricing be employed to rationalize road space and urban space.

However, in a nuanced way government-sponsored automobility also undergirds the alignment of conservative views toward personal responsibility with the possessive individualism of neoliberalism. Personal responsibility toward one's family can translate into lack of interest in collectively solving larger-scale problems like congestion, pollution, and the inequality that stems from automobility. The supposed community in which conservative values are synthesized moves inside, secedes to the private spaces of home, churches, and clubs, which exclude the undesired. Everyday interaction is homogenous, church and family comprising the whole extent of ideas about community, instead of a broader multicultural, ethnic, or religiously diverse concept of community. Then, as happens with neoliberal spatial outcomes, private consumption of the home and by the family takes precedence over public consumption, stimulating market demand for private yards and private malls instead of public parks and civic spaces, and, most important, for private automobiles over public transport.

As noted, the SUV model of citizenship centered on privatized, unhindered, cocooned movement through public space allows conservatives to exercise the right not to be burdened through interaction with anyone or anything they wish to avoid. It is "responsible" to move the family away from problems—to secede—and fulfill daily needs atomistically. Although largely absent from San Francisco, throughout parts of the United States, including California, there is an extreme evangelical religious worldview in some populations that translates into a strong antiurban rhetoric about mobility.[39] The religious ethos holds a pessimistic view of human nature, and therefore people, especially strangers, are not to be trusted. In a dense city, where the presence of strangers is more pronounced than in small locales, the possibility of vice is amplified. Automobility enables one to circumvent, if not remove oneself from, the perceived evils of the city.

Spatial secession is not simply religiously motivated but is attached also to a broader conservative ambivalence toward cities, including an antiurban image of the city as a place of vice and immorality.[40] For example, a common argument deployed in San Francisco is that the city's public transit system is dysfunctional and unreliable and that the city streets are unsafe for children to walk or bicycle owing to homeless people and child predators. While these may be true to an extent, the conservative approach, rather than working to systematically fix these problems, emphasizes personal responsibility toward one's family, which results in the necessity of driving in order to circumvent hostile strangers and potentially dangerous spaces.

Conservative discourses about automobility have been empowered, even among low- to moderate-income conservatives, because automobility has been historically inexpensive. That conservatives can secede through driving is engendered by the relatively low out-of-pocket expense of automobility, resulting in a trade-off of distance for other costs.[41] Government must maintain the armature for secession through generous subsidies to automobility. When fuel prices rise, the outcry from many conservative motorists is that the government should intervene to reduce costs. To many this is also a call for government to preserve the car as a means of physically separating oneself from perceived hostile urban spaces.

Beyond fuel prices, the livability agenda is, in many ways, a threat to the relationship between conservative values and automobility. While progressives seek to reduce automobility through the livability agenda and neoliberals seek to price automobility using the same agenda, conservatives deploy the rhetoric of culture war and believe that contesting automobility is a political nonstarter in the United States. Critics of the automobile are lambasted as being out of touch or as a set of exclusive urban elites.[42] For example, an "anti-auto vanguard" of academic elites, environmentalists, and urban advocates are delusional because they think they can actually roll back the influence of cars over cities.[43]

The socially conservative Heritage Foundation has led this national culture war over mobility and specifically against the livability agenda.[44] This unfaltering conservative think tank warns that the livability agenda is an attempt to create federal legislation to control growth that would usurp local control, a key conservative land use policy, and socially engineer individual behavior. Automobility is conceptualized as part of a benign culture centered in gardenlike settings with wide open spaces and expansive views in crime-free, low tax, and fully served environments.[45] Using culture war rhetoric, defenders of automobility make it appear inevitable. Most important, automobility is "essentialized" in conservative political discourse.

To essentialize is to assume that a group of people, institutions, or objects have a universally shared set of attributes as well as certain fixed identities that produce fixed, determined outcomes.[46] Essentializing assumes there are naturally inherent cultural characteristics tied to national and regional geographies. For example, it is assumed that Californian or American identity is inextricably bound with automobility, that California is a car culture, and that the car is natural, inevitable, and embodied in state and national identity. A feedback loop is in motion, whereby politicians carefully avoid using their bully pulpit to critique automobility while prominent research on automobility concludes there is no political will to contest automobility. It is the path of least resistance to conclude simply that Americans have a love affair with automobility—end of discussion.

Essentialism pervades academia and policy making. Many transportation experts, politicians, and pundits who are otherwise sympathetic to livability lament that restrictions on automobility, such as taking away the space of automobiles, are a political dead end in the United States.[47] The conclusion is that the only sustainable transportation policies that are politically feasible in the United States are those that can be achieved not through travel behavior and lifestyle changes that would accompany the reallocating of street space but through technological change. For example, in *Two Billion Cars* Daniel Sperling and Deborah Gordon concede that the best option for addressing global warming and oil depletion is to reduce dependency on automobiles and promote alternatives, but they state that political paralysis and lack of political will are blocking that option at present. Vested interests are too powerful, and there is too much profit in automobility.[48] Sperling and Gordon conclude that "cars are here to stay and that the car is firmly entrenched in our culture and way of life."[49]

Similarly, the transportation historian David Jones promotes "sustainable motorization" because automobility's global rise is an economic inevitability, that people, when given the choice, "vote with their wheels and checkbooks."[50] The logic is that as wealth increases, so does automobility, and as wealth increases globally, so must automobility. The fact that as China grows wealthier some two thousand new cars take to the streets every day in Beijing strongly supports this argument. The obvious essentialist conclusion is that public policy should emphasize cleaner engines and, in the long term, use of hydrogen fuel cells rather than try to stifle the inevitable demand for automobility. The essentialized automobility narrative is hegemonic, projecting automobility as natural, common-sensical, and inevitable. It creates a veil of consensus and severs the automobile from the conditions of its production and consumption, thereby making automobility appear to be nonideological.

Although San Francisco may not occupy a central place in American conservative thought, conservative discourse does shape the city's politics of mobility. With its increased affluence and demographic changes, San Francisco may be turning slightly more conservative, but there has always been a conservative element in the city's politics. Political conservatives on the west side have been known to oppose the pro-growth agenda of business elites in the downtown. In the 1980s conservative politics were part of a broader backlash against the rapid "Manhattanization" of the downtown. Conservatives believed that high rises were subsidized by such public services as emergency response and public transit and yet did not bring in enough tax revenue to pay their way. They feared that homeowners and small businesses would be asked to pay more in property taxes and fees to underwrite growth.

To conservatives, identity politics also emerged in the debate over growth control of the 1970s through the 1990s. Some conservatives felt they were forgotten as the city, including neoliberal business elites, tolerated new ideas and lifestyles such as gay rights and locally based social programs like affirmative action in city employment. While conservatives and progressives shared very little in their identity politics, both political factions opposed the business elite's agenda for land use in the broadest sense during the eighties and nineties. This pushback culminated in the passage of a local growth control measure, Proposition M, in 1986. Proposition M limited the spread of commercial real estate development and high rises but also imposed rigid height limits in most of the city, solidifying them as lower-density, automobile-oriented districts. Broadly, political progressives and conservatives agreed on the specific desire to preserve what they saw as their own distinctive visions of the city, which were being compromised by neoliberal real estate developers and business elites.[51] They subsumed their differences in order to circumvent the power of the business elites that controlled the local political system.

Today, discourses about family values are commonly deployed in debates about mobility in San Francisco in ways that project an essentialization of automobility. For example, a former supervisor representing the Marina and Pacific Heights neighborhoods in 2003–10, in discussing the need for more parking, that automobiles are an "important resource to families" and that as an advocate for families she believed more car parking was needed. Families with children are said to need cars to transport their children and run errands. Similarly, the conservative-leaning civic organization Coalition for San Francisco Neighborhoods states that "families with children cannot function without a car."[52]

The relationship between families with children and automobility is perhaps one of the most emotionally charged dimensions of San Francisco's politics of mobility and is not simply a conservative mantra. Political thought is complex, and people cross over depending on the issue or the stage of life they are in.[53] Self-identified progressives frequently insist that once children enter the scene, an automobile becomes a necessity. A major factor is the school system, which has a ranked-choice lottery that does not guarantee parents can send their children to nearby schools; at the same time, some progressives seek to avoid poorly performing neighborhood schools and opt to send their children to schools that are further away. This leads to a difficult conflict for progressives with children, who support reducing automobility but also seek convenient transport for their children.

There are, nevertheless, important nuances between the progressive and the conservative outlooks. Progressives remain committed to transforming the city to make it possible to live without a car. In the immediate term this may not be easy to do, but the vision includes creating safe spaces for bicycling and a more family-oriented public transit system. It also includes slowing cars down through traffic-calming measures and the reconfiguring of street space. Generally, progressives who drive tend to support such policies even if it means some inconvenience to their immediate mobility. Progressives are willing to slow down.

For conservatives, however, the politics are not susceptible to reform. The conservative emphasis on personal responsibility toward one's family results in a minimal level of civic and social responsibility toward public space and notions of community.[54] Revamping public transit and densifying around transit are anathema to the conservative goal of spatial secession. Slowing down automobile traffic is inconvenient and to be avoided except on lightly traveled neighborhood streets. Adding bicycle lanes instead of car lanes or parking is also to be avoided when it affects higher-speed automobile movement. The physical manifestation of this is the need for a built environment of roads and parking garages. On the whole, conservatives do not want cars to slow down, except perhaps on their own neighborhood street.

Some among San Francisco's small business merchant class also deploy a somewhat conservative rhetoric about mobility. Many small business owners in neighborhood commercial districts are vocal proponents of public policies increasing the availability of inexpensive, easily accessible off-street parking. Merchant organizations such as the Council of District Merchants, which claims to represent twenty business associations in San Francisco, argue that small business must have unfettered automobile access to survive.[55] They, too, employ a discourse that essentializes automobility. Even merchants in gay neighborhoods like the Castro, far removed from conventional American conservative political thought, nevertheless evoke conservative rhetoric when arguing that more parking is needed and that their customers are forced to drive.[56]

What's more, since the 1990s a new Chinese American property-owning class has asserted itself in city politics, a faction that holds a low-tax, less-government position and has mounted challenges to the progressive vision of restricting automobility.[57] Like that of traditional white conservatives, the Chinese-American politics of mobility often upholds rigid cultural arguments such as the contention that automobility is American or Californian, considers automobile usage a natural right, and insists that government require abundant space for automobility throughout the city in order to accommodate people's love affair and need for automobiles. This cohort was instrumental in shaping the outcome of San Francisco's debate over removing the Central Freeway in the 1990s (see chapter 3).

Ideology and Mobility

It is sometimes difficult to pin someone down on their ideology vis-à-vis the politics of mobility. For example, in San Francisco many progressives own cars and get impatient when a bicyclist appears in the roadway in their path. Still other progressive motorists insist they must have a car to transport their children, and they simply will not take transit or bicycle because of distance and time constraints or safety concerns. They may drive perceived cleaner cars, but they drive nonetheless and have an expectation that the infrastructure and built environment of automobility are in place for their convenience. While these progressives may share the broad political project of an activist government, they may be unaware they are expressing a conservative or neoliberal politics of mobility.

The presence of ideology, although people may not be aware of it, means that ideology may not always be exerted through visible force but through the willing acquiescence of people in accepting their status via their endorsement of cultural, social, and political practices and institutions. As I stressed at the beginning of the chapter, automobility is so ubiquitous and universal in San Francisco and the United States that it seems as if the act of driving has no meaningful ideological dimension. Automobility seems to be not historically contingent but inevitable: it is essentialized. Yet, as I intend to show in the remainder of this book, automobility is not inevitable, and San Francisco is a dramatic canvas by which to analyze how automobility has been challenged.

CHAPTER TWO

San Francisco's Mobility Stalemate

A Historical Geography

Traversing san francisco's sunset district on the west side of the city is 19th Avenue, a mundane six-lane arterial roadway. To the south, it is the gateway to the regional freeway system in suburban San Mateo County. To the north, 19th Avenue enters Golden Gate Park and becomes Crossover Drive and then Park Presidio Boulevard before merging onto the Golden Gate Bridge and suburban Marin County. The avenue is designated as Highway 1, and the California State Department of Transportation (Caltrans), owns and operates it as a regional highway. About eighty-five thousand vehicles a day use the road, passing through unassuming middle-class neighborhoods, yet since Caltrans views it as a regional highway it considers maximum throughput and speed a priority.[1] This makes 19th Avenue one of the busiest thoroughfares in San Francisco, but it is also sometimes pejoratively lamented as a car sewer.

Three Muni bus lines also ply 19th Avenue, carrying up to fourteen thousand passengers daily, and the Muni Metro M light-rail line merges with the southern segment of the roadway. Thousands of transit passengers use these lines to access San Francisco State University (SFSU) in the southwestern sector of the city, and other transit lines pass across the corridor, adding significant pedestrian activity at key intersections. A few relatively walkable neighborhood commercial streets, which could qualify as livable, run perpendicular to and intersect the roadway, with upward of eighty thousand pedestrian trips in the corridor daily. Despite functioning as a regional highway, in reality the roadway is also an urban street, with parallel-parked cars in front of residences with no setback from the street. With all of that, the performance of the road is dismal.

Muni's on-time rate in the corridor is poor, as buses are slowed in mixed traffic. Bus passengers line up on narrow, dehumanizing sidewalks and in the driveways of gasoline stations, and they scramble around cars parked with two wheels on the sidewalk (local residents park their cars on sidewalks to avoid getting sideswiped by the traffic). The situation is no better for frustrated motorists navigating the route. Automobiles and trucks crawl slowly through signalized intersections but then speed up to thirty-five, forty, and fifty miles per hour midblock, only to come to a halt at the end of the next block.[2] Many vehicles do not stop, instead accelerating through yellow and red lights. During peak periods some intersections are routinely blocked, tying up cross traffic and transit lines and making it more dangerous for pedestrians as they avoid cars blocking the crosswalks. Pedestrian fatalities and injuries are notorious, mainly owing to speeding, red-light running, and careless turning. Most bicyclists avoid the road, using parallel side streets instead and entering 19th Avenue only when necessary. Sidewalk cycling, another pedestrian hazard, is common around SFSU, where twenty-five thousand faculty, staff, and students crowd the sidewalks and transit stops while cars whizz by.

Nineteenth Avenue exemplifies a mobility stalemate, whereby everyone using the street has an unpleasant experience, but any improvement to one mode of transport comes at the expense of others. Nearby residents despise the road but have voiced opposition to proposals for tunneling a new express roadway beneath 19th Avenue to remove regional thru traffic from the surface. Building sunken underpasses at major intersections has also been proposed but rejected as too disruptive to local businesses and subsuming the needs of local neighborhoods to regional traffic needs. The City of San Francisco has sought to improve the flow of bus transit by proposing bus bulb-outs (an extension of the bus stop and sidewalk into the parking lane, allowing the bus to stay in the traffic lane and avoiding time-consuming maneuvering back into traffic) and implementing special pedestrian signal-priority at intersections. Caltrans views these steps with skepticism because they come at the expense of automobile throughput and threaten the regional bypass function of the roadway. Some locals

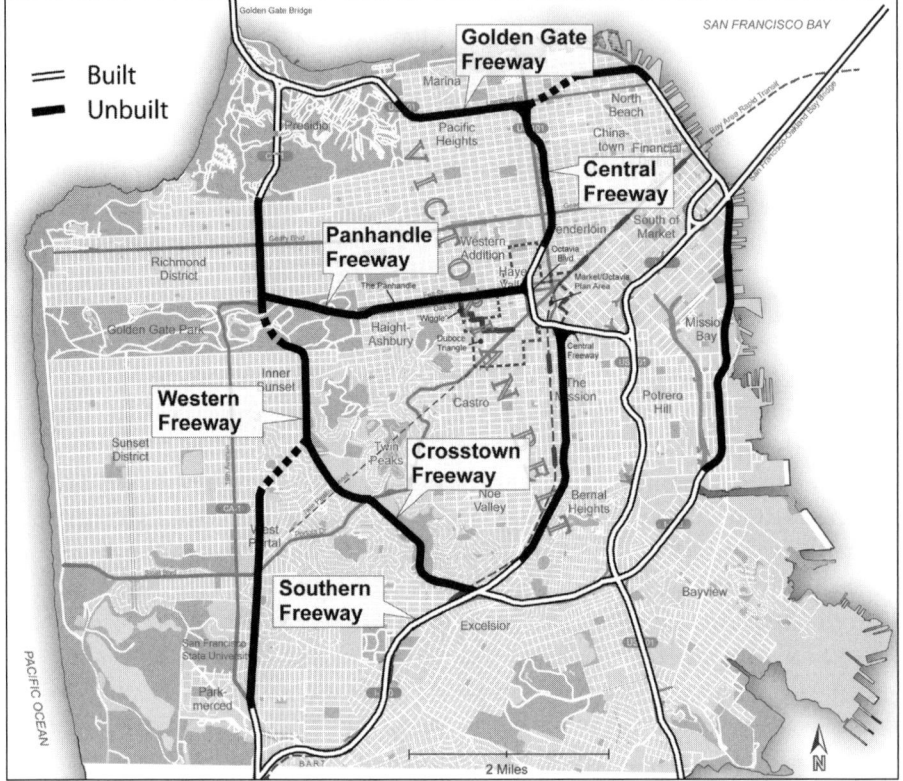

Figure 2. Proposed freeways and the freeway revolt in San Francisco, 1959–66. The map is a hybrid of freeway proposals, drawing from the city's *Trafficways Plan of 1951* and William Lathrop, "San Francisco Freeway Revolt," *Transportation Engineering Journal* (February 1971): 134. Cartography by Michael Webster.

would prefer that 19th Avenue have more left-turn pockets at intersections, but Caltrans objects because this would add delay to oncoming traffic and reduce overall vehicle throughput. Therefore 19th Avenue has few left-turn options. The state has also rejected repeated attempts by the city to increase traffic fines for red-light running and speeding, which the city deems necessary to improve pedestrian safety.

To an outsider, the role of 19th Avenue as both a major regional highway and a local urban street—and the mobility stalemate that derives from that fact—may appear accidental and illogical, the result of poor planning and lack of foresight. Looking at a map of Bay Area highways, one can discern a glaring omission in the freeway system along the route of 19th Avenue (figure 2). Indeed, in the middle of the twentieth century such a regional bypass freeway was proposed, vetted for over a decade, and finally rejected in San Francisco's famous freeway revolt. For better or for worse, the mobility stalemate on 19th Avenue stems in part from the rejection of a western bypass freeway that would have carried regional traffic between I-280 and the Golden Gate Bridge. The contemporary politics of mobility in San Francisco are rooted in this freeway revolt.

The freeway revolt established the city as a bellwether in the national politics of mobility because it was the longest, most expensive, and most comprehensive rejection of freeways to ever occur in the United States.[3] Yet however messy the traffic conundrum has become on streets like 19th Avenue, the freeway revolt resulted in the preservation of a pattern of livability in other parts of San Francisco because dense, walkable, transit-oriented neighborhoods were not torn down to make room for freeways. But the freeway revolt, while important, is only half of the story. In conjunction with the freeway revolt, proposals for rapid transit to San Francisco's west side were also resoundingly rejected, effectively condemning this part of the city to a mobility stalemate and large subsequent increases in automobility. The historical rejection of both freeways and rapid transit contributes to a paradox in that San Francisco has both a solid template for livability and a very high density of automobiles that choke much of the city.

Freeway Revolts

The conventional narrative of American freeway revolts, including San Francisco's, says that after the Second World War there was a national consensus about automobility, and across the nation business elites, labor, politicians, and urban planners organized a political agenda around the idea that automobility was inextricably linked to growth and prosperity.[4] In San Francisco, as elsewhere, business and labor elites established local think tanks and advocacy organizations and actively promoted a vision of freeways as well as high-speed, commuter-oriented rapid transit, airports, bridges, and heavy industry, while making downtown San Francisco a Pacific-rim agglomeration of finance and corporate headquarters.[5] The San Francisco Chamber of Commerce, the San Francisco Planning and Urban Research Association (SPUR), construction trade unions, and the entire political establishment unanimously embraced automobility, centered on a concern that without investment in freeways the city would experience devaluation. There was no politically viable countervision for the city.

This political consensus summoned a Keynesian ideological support for public works and modernist rational planning. Invoking early twentieth-century Progressivism, government could be used to provide a public good while also meeting the needs of capital to stimulate economic activity, but the ultimate goal was wealth generation, not the broader ambitions of contemporary progressives.[6] Keynesianism as an ideology departs from today's neoliberal mobility vision, which has less faith in central planning and public ownership, but the goals of the two philosophies were similar: to use the state to accumulate wealth. Like that of today's neoliberal ethos, the goal of Keynesian capitalist ideology was to optimize mobility, accommodate high-speed transport, and expand the spatial range of capitalist land development. The means of achieving this goal was to establish and then control the planning functions of city, regional, and state government.

Enjoying a local political consensus around freeways, San Francisco and the California Division of Highways entered the honeymoon years of the late 1940s and early 1950s.[7] The state raised gasoline taxes and dedicated a portion of the new tax revenue to urban freeway building, creating the nation's most far-reaching commitment to urban freeways. Next, urban freeway construction accelerated with the passage of the Federal Interstate Highway Act of 1956, which, having been enacted by a 388–19 vote in the U.S. House and unanimous voice vote in the U.S. Senate, symbolized a national political consensus for automobility. No major group organized opposition to urban freeways on a national scale.[8] The act established a new funding ratio by which the federal government would provide 90 percent of the cost of building new urban freeways, and state and local governments were obliged to provide 10 percent in matching funds.

San Francisco's extensive freeway vision was poised to be realized, and local politicians barely considered the costs since they were borne by the state and federal governments. Cooperating with the Division of Highways, city planners in San Francisco eagerly mapped multiple iterations of freeway plans that optimized speeds and expanded the spatial range of automobiles in the city (see figure 2). As was the case throughout the United States, initial segments of urban freeways were built in industrial areas, along railway corridors, and in parts of the city that wielded little political power. When the first segment of the Bayshore Freeway (US Highway 101) was constructed in southeastern San Francisco, it followed former railroad right of way, bifurcated light industrial areas, and flanked lower-income marginal neighborhoods that had little political voice. In the mid-1950s the removal of the first homes in the path of the Bayshore Freeway got scant media attention and little understanding from the public.[9] Once freeway construction approached denser, more established, and politically influential parts of cities, the freeway revolts flared up, in San Francisco and eventually in cities around the nation.

The storyline of urban freeway revolts during the fifties and sixties points to strong grass-roots opposition with politically progressive inclinations. Historical accounts of freeway revolts in Boston, New York City, and Washington, D.C., resonated with this observation.[10] Freeway revolts were spearheaded by localized coalitions of white, upper-class urban professionals, environmentalists, historically established African American neighborhoods and civil rights advocates, historic preservationists, and architects with urban allegiances. The historian William Issel refers to the politics of San Francisco's freeway revolt as a new, environmentally informed liberalism.[11] A lasting impact of the freeway revolts was, in fact, decidedly progressive. In response to freeway revolts and the emerging environmental movement in the late 1960s, the federal government and the California state government democratized transportation planning by creating environmental laws that required extensive analysis, public disclosure, and public participation in highway building. That development made it harder to plan further urban freeways. In an era of white flight, urban strife, and rapid suburbanization, the progressive angle of the freeway revolts also heralded a new discourse about cities as places worth preserving and making more livable. However, while an emergent urban progressive politics and environmentalism mattered to the freeway revolts, San Francisco's freeway revolt was more ideologically nuanced than this conventional narrative, and this has considerable bearing on how San Francisco arrived at today's mobility stalemate.

West Side Story

San Francisco's first successful freeway revolt began when middle-class property owners and small business owners on the west side were informed that closed-door meetings between state highway officials and local officials and engineers had taken place without their knowledge.[12] Those meetings focused on planning a Western Freeway that would act as a regional bypass linking the suburbs of northern San Mateo County to the Golden Gate Bridge in a corridor roughly paralleling today's 19th Avenue.[13] Objecting to the freeway's alignment, west-side neighborhoods organized to protest the freeway, expressing frustration with the culture of the California "highway machine."[14] As influential voting districts and neighborhood organizers deployed innovative direct mailing and house-to-house canvassing techniques, two thousand people came to the first organizational meeting and sixteen hundred to the second, including seven members of the Board of Supervisors. And although there was certainly discussion about preserving the environment and about what kind of city San Francisco should become, there was also a focus on personal property values and subtle identity politics about white, middle-class neighborhoods being destroyed by the freeway. The leadership of the local Catholic Church hinted that the Western Freeway would ruin a good Christian neighborhood.[15]

White, middle-class, Catholic, often unionized conservative politics were strong in many of the city's outer neighborhoods in the postwar era.[16] During the fifties and early sixties such politics made San Francisco a Republican city, with a Republican mayor and a Republican majority on the Board of Supervisors. However, while political conservatives may have aligned with business elites on a fundamental belief in capitalism, they departed from them at the local level over specific development agendas. In San Francisco, Republican-leaning working-class political conservatives had a mildly populist tradition of conflicting with business elites over development and land use policy, for example, an attitude that continues to this day. These politics centered on property rights and property values, an emphasis that arises in several detailed studies of the revolt.[17] For example, Issel hints that property values were the most important factor when the Board of Supervisors, in its resolution of 1963 against freeways, stated that "all future transportation plans [must] be compatible with the protection of *land values,* human values, and the preservation of the city's treasured appearance."[18] The urban historian Seymour Adler describes the colorful, apocalyptic language emanating from small-scale merchants and homeowners characterizing the Sunset as a "first-class" residential neighborhood with "rugged individualists," and homeowners "threatened by big business and freeways."[19] Putting that disposition on full display, politically cogent conservative neighborhood activists fired the first effective and resonant volley in America's urban freeway revolt.

As the deliberation over the alignment of the Western Freeway continued in the late 1950s, more neighborhoods organized throughout San Francisco, and the *San Francisco Chronicle,* publishing editorials couched in terms of neighborhood identity and preserving family housing, began championing a broader, citywide freeway revolt and provided ample space for neighborhood groups to make their case.[20] Neighborhood associations, individual homeowners, and small business owners wrote letters to the editor that were published widely in the *Chronicle.* The initial upwelling of rebellion culminated in December 1959 when seven of the nine proposed freeways were blocked by the Board of Supervisors, the first successful rebuff of urban freeways in the nation.

Not easily discouraged, freeway proponents persisted, and several canceled freeway proposals were resuscitated and remained in the city's highway-building pipeline. The mayor and business elites were resolute in their belief that freeways were necessary for economic growth and competitiveness, and they convened a citizen advisory committee to rethink freeway alignments—but not the concept of freeways themselves.[21] Leaders of the west-side revolt were placed at the head of the committee, and this tactical maneuver exposed the limits of the revolt, as the dissenters by and large looked at freeways not systematically, but on an ad hoc, neighborhood-by-neighborhood basis. For example, west-side neighborhood leaders and merchants urged quick construction of the massive, eight-lane Southern Freeway (now I-280), which gutted parts of the Excelsior, Outer Mission, and Portola, neighborhoods with weak political clout.[22] Adler quips that the Southern Freeway was approved because it did not disrupt any first-class neighborhoods.[23]

Moreover, as west siders turned a blind eye to the Southern Freeway, their housing was largely designed around automobiles. Many homes had garages rather than pedestrian stoops as their façade and were fronted by wide driveways rather than gardens, stoops, or pedestrian-scale amenities. A new automobile-oriented shopping mall had just been built on 19th Avenue, drawing nearby residents with its ample free parking and diverting shoppers from downtown San Francisco. Small neighborhood-serving merchants might have opposed a west-side freeway, but they also advocated more parking near their stores, to be provided by the city.[24] Neighborhood and business activists scoffed at the intrusive nature of a west-side freeway but were otherwise not opposed to automobility. The point is an important one because, their opposition to freeways notwithstanding, west-side neighborhoods remained oriented toward the automobile (see chapter 3), and today the political discourse of the west side insists on high-speed automobile access to other parts of the city even as the city has put into place policies discouraging automobile use.

In that ad hoc, politically fragmented, and somewhat clumsy and confusing manner, the San Francisco freeway revolt lasted until 1966. The last round of the freeway revolt focused on the Panhandle Freeway, which would have traversed an east–west axis from the downtown to Golden Gate Park and then curved northward toward the Golden Gate Bridge. It would have bifurcated the mixed-race, lower-income Victorian neighborhoods of the Western Addition, slated for redevelopment and itself a flashpoint in San Francisco politics in the 1960s. Though encouraged by the successes of the revolt in 1959, the politics of the Panhandle debate were

different. Instead of a conservative discourse, it galvanized a new, environmentally informed liberalism more in line with the narrative described by
Issel and other scholars of the freeway revolts.[25]

Centered in the eclectic Haight-Ashbury neighborhood, progressive
neighborhood and environmental activists sought to reform the local
Democratic Party by fusing it with environmentalism, urging the use
of government to limit the negative impacts of economic growth on the
environment and quality of life. San Francisco's evolving environmental
movement was in the early stages of developing an urban-focused land
use, transportation, open space, and historic preservation agenda—one
that actually did begin to question automobility itself. Opposition to the
Panhandle Freeway expanded as the local AFL-CIO became internally divided and shifted position from support to objection and then back to
support.[26] Next, the International Longshoremen's Union opposed the
freeway, and, last, some of the business elite, notably SPUR, switched
sides in 1966 and became an opponent of the freeway. In 1966 the Board
of Supervisors voted six to five to stop the Panhandle Freeway. At long
last a combination of progressive and conservative political activity ended
San Francisco's freeway revolt, even though five supervisors voted in favor
of the Panhandle Freeway, and at least one attempted to put the freeway
question on the ballot. The politics were far from unanimous.

Nevertheless, as the site of the most far-reaching freeway revolt in the
nation, San Francisco inspired freeway revolts throughout California and
the United States. A California Citizen's Freeway Association formed and
claimed a quarter of a million members.[27] It fought freeways in Monterrey,
Chico, and Santa Barbara. Freeways were also debated in Bay Area suburbs in Marin and San Mateo counties, and in Southern California activists in Beverly Hills, Pasadena, and Watts stopped or truncated proposed
freeways.[28] Participants in the San Francisco freeway revolt were invited to
New Orleans to advise local activists on how to fight the proposed Riverfront Expressway, which would have disrupted the French Quarter.[29] Portland canceled the Mt. Hood Expressway, and activists mobilized against
freeways in Atlanta, Baltimore, Nashville, Miami, and Philadelphia.[30]

Transit Revolts

In view of the canceled freeways it might have seemed obvious that San
Francisco would embrace transit as an alternative. For example, the freeway revolt in Washington, D.C., which paralleled San Francisco's, con-

cluded with the expectation that the Metro subway system would substitute for the missing roadways.[31] Indeed, on the heels of the freeway revolt in San Francisco political leaders and downtown elites proposed rapid transit for the city. The proposals included converting the existing Twin Peaks Tunnel to rapid transit and extending the tunnel further westward to 19th Avenue, in the vicinity of SFSU. Another plan proposed rail rapid transit on Geary Boulevard into the Richmond District. The proposals emphasized placing the downtown within twenty minutes of the far western reaches of the city.[32]

San Francisco's rapid transit lines were to dovetail and complement the regional Bay Area Rapid Transit System (BART), which was to commence construction in the late 1960s and, like the freeways, was to be a signature project of the business elites centered on the downtown.[33] BART, like the freeways, maneuvered the political process through the Keynesian political coalition centered on land development and linked to labor unions, urban renewal, real estate, and regional economic growth. Led by the Bechtel Corporation, then and now one of the largest mega-engineering companies in the world, San Francisco's business elites lobbied for the creation of BART, initiated studies that justified the system, and steered money to the ballot campaign in 1962 to publicly finance it. Given Bechtel's power and influence in California politics, there was little organized opposition to early iterations of BART, and it was supported by key politicians, all four major Bay Area newspapers, most civic groups, and an impressive 67 percent of voters in San Francisco.[34]

Like San Francisco's freeway revolt, the success of the BART referendum in 1962 was unprecedented in the United States. At the time there was no federal funding for public transit and only trivial state funding. There was no popular, citizen-based transit advocacy coalition in the Bay Area in the forties, fifties, or sixties, as there is today. Instead, the business elite hammered down deals to acquire part of the Bay Area's bridge tolls, county sales taxes, and property taxes for BART and pushed further and faster for BART than any other similar effort in the United States at that time.[35] The elite achieved political success by merging its interests with those of modernist planners and by tapping into a broader Bay Area political culture that held an appreciation of rational planning but that was generally lacking a leadership attuned to transit.[36] Meanwhile, in San Francisco the opposition to freeways was accompanied by rhetoric endorsing BART, but BART's alignment was through the downtown, the Mission, and then in the median of the Southern Freeway. BART did not go to the city's west side, and once rapid transit was planned to serve the west side, a transit revolt ensued.[37]

In 1966, the year the freeway revolt ended in San Francisco, a ballot initiative to build subways to the west side failed to get the necessary two-thirds majority votes.[38] There was no single reason for the failure of the rapid transit proposal, and, as in the case of the freeway revolts, an array of ad hoc reasons can be attributed to the shortfall in yes votes. Some neighborhood groups were opposed to the proposal because the plan included restructuring of the bus routes so that the buses fed into the rapid transit trunk lines. Passengers' actual travel times would be higher with the transfer and restructuring of routes. The transit plan of 1966 discontinued almost all electric trolley bus service, replacing it with a diesel bus fleet. Some neighborhood groups opposed the proposal on these grounds because in San Francisco, with its many hills, diesel buses performed especially poorly and were extremely noisy compared to electric buses. The plan also discontinued all remaining streetcar service and replaced surface streetcars with three rapid transit trunk lines. These rapid transit lines would have put the furthest corners of San Francisco within a twenty-minute commute of the downtown, but only for residences proximate to the rail lines. Everyone else would need to access the lines via feeder bus, increasing commuting times for many.

Moreover, the land adjacent to the new rapid transit lines would be coveted by real estate developers, who saw the lines as a potential boon to high-density redevelopment. There was substantial resistance to this potential densification on the west side of the city. In the Richmond District, residents worried that high-rise development would follow rapid transit from downtown along the Geary Street corridor. An antidensity movement was germinating, and rapid transit was characterized by some as part of a scheme to Manhattanize San Francisco. Last, some voters objected to the tax increases necessary to pay off the bonds for the rapid transit scheme. For all of these reasons and perhaps more, the last real attempt at rapid transit in San Francisco failed at the ballot box in 1966. Although the downtown Central Subway was included in the voter-approved sales tax referendums of 1989 and 2003 (see chapter 7), no ballot measure for a west-side subway has been introduced since.

After the defeat of the rapid transit bond in 1966, proponents attempted one last rapid transit expansion, which was also defeated by neighborhood groups on the west side. Briefly, the official BART plan approved by voters in 1962 included a bi-level tunnel running the length of Market Street to the Twin Peaks Tunnel, a major renovation of the tunnel itself, and further tunneling through west-side neighborhoods toward SFSU on 19th Avenue.[39] The tunnel was part of the now-defunct rapid transit plan of 1966, but since it was technically funded by BART it was still financially feasible, and Muni continued to push for the extension of a tunnel southwestward. West-side merchants and homeowners convinced the city to abandon the plan, just as they had convinced it to block the Western Freeway in 1959, mainly because they saw rapid transit as disrupting neighborhood identity and small businesses and eventually drawing high-density development to the area. The city canceled rapid transit to the west side, and BART reallocated the money. The west side of San Francisco, left with no rapid transit, was characterized instead by a generally automobile-centric built environment.

In sum, in the late fifties and early sixties a convergence of political support and funding for freeways and BART laid the foundation for a Keynesian-capitalist vision of mobility in the Bay Area. Powerful business organizations had deep pockets and a commanding influence in the shaping of public policy in favor of this vision. It seemed there were no other possibilities. Yet no sooner had the political consensus for freeways and rapid transit been established than it unraveled. Conservative and progressive political discourses were used to stop much of the freeway vision promoted by business elites, and soon thereafter the rapid transit vision was also scaled back. San Francisco's freeway and transit revolts showed how countervailing but disparate political ideologies contested the demands of business elites, who were the antecedents of today's neoliberal class in San Francisco.

But the revolts were not revolutionary. Progressives were not able to institutionalize a substitute vision of mobility to counterbalance that of the freeway and rapid transit vision promoted by business elites, and conservatives had no alternate vision to offer either. One pundit observed at the time that an unprecedented coalition dissolved after the freeways were beaten back.[40] The political scientist Richard DeLeon suggested that ad hoc neighborhood groups and merchant associations had the power to stop projects but not to build them.[41] The politics of freeways and transit exhausted many citizen activists, while others shifted to the political debate over high-rise buildings and density in residential neighborhoods. The overall movement opposing freeways was not able to remain cohesive around an alternate mobility vision, and there was no consensus about how to shape mobility in San Francisco. Instead there was an ambivalent atmosphere of "disjointed incremental decision making."[42]

The Stalemate in the Streets

The political ambivalence about mobility was coupled with a very real physical stalemate on city streets, where there was a visible increase in traffic while transit got stuck and delayed in that traffic, and pedestrians were forced to navigate around blocked crosswalks and a surge of parked cars jammed onto sidewalks. Between 1950 and 1970 the city's population declined substantially, but automobile and truck registrations increased by 60,000, to 288,000.[43] As the raw number of automobiles increased, so did automobile density. In 1950 there were 4,815 automobiles per square mile.[44] By 1970 there were over 6,000 automobiles per square mile. By comparison, New York City had 5,000 vehicles per square mile and Los Angeles 3,000.[45]

After the freeway and transit revolts there was also a massive increase in automobility in the rest of the Bay Area. Over 2.6 million cars and personal-use trucks were added to the region between 1960 and 1990.[46] Even if the city had stemmed the tide of automobility within its own boarders, which it did not, it was nevertheless overwhelmed by the numbers of new cars proliferating in the Bay Area at large. Every day many of these suburban-based automobiles added to the already high density of automobiles in the city, and the city tried to accommodate them.

By the early 1970s a system of multilane, one-way arterials called one-way couplets radiated from downtown San Francisco and permeated many of the areas adjacent to the downtown. Originally intended to complement the freeways as part of a holistic automobility network, the city's one-way couplets, like 19th Avenue on the west side, eventually came to substitute for freeways. For example, the Fell and Oak Street one-way couplet was a de facto substitute for the Panhandle Freeway, and the Franklin and Gough Street one-way couplet became a substitute for the canceled northern segment of the Central Freeway. The gradual conversions and steady increase in traffic were not accompanied by large-scale removal or eviction; instead, sidewalks were narrowed, and public space usurped one block at a time with new driveways and traffic lanes.

In the eastern part of San Francisco, along the Market Street corridor, one-way couplets smoothed automobile movements between three differently aligned grid patterns that met along Market Street, with Market Street itself diagonal to two of the gridiron patterns (see figure 1). The streets north of Market Street intersect it at a roughly forty-five-degree angle and have no continuity to the south of the Market Street grid or the Mission District street grid. Originally, two-way streets converged at these five-point intersections, slowing car traffic with a welter of confusing flows and turns. Reconfiguring many of these streets to one-way couplets eliminated conflicting left turns, enabling traffic signals to be tweaked for shorter wait times. Vehicular capacity on these streets could increase by upward of 50 percent over the two-way configuration because of fewer turning conflicts and smoother flow.

The price for optimizing automobility with one-way couplets was that previously narrow, human-scaled walkable streets with neighborhood-serving businesses were widened, eviscerating the type of livability promoted today. To accommodate automobility dozens of bus routes east and south of downtown were either detoured, lengthening travel times, or made to sit in long traffic queues. The flow of transit on Market Street itself was secondary to the cross traffic on the one-way couplets, and so surface transit on Market Street was also crippled. Today, planners lament that the confluence of the three incongruent grids creates a disorienting situation in which misshapen buildings are overwhelmed by cars trying to access the regional freeway system via confusing jogs between one-way couplet streets.[47] As the city absorbed more infill residential development in these corridors, the one-way couplets became further divisive flash points in today's politics of mobility (see chapter 3).

While it converted streets, the city also required off-street parking for cars for every new housing unit and virtually every new commercial development. New surface parking obliterated ornate Victorian houses and other stately buildings. For example, several new McDonald's restaurants, including one in the Haight-Ashbury at the entrance to Golden Gate Park and one in the Western Addition on Fillmore Street, were allowed to build large surface parking lots in ostensibly walkable neighborhoods. At one point in the mid-1970s the city proposed leveling many historic buildings in the Mission District to accommodate parking behind stores fronting Mission Street. That proposal was halted after vocal protests, and an isolated bombing of a bank building ended the discussion.[48]

The retrofit of San Francisco for automobiles did not bode well for Muni. After a steady ten-year stabilization and rise in ridership between 1958 and 1968, the system's daily ridership began to plummet in 1969, when Muni fell into a vicious cycle of decline.[49] Muni was consistently plagued with aging buses and streetcars, neglected tracks and overhead catenary, and antiquated storage and maintenance facilities. Bus operations, delayed in traffic, experienced "bunching," whereby busses on five-minute headways arrived twenty minutes late, immediately followed by another bus, leaving many Muni riders disgruntled. Muni's reliability problems have continued

to dog the system up to the present. In the early 1970s the Board of Supervisors established an official transit-first policy meant to improve reliability and efficiency. In response Muni proposed, as part of the city's long-
range plan, a grid of transit-preferential streets with exclusive bus lanes,
signal prioritization, and restrictions on right turns for automobiles. This
physical reallocation of street space was sparingly deployed and remained
mostly incomplete by 2012. In 2006 Muni planners noted that the system's
average speed had declined by 1 percent annually over the previous twenty
years.[50]

San Francisco had a relatively well preserved transit network compared
to many cities, however, and ridership on Muni did not deteriorate to the
dismal levels found in other American cities. Yet as of 2012, despite the
modernization of rail vehicles, it took over forty-one minutes to travel
seven miles on Muni's N-Judah light-rail line between Ocean Beach and
the Embarcadero Station in the downtown, about the same travel time as
in the 1920s, when the line was built. By comparison, it takes thirty-four
minutes to travel twenty-three miles on BART between Embarcadero Station and suburban Walnut Creek in the East Bay. Muni light rail crawls
across the city at roughly ten miles per hour, even with extensive tunnels
on the east side separating it from traffic, while BART travels swiftly from
far-flung suburbs to downtown. Put another way, had rapid transit been
constructed to the west side, it might now take less than twenty minutes
to travel from downtown to Ocean Beach. Instead, many on the west side
opt to drive in the city, further contributing to Muni's slow pace and also
congesting the streets.

In an oft-cited study of San Francisco residents' perceptions of traffic
in the 1970s, Donald Appleyard found that a prevailing attitude of those
surveyed was that automobile traffic was an inevitable part of city life.[51]
Among the main complaints of the residents surveyed were that increased
traffic made it harder to back out of their driveways, that residents had
to frequently wash their cars because of traffic pollution, and that there
were too many on-street parking conflicts.[52] Residents expressed anger
at suburban commuters for driving through their neighborhood but also
said they were considering moving to the suburbs to escape traffic.[53] Many
residents stated that they drove their children to playgrounds because they
thought it was unsafe to walk or bicycle. Although most people were concerned about traffic, they did not support measures to create cul-de-sacs
or to barricade streets or to build neck-down intersections (narrowing
travel lanes with bulb outs or curb extensions) to slow traffic because such
modifications would make their own driving less convenient.[54] Residents

complained about the impact that other people's automobility was having on their own convenience of driving, but those surveyed did not question the concept of automobility itself.[55] Traffic increases were seen as part of urban life, and increasingly urban residents were car drivers too. These outlooks amounted to an essentialization of automobility in San Francisco.

The essentialization of automobility in San Francisco dampened enthusiasm for envisioning or implementing other possibilities and created self-fulfilling prophecies of a city that, while at once considered livable in some respects, today chokes on one of the highest densities of automobiles in the nation and perhaps the world. Streets like 19th Avenue and the system of one-way couplets became tolerable background noise. Muni has remained financially unstable and unreliable for many. With the exception of a very narrow corridor of BART though the Mission and on Market Street, San Francisco was frozen in the transportation network of the 1950s.

CHAPTER 3

The Second Freeway Revolt

Removing the Central Freeway

On October 17, 1989, the magnitude 6.9 Loma Prieta earthquake shook down several Bay Area freeways. The Cypress Freeway, a double-deck, 1960s-era freeway in the working-class neighborhood of West Oakland, collapsed, and forty-two people were killed. A section of the upper deck of the Bay Bridge collapsed onto the lower deck, killing one motorist. In San Francisco the Embarcadero Freeway and sections of I-280 in Mission Bay were damaged, and in Hayes Valley the Central Freeway was shut down.

The loss of life and the destruction were devastating, but to many people in San Francisco the disaster had a silver lining. It was an opportunity to consider removing some of the vestigial freeways that slipped past the freeway revolts of the fifties and sixties. Whereas in Oakland the Cypress Freeway was rebuilt, in San Francisco some damaged segments were removed in what I call the second freeway revolt. The earthquake so badly destabilized the Embarcadero Freeway that it had to be razed quickly. The mayor, a progressive who was open to rethinking the waterfront, expedited the decision to replace the freeway with a surface boulevard. Previous political efforts to remove the Embarcadero Freeway had failed, but the earthquake redefined the possibilities.[1]

It took longer—ten years—to determine the fate of the Central Freeway. After the quake, parts of the freeway that were beyond repair were removed, but other segments reopened. An acrimonious debate included ballot initiatives in 1997, 1998, and 1999 and was resolved with only partial removal and replacement with a short surface boulevard. The decade-long debate about removing the Central Freeway represented a cautiously hopeful juncture in the politics of mobility in San Francisco. It signified a political maturing of progressive transportation advocacy and also a subtle rapprochement with neoliberal real estate and development interests, who shared in promoting reurbanization of housing and voiced some of the principles of livability.

The city's conservatives were less optimistic. They opposed removing the freeway and took the matter to the ballot. Their concern was the loss of easy freeway access to the Fell–Oak and Franklin–Gough one-way couplets which linked to the west and north sides of the city. Caltrans also wanted to rebuild the Central Freeway because, like 19th Avenue on the west side, it was a vital, albeit incomplete, regional link connecting the Bay Area freeway network to the Golden Gate Bridge. But the end result, partial removal, was an incremental nudge toward livability in Hayes Valley, where the freeway once ran overhead. This outcome is far from perfect, however, and traffic remains a major problem.

The debate over the Central Freeway has implications for the national discourse about urban transportation and livability. It offers a glimpse of how progressives were able to redefine the politics of possibilities and begin unshackling the previous paradigm that essentialized automobility. This redefinition of the politics of possibilities comes at an opportune moment. Much of the nation's aging urban freeway system is approaching fifty, sixty, and even seventy years of service. The roadbeds and the vast systems of viaducts and bridges that crisscross cities will have to be retrofitted or rebuilt. The American Society of Engineers warns that one-third of the nation's major roads and freeways are unsound and that 26 percent of bridges are structurally deficient.[2] Much of the nation's urban freeway infrastructure, especially bridges and elevated freeways, must be overhauled, and this will bring disruptions to traffic flows while also being very costly.

Given this gloomy picture, some people are asking, why not just tear down the old freeways and rethink urban transportation?[3] The politics of possibilities for removing freeways is gaining traction. The mayor of Milwaukee replaced a freeway stub with a boulevard similar to the Embarcadero. In New Orleans there is a movement to remove an aging elevated freeway that blighted a once-thriving African American neighborhood. In Seattle there is a debate about removing the crumbling Alaska Way Viaduct on the city's waterfront. In Washington, D.C., and in the Bronx, New York, there is discussion of removing segments of freeways. Elsewhere, including Syracuse, Louisville, and Providence, tunneling or realigning of freeways has been proposed. In San Francisco the remainder of the Central Freeway may be considered for removal, and the northern segments of I-280 are also questionable. In light of these developments, there are lessons to be learned from the Central Freeway debate that can inspire, inform, but also caution the new politics of possibilities for freeway removal.

Hayes Valley and the Central Freeway

The removal of the Central Freeway took place in Hayes Valley, in the center of the city just west of City Hall and one of several Victorian-era neighborhoods in the original alignment of the freeway (figure 3). After the earthquake and firestorm of 1906, which burned down much of San Francisco, Hayes Valley densified because it was largely spared by the fire and had solid housing that could be subdivided. In the 1920s and 1930s Hayes Valley was a choice area for apartment development because of its proximity to downtown. With its streetcars and dense, mixed-use, walkable neighborhoods, the built environment of Hayes Valley mirrored much of what is promoted in livability discourse today.

Because of its central location Hayes Valley was the confluence of major automobile routes through the city. After the earthquake in 1906, Van Ness Avenue (present-day U.S. Highway 101) was reconfigured as a key north–south automobile route that bypassed the west flank of downtown. In the 1930s Van Ness Avenue was extended south of Market Street and penetrated the incongruent grid that now complicates movement through the city. Later, Gough Street, albeit at a different angle, also penetrated the incongruences. Parts of Hayes Valley were transformed into a bypass for cars and a de facto node in the regional highway system. Many new businesses catered to automobiles, including automobile dealerships, service stations, and automobile-oriented retail and commercial establishments. The juxtaposition of dense housing and a thruway for automobiles is a quandary residents and planners have spent decades trying to solve and reflects the paradoxical mobility stalemate described above (see chapter 2).

During the Second World War, African Americans moved into the area, and Hayes Valley experienced white flight and declining maintenance of the housing stock. After the war, planning was biased toward incremental

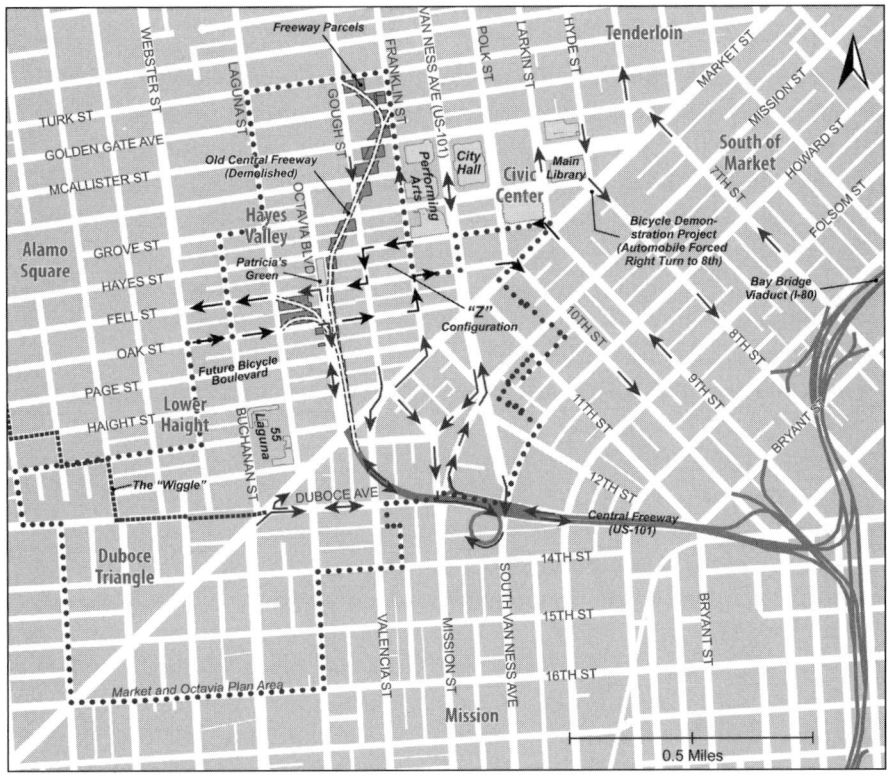

Figure 3. Central Freeway and vicinity, including the Market and Octavia Better Neighborhoods Plan area and primary flows of automobile traffic to and from the freeway. Cartography by Michael Webster.

conversion of the area into a major automobile thruway. By the mid-1950s, streets like Fell, Oak, Franklin, and Gough were converted into major one-way couplets, while city planners considered the neighborhood blighted, pathologically disorganized, and in need of "social surgery."[4] Freeways could do more good than harm, the logic followed, and so the city and state agreed on building the Central Freeway in Hayes Valley, with the corollary network of widened one-way couplets also radiating outward. The alignment of the Central Freeway paralleled Van Ness Avenue, linking the Golden Gate Bridge to the Bay Bridge and to the Bayshore Freeway to the south. Like the Western Freeway (see chapter 2), the Central Freeway was a strategic regional highway link.

In 1959 the Central Freeway was completed from the junction of the Bay Bridge Viaduct and through Hayes Valley north to Turk Street, but the remainder of the route was canceled during the freeway revolts. Hayes Valley was considered marginal and had little voice in the freeway debates, but the neighborhoods to the north, including Pacific Heights and the Marina District, were active in the revolts and objected to the northern extension of the Central Freeway. This meant that freeway traffic was delivered to the surface streets in Hayes Valley. As on 19th Avenue on the west side of the city, this created an intractable traffic mess, making Hayes Valley a less desirable part of the city.

Adding to this, in 1955 traffic engineers established the Hayes–Fell–Oak Z configuration (see figure 3). Briefly, the Z configuration shifts the Fell and Oak Streets one-way couplet north by one block to Hayes Street, utilizing the perpendicular Franklin and Gough one-way couplets. The Z jog effectively aligned the east–west traffic flow to the South of Market grid, enabling large volumes of traffic to cross Market Street on the 9th and 10th Street one-way couplets, which also fed the 101 Freeway to the south. Additionally, the shifting of the couplet northward to Hayes Street enabled elimination of the five-point intersection at Oak Street, Van Ness Avenue, and Market Streets. The Z configuration solidified Hayes Valley as a conduit for cars.

In 1966, as noted earlier, San Francisco's freeway revolt finally ended with the cancellation of the Panhandle Freeway, which would have extended from the Central Freeway westward along the Fell–Oak axis. Touchdown ramps built directly to Fell and Oak Streets became permanent, feeding the freeway to the cross-town one-way couplet. By the late sixties more than 150,000 vehicles per day were traveling through Hayes Valley.[5] The intense traffic, wide one-way streets, and confusing Z jog led to the further decline of Hayes Valley, and by the 1970s the underside of the Central Freeway was notorious for prostitution and drug dealing.

Despite the neighborhood's historic decline, parts of Hayes Valley underwent limited residential revitalization in the 1970s. Gentrification spilled into parts of Hayes Valley from neighborhoods further to the west, such as the Castro and Duboce Triangle. In the 1980s the opening of Davies Symphony Hall stimulated small business and new restaurants along Hayes Street. This gradual revitalization lay the foundation for organized advocacy for freeway removal after the earthquake in 1989. New merchants were particularly fond of the idea of day-lighting Hayes Street, and many residents experienced what it was like to see traffic density plummet, as it did immediately after the earthquake. They did not wish for it to return.

The idea of removing the freeway was complicated by the debate over the Embarcadero Freeway. In 1991 Mayor Art Agnos, a progressive, faced a political backlash from merchant organizations in Chinatown that believed the Embarcadero should have been rebuilt to sustain freeway access to Chinatown.[6] They charged that Agnos acted too hastily and without their input. While many of the merchants lived outside of Chinatown, prior to the earthquake they drove into Chinatown via the ramps from the Embarcadero Freeway, which also fed automobile-oriented tourists into a five-hundred-stall parking garage. The Chinatown backlash slowed early political momentum for removing the Central Freeway. Agnos lost his reelection bid in November 1991, in part owing to political organizing against him from Chinatown. For progressives, the second freeway revolt had political costs.

However, just before Agnos failed in his reelection bid, the segment of the Central Freeway north of Fell Street was dangerously unstable, and engineers concluded it had to be removed and rebuilt later. Agnos and the Board of Supervisors concurred, and it was demolished, thereby day-lighting Hayes Street and attracting more investment. Hayes Street transformed into a hip bohemian shopping and art studio enclave, while the remaining section of the freeway to the south was braced for interim seismic support and kept functioning. By 1992 the volume of traffic using the remaining segment of the Central Freeway dropped from one hundred thousand vehicles per day to eighty thousand.[7]

The post-earthquake traffic was distributed unevenly, and some parts of Hayes Valley were overwhelmed. For example, the newly truncated configuration increased traffic by 70 percent on the Fell and Oak couplet as many cars that once proceeded north to the Franklin and Gough couplet now exited there.[8] There were rumblings of dissent from that section of Hayes Valley. Moreover, everyone in the neighborhood saw the benefit of freeway removal over Hayes Street, and the idea of further removal spread among the local residents. The Board of Supervisors established a citizens' advisory task force to advise the board on what to do about the remaining segments of the freeway, and the San Francisco Planning Department (SFPD) investigated the potential for urban infill on the former freeway parcels north of Hayes Street. Members of the task force called for the remaining freeway to be torn down. Yet by the time the nascent task force made its recommendation, the political pendulum of the city had swung in a more conservative direction, and the recommendation was ignored.

Agnos lost the mayor's race in 1991 to the conservative Frank Jordan, a Republican who ran on a law-and-order platform and who was the former police chief of San Francisco.[9] To Jordan, the Central Freeway was an annoyance and a political third rail. His constituency was on the west side of the city, and so he did not want to see it removed, but his lack of political capital (he was considered dysfunctional and bumbling) meant he could not push the rebuilding of the freeway aggressively. Doing nothing became the temporary default position—a mobility stalemate. The hope was that Caltrans would sidestep local political debate and simply rebuild the freeway.

However, state law limited Caltrans's ability to decide the ultimate fate of the Central Freeway. This was significant because Caltrans, viewing the freeway as a strategic regional roadway, would have likely rebuilt the entire damaged freeway regardless of local objections. Instead, state law obliged Caltrans to cooperate with the city and explore various alternatives to fully rebuilding the freeway. This process required both public input and environmental evaluation of air and noise and spelled out that Caltrans could proceed on the Central Freeway project only if the city approved. In the early 1990s it became apparent that the question of what to do about the Central Freeway would become a prolonged political struggle. The delay allowed more time for Hayes Valley residents and merchants to organize and for progressive transportation ideas to inform the debate.

Two themes characterized progressive organizing around freeway removal in the 1990s. First, the demographics of the area changed as a result of gentrification. Hayes Valley was being transformed by a new stratum of well-educated middle-class residents from outside of the neighborhood who were seeking inexpensive urban housing or were willing to invest some sweat in renovating properties. Many of these new residents were renters, not homeowners, and many of the homeowners were not speculators. As we shall see in subsequent chapters, later waves of gentrification focused more on speculation and commodification of neighborhoods, reflecting a pronounced neoliberal perspective on mobility rather than a progressive one.[10] Meanwhile, accompanying the first wave were small businesses that lined Hayes Street with arts and crafts, clothing, and other shops. Many of the new residents and business owners self-organized to promote removal.

Second, a newly invigorated, citywide progressive mobility discourse, led in part by a vocal bicycle advocacy movement, was gaining traction and by the mid- to late 1990s had achieved political parity with other progressive causes. Most pronounced in the city's Victorian belt, this new progressive discourse about livability, urbanism, and mobility strengthened the arguments of Hayes Valley residents who were seeking freeway removal.

The Hayes Valley neighborhood activists who eventually took down the freeway first began to organize around the prostitution and drug dealing taking place underneath the freeway.[11] Where the freeway crossed over Haight, Page, and Waller Streets two small groups coalesced in early 1994 and began to develop a leadership structure with officers, committees, and regular meetings. Significantly, many of these Hayes Valley residents did not secede from their space in response to the public safety concerns. Instead, the activists were eager to develop solutions that were realistic and believed that simply pushing prostitution and crime out of the neighborhood would not suffice. They held safety outreach events for prostitutes, worked with the police in identifying pimps, and lobbied for community policing. The group advocated that prostitutes receive treatment and reform rather than jail.

The Hayes Valley activists would gradually gain a reputation among city bureaucracies as being constructive and proactive rather than reactive law-and-order or not-in-my-back-yard (NIMBY) activists. This was important over the next decade as the neighborhood confronted major transportation and development issues. The group interacted positively with the local media and got favorable press coverage on how it approached prostitution. It also worked with a broader, citywide group called the Coalition of San Francisco Business and Neighborhood Communities Impacted by Prostitution to ensure that the problem was approached holistically and not simply moved from one neighborhood to another. The Convention and Visitors' Bureau and downtown hotels supported the coalition because it also focused on the Tenderloin, which was adjacent to the downtown hotel district. The coalition provided some beneficial networking between the neighborhood group and larger political forces and put activists in Hayes Valley on the political map, at least on issues of social service and public safety. By 1996 neighborhood crime had been reduced by 85 percent, although a persistent safety problem underneath the freeway accentuated neighbors' support for removal.[12]

While organizing around public safety, Caltrans put forth a plan for a new replacement freeway viaduct from Mission Street to the remaining Fell and Oak Street ramps. In a nod to Hayes Valley, the Board of Supervisors adopted a resolution urging Caltrans to delay the retrofit process until other alternatives were studied. The board then appointed several Hayes Valley residents to a newly reconstituted Central Freeway Citizens' Advisory Task Force (CFCTF), which became the formal platform for shaping local rethinking of the freeway. Members of the CFCTF asked that an option of complete freeway removal be included among the alternatives Caltrans would study. The CFCTF also suggested that if there was to be a rebuilding, a new freeway touchdown ramp should be located somewhere south of Market Street rather than at the Fell and Oak Street couplet.

The CFCTF met frequently in 1995 and 1996 and held several citywide public meetings. It drafted guidelines for how it would approach the freeway question, including many of the tenets of livability, such as promoting the city's transit-first policy and emphasizing walkability and affordable housing. The CFCTF guidelines also had a clause stating that no single neighborhood should absorb the burden of freeway traffic. These guidelines hinted of progressive values, including a strong sense that government should ensure environmental and social justice as part of the public interest.

Hayes Valley's organizing around freeway removal shared in the broader zeitgeist of rethinking mobility in San Francisco, the Bay Area, and nationally. During the mid-1990s congestion and sprawl became leading political issues in the Bay Area.[13] Congestion and sprawl were also national concerns. From Atlanta to Portland and across the nation new urbanist and smart-growth advocates organized to offer an alternative vision of cities that invoked much of the livability discourse.[14] Even in Southern California, long regarded as a region where the car was idolized, citizens bemoaned smog and protested the last segment of I-710 through Pasadena.[15] Neighborhood activists succeeded in halting a short segment of freeway that would have split cohesive neighborhoods east of downtown Los Angeles.

Distrust of highway engineers and the highway lobby was widespread. The Public Broadcasting Service (PBS) aired *Taken for a Ride,* a documentary which contended that General Motors destroyed a once-extensive and viable transit system in a vast conspiracy.[16] Regardless of the accuracy of the film, it resonated strongly among sustainable transport activists, and prominent figures in the livability movement propelled the idea that something sinister had produced the system of automobility. In Hayes Valley, as activists circulated the video among themselves, distrust of the highway lobby spread and reinforced enthusiasm for tearing down freeways.[17]

In suburban San Mateo County, the so-called Devil's Slide highway and tunnel controversy fed into the Central Freeway debate and suggested to Hayes Valley activists that Caltrans bullied communities into accepting freeways.[18] In this case Caltrans was found to be withholding evidence from opponents of an inland freeway bypass, while diluting evidence of the benefits of a tunnel option along the San Mateo County coastline.

Eventually citizen activists put the tunnel option on the ballot and won. The high-profile Devil's Slide controversy reminded many of the long-standing tension between Caltrans engineers and local control of transportation, which in San Francisco went as far back as the first freeway revolts in the 1950s and 1960s.

In San Francisco, Critical Mass bicycle rides challenged not only automobility but also capitalism and compelled many to rethink the role of automobility in cities. Initiated in September 1991, Critical Mass had generally been a relaxed affair until the mid-1990s, when it started to get popular, larger, and more disruptive to automobile traffic.[19] Angry motorists complained to local politicians, and the police began to steer Critical Mass to streets where there would be less of a traffic impact. Bicyclists protested, and a violent upheaval followed in the summer of 1997. The crackdown on Critical Mass got ample media attention, and the bicycle protest movement became conflated with the anti-freeway movement, no doubt because the two groups were not only sympathetic but shared participants. Notably, the controversy over Critical Mass attracted even more cyclists to subsequent rides, with thousands of participants on warm summer evenings in the late 1990s, just as the Central Freeway debate would come to a crescendo (see chapter 5).

In this broader context Hayes Valley activists formed the Association to Simplify Traffic and Abate Congestion (ASTAC). ASTAC tapped into the broader politics of mobility of San Francisco's Victorian Belt and used political connections to lobby for complete or near-complete removal of the Central Freeway north and south of Market Street. ASTAC's members had considerable linkages to progressive advocates outside of the neighborhood, including the Sierra Club, San Francisco Tomorrow, the San Francisco Bicycle Coalition (SFBC), the Harvey Milk Club, the American Institute of Architects and Urban Ecology. The group also had connections and support from merchants in Hayes Valley and other nearby neighborhood organizations.

ASTAC activists proposed to fully remove the entire length of the freeway and suggested not replacing it with anything. They showed their removal proposal to various community groups and organizations around the city and got a largely positive response, implying that this option should at least get a fair hearing. Yet the full-removal proposal was dismissed outright by the consultant hired by Caltrans and the city to study the options. City traffic engineers and the city's consultants literally laughed at the Hayes Valley activists. The city therefore never had the information

or data to adequately consider a full-removal alternative. A fair hearing
on the full-removal alternative did not happen, and this immediately narrowed the politics of possibilities.

While progressive transportation advocates such as ASTAC could not
get everything they wanted—full removal with no replacement surface
boulevard funneling cars through their neighborhood—they were able to
contribute to removing part of the freeway. Their main contribution was
to achieve a political redefinition of the possibilities away from the other
extreme of fully rebuilding the freeway. But the struggle for freeway removal was far from over. Complicating progressive visions was a conservative movement to fully rebuild the freeway.

Conservative Backlash

In 1994 the Northridge earthquake in Los Angeles damaged part of that
city's freeway system. There was little public debate about rebuilding the
freeways, and the damaged I-10 in Santa Monica was quickly rebuilt. In
San Francisco proponents of rebuilding the Central Freeway were awed by
the speed of post-earthquake rebuilding in Los Angeles. Across the bay in
Oakland, the Cypress Freeway, also shaken down by Loma Prieta in 1989,
was under reconstruction by the mid-1990s, despite protests and mixed
reviews from some neighborhood residents. Protests in Oakland did not
stop the rebuilding of the Cypress Freeway, and this fact was not lost on
proponents of rebuilding the Central Freeway. In San Francisco, conservatives were none too thrilled with the city's second freeway revolt. Against
that backdrop, a group of pro-freeway business interests formed a Central
Freeway Coalition in 1996 to counter progressive organizing. The Central
Freeway Coalition was a business group and included all of the automobile dealerships in the vicinity of the Van Ness Auto Row as well as businesses and institutions that considered automobile access by freeway to be
crucial, such as the San Francisco Ballet, hotels on Van Ness Avenue, and
a number of real estate agencies, law firms, restaurants, and local shops.

The Central Freeway Coalition advocated for Caltrans to fully rebuild
the freeway as an elevated, single-deck crossing over Market Street and
connecting the Fell and Oak couplets with new ramps. In an op-ed in the
San Francisco Chronicle the Central Freeway Coalition argued that San
Francisco's sales tax base would decline because auto-oriented costumers
would shop elsewhere and that this in turn would kill the retail viability
of the Van Ness corridor and the downtown.[20] The group claimed that
retail jobs would then be lost and that the performing arts institutions at

the Civic Center would lose patronage. They lobbied the city's political establishment and sent representatives to public hearings on the freeway. The Central Freeway Coalition also allied with the California Academy of Sciences, which was located in Golden Gate Park and was dependent on regional automobile access via the Fell and Oak couplet, as well as with some residents and businesses of the Sunset and Richmond Districts. These west-side interests wanted to preserve automobile access to the freeway via the Fell and Oak one-way couplets. The coalition's reasoning was that cars were natural, necessary for economic activity, and not going away, invoking a conservative essentializing discourse about automobility and the freeway.

Freeway proponents sought to spin the livability discourse to favor the freeway. They reasoned that a rebuilt elevated freeway would keep traffic off local streets, making it safer to walk, and that the elevated structure would minimize disruption to Muni operations on Market Street and Haight Street, two key transit routes. Some also promoted a tunnel variation that had aesthetic appeal, although it was extremely costly compared to an elevated structure. Members of the Central Freeway Coalition wrote letters to the editor of both dailies, the *San Francisco Chronicle* and the *San Francisco Examiner,* accusing Hayes Valley neighborhood activists of being NIMBYs concerned only about property values at the expense of citywide mobility needs and framing progressive transportation advocates as obstructionist.

A second front in the movement to rebuild the freeway came out of a new west-side Chinese American faction with a conservative politics toward automobility. Beginning in the 1980s and through the 1990s, Chinese Americans moved into the west side, using their frugal savings and pooling their incomes to buy homes, and, as they moved, many of these households enthusiastically adopted automobility. Politically active white conservatives courted the new Chinese American property-owning class on the west side as early as 1991.[21] White conservative organizations financed voter registration drives among the Chinese American electorate, and conservative Chinese voters defected from the politically liberal Chinatown establishment that had been in power since the late 1960s.

The new conservative, home-owning and car-driving Chinese electorate voted for the conservative Jordan for mayor in 1991, aiding in the defeat of the progressive Agnos. Chinese American conservatives were pro-growth and antitax, and they favored less government and reductions in social services. Jordan returned the favor of this voting bloc by getting the planning commission, which he appointed, to change the planning code to allow more housing on the west side, albeit not the kind of high-density housing found in eastern parts of the city. The San Francisco Neighbors Association coalesced out of this politics. It promoted new family homes with abundant parking and often characterized by large, unsightly garage doors facing the street and commanding the entire width of the front of the house.

At the time of the Central Freeway debate, there were two ideological factions within the Chinese American voting bloc.[22] There was an established progressive politics centered in Chinatown with ties to the local Democratic Party. These progressives usurped the power of the Six Companies, which had operated as Chinatown's political voice for a century.[23] They linked to federally funded social service programs for assimilating immigrants and were part of a cluster of nonprofits with strong bonds to the civil rights movement. These nonprofits organized lower-income Chinese immigrants and helped them settle in Chinatown as well as in Visitacion Valley and the Excelsior on the south side of the city.

On the other hand, middle-class Chinese American property owners tended to be more conservative and ally with traditional west-side conservative politics, particularly on transportation. Through the San Francisco Neighbors Association, these conservatives were politically organized and sought to usurp power from the progressive Chinatown faction. They used a Cantonese-language radio program as an organizing tool because many of the new Chinese homeowners were not proficient in English. Conservative advocates used the radio forum to agitate and stoke the anger of their audience over the proposal to tear down the Central Freeway. Many of the listeners were personally indebted to Chinese American leaders who had helped them buy property, often at low prices relative to the east side of the city, and so they trusted and deferred to this leadership in local politics.

Since many in the Chinese American community did not speak English fluently, they heard only one side of the debate, and they heard that the American dream included owning a home and a car. The pro-freeway advocates took it a step further, pontificating that Hayes Valley radicals were going to make it impossible for them to use their new automobiles. An angry subset of an ethnic community was now organized to fight freeway removal. The anger spread, leading to the formation of another grassroots organization called the Coalition to Save the Central Freeway, which included white and Chinese American conservatives.[24]

In the meantime Caltrans gave the debate added momentum in 1995 and 1996. Just as progressives pushed harder for removal and conservatives pushed back, Caltrans circulated an internal memorandum stressing that the freeway segment from Mission Street to Fell Street was in danger of imminent collapse.[25] The memo urged Caltrans to immediately undertake a complete rebuilding or retrofitting of the freeway from Mission to Fell, irrespective of the more deliberative planning process then under way. It warned that the upper deck of the structure would collapse in the event of an earthquake and that the probability of another earthquake occurring was high.

ASTAC activists responded that here was evidence that the entire freeway should be promptly removed. Caltrans, using traffic data, instead insisted that the freeway be rebuilt expeditiously in order to avoid a regional "traffic nightmare."[26] If progressive advocates had their way, Caltrans reasoned, queues of vehicles waiting to exit the freeway westbound at the new Mission Street off-ramp would extend onto the mainline freeways of I-80 and US 101 and impede Bay Bridge and Peninsula traffic. Caltrans predicted that all motorists heading to the Central Freeway from the south would experience a thirty-minute delay.[27]

Embellishing the prophecy of a traffic nightmare, the Department of Parking and Traffic (DPT) floated a traffic management proposal to convert some residential streets in Hayes Valley into one-way arterials to detour traffic through the area. The DPT asked Caltrans to open vacant lots adjacent to the freeway for residential parking so on-street parking could be removed to create additional travel lanes. The DPT's position was that if the freeway was removed, city surface streets had to be reconfigured to accommodate the corresponding increase in the amount of traffic, reflecting the logic that created one-way couplets throughout the city in the 1950s and 1960s.

DPT's proposal was beat back by ASTAC. The structurally compromised segment of the Central Freeway, from Mission Street to Fell Street, was shut down on August 26, 1996, as Caltrans peeled off the upper deck. The predicted traffic nightmare did not occur. Instead, traffic volumes actually dropped on some streets in Hayes Valley. The Fell and Oak couplet obviously saw deep reductions in traffic. Since they fed into Golden Gate Park, reductions occurred there too. Caltrans acknowledged that the mainline 101 and I-80 flowed smoothly, not worse, as predicted. By the week after Labor Day, Caltrans reported that 30 percent of the Central Freeway traffic had disappeared.[28]

In a follow-up study of the freeway closure, traffic counts, surveys of motorists, and focus groups of former freeway users revealed that 76 percent of drivers used another ramp to access the regional freeway system, including 19th Avenue.[29] Up to 11 percent of motorists shifted their trip entirely to city surface streets, 2.2 percent of drivers shifted to transit, and 2.8 percent of drivers no longer made the trip previously made on the freeway. Caltrans concluded that a public information campaign alerting drivers of alternatives was a success and that drivers experimented with options and learned new ways to navigate the city by car. The evidence was that a traffic nightmare did not ensue after a segment of urban freeway was removed without a replacement boulevard. This reinforced progressives' arguments for full freeway removal, but that in turn alarmed the proponents of rebuilding, compelling them to act more aggressively.

In March 1997, nine months after closure, pressure to reopen the Fell Street ramp mounted. The California Academy of Sciences urged its members to write to the mayor and the Board of Supervisors to support the rebuilding of the Central Freeway.[30] The academy alleged that its attendance was suffering because the Central Freeway was not yet rebuilt. Merchants in the Upper Haight claimed that their businesses were suffering because the freeway was down. The *San Francisco Chronicle* lamented that Hayes Valley was dictating the terms of the discussion and called for citywide participation in the debate.[31] A new transit advocacy organization, Rescue Muni, established to advocate from a neoliberal, businesslike perspective for improvements to Muni, weighed in, suggesting that Muni was stuck in the traffic of the closed freeway.[32] Yielding under all of that pressure, city officials reopened the Fell Street ramp in April 1997.

Complementing the reopening of part of the freeway, a new environmental impact assessment, required by the Federal Highway Administration and heavily influenced by Caltrans and city traffic engineers, provided more ammunition for proponents of rebuilding the entire freeway.[33] The environmental assessment used conventional traffic engineering techniques that predictably forecast congestion and assumed that automobile use would grow. It warned that freeway removal would cause widespread congestion at intersections throughout the Market and Octavia area and add an average of five minutes' travel time for a motorist previously using the Fell Street ramp. It warned that businesses in Hayes Valley, Japantown (to the north of Hayes Valley on Geary), and in the Haight-Ashbury would decline owing to the removal of the Fell Street ramp and the increased travel times for motorists.[34] It cited self-reported anecdotal evidence from west-side businesses that claimed delays in daily deliveries and stated that the Academy of Sciences and the Exploratorium in the Marina District had a decline in patronage attributable to ramp removal. Last, the report reiterated Caltrans's position that freeway removal would cause a traffic nightmare on the mainline US 101 and I-80.

The environmental impact assessment essentialized automobility, characterizing increased automobility as inevitable. The language and tone of the report clearly advocated the rebuilding of the freeway. The report did not consider that in the future there could be less traffic and more bicycling and transit use. Fundamentally the analysis presumed the continued dominance of automobility and never entertained the idea of transit-first treatments to streets and increased walking or bicycling; it looked solely at the traffic impacts in the immediate area, assuming that all the existing freeway users would converge there, despite contrary evidence that traffic dispersed after the entire freeway was temporarily shut down months before.

Not surprisingly, public hearings on the draft environmental assessment were highly polarized. The emotional nature of the issue led people in the audience to boo and jeer at the hearing on April 23, 1997, held in the Veterans Memorial Building, a large hall in the Civic Center area that accommodated the boisterous audience.[35] A few days after the hearing the Board of Supervisors held a unique Saturday hearing to vet public sentiment about the environmental assessment. Both hearings, though highly charged, were inconclusive. The proponents of rebuilding felt vindicated by the environmental assessment and used it to rally citywide support to quickly rebuild the freeway. Advocates of removal argued that the data were flawed and that the fundamental assumptions in the environmental assessment skewed the results toward rebuilding. They asked for a second opinion, requesting that the Board of Supervisors direct its in-house transportation agency to conduct its own analysis of the alternatives.[36] Supervisor Sue Bierman, a progressive of freeway revolt fame in the sixties, and other board members requested that the city undertake its own review, and the resulting report was skeptical of the conclusions drawn in the environmental impact assessment promoted by freeway proponents.

The second opinion, by the San Francisco County Transportation Authority (SFCTA), suggested that the environmental assessment and other Caltrans reports on traffic were confusing and conflicting.[37] It highlighted that full removal was actually the cheapest of the alternatives analyzed and that removal would distribute traffic in such a way that it was more dispersed and thus equitable because no single neighborhood was absorbing the brunt of automobility. The SFCTA's second opinion also argued that even though more intersections would be congested by removing the freeway, the congestion was really acute only during rush hour while at most other times of the day freeway removal would not cause traffic. The report hinted that Hayes Valley was being sacrificed for rush hour traffic.

The SFCTA warned that regardless of which alternative was chosen there would be cost overruns and a lengthy construction period. The full rebuilding of the freeway would take four to five years and thus be the most disruptive option. As was the case with the temporary shutdown of the freeway in 1996, traffic would have to be rerouted and dispersed throughout the city, but this time for up to five years. Motorists would behave rationally, as they had before, and find detour routes and establish new patterns that exhibit that the freeway was not necessary. Full rebuilding was also the most expensive of the options in overall engineering and construction costs and would have a major funding shortfall because emergency funds set aside after the earthquake in 1989 were depleted and no other funds identified. The SFCTA report did not explicitly select a preferred option, but the comparison of the alternatives was least enthusiastic about rebuilding an elevated freeway to Fell Street.

There were now two sets of evidence in front of the public. One, the environmental impact assessment conducted by the Federal Highway Administration with the collaboration of Caltrans and city traffic engineers stressed that if the freeway to Fell Street were not rebuilt a traffic nightmare would engulf much of the eastern half of the city. The second report, requested by progressives on the Board of Supervisors and conducted by the board-controlled SFCTA, suggested that not rebuilding the freeway would be manageable and that traffic would disperse. Both sides dug in. Progressives were armed with both a report and physical evidence from the temporary shutdown that a traffic nightmare would not occur with removal. Conservative activists had their own evidence and data that warned that continued future growth in automobility would overwhelm the city unless the freeway was rebuilt. This pushed conservative activists into a deeper political commitment to rebuild. In the meantime, neoliberals, the heirs to the Keynesian business elites, etched out a role in the debate as well.

Neoliberals and Freeway Removal

After the earthquake in 1989 part of the decision to tear down the Embarcadero Freeway had a neoliberal hue, that is, using market forces to shape transportation policy in what was ostensibly a privileged space along the waterfront. Special legislation was crafted that required the city to provide an adequate surface street to handle the traffic previously carried by the freeway, today's Embarcadero Boulevard and Promenade. Built into the legislation was a financing scheme stipulating that the land parcels beneath the former freeway be sold at market rates and that the proceeds be used to help finance construction of the boulevard. Real estate speculators and global corporations like the apparel giant the GAP would purchase signature waterfront properties on some of the former freeway parcels, a beautifully landscaped waterfront promenade and boulevard were constructed, and those same parcels, now privatized, doubtless increased even more in value. A few blocks inland, other former freeway parcels were part of this approach, eventually including a handful of luxury high-rise condominium projects.

This financing scheme reflected an emerging neoliberal turn in cities and signaled a retreat from Keynesian policies for public finance. Neoliberalism accompanied a substantial retrenchment in federal funding of urban programs during the 1980s, forcing localities to take on more of the burden for providing local needs like transportation. In California this retrenchment was accentuated by the passage of Proposition 13 in 1978, which froze local property taxes to 1975 values, limited the rate for reassessing property values, and required a two-thirds supermajority vote in a plebiscite for any local special tax increases, such as for transportation. The combination of federal and state defunding of urban infrastructure meant that cities like San Francisco had scarce resources to take on the removal or replacement of a freeway. To compensate for the loss of public finance, the land, some of which was held by the city redevelopment agency, was sold at market rate.

As the Central Freeway was debated in the mid-1990s, the neoliberal financing arrangement gained traction among some progressives, signaling a rapprochement with the city's neoliberal land development class. Progressive advocates recognized that money, not just conservative opposition, stood in the way of freeway removal. Activists in Hayes Valley and in the broader sustainable transportation movement came to cautiously accept the notion that adopting the neoliberal approach of land sale could be the best way to achieve their vision of removal. However, while progressives were overwhelmingly in favor of eliminating the freeway and conservatives adamantly opposed to it, the neoliberal land development class had a disjointed, ambivalent view of the matter, reflecting a broader ambivalence toward automobility.

On the one hand, the Central Freeway provided high-speed, high-volume automobile access to specific locations important to the neoliberal class, such as the Civic Center performing arts venues, which were adorned by the philanthropic wealth of capitalist elites. The Civic Center was a major regional destination, and the elite did not take the bus to the symphony or the opera. Recognizing this, the SFPD characterized the freeway as a significant factor in the array of components supporting the Civic Center area and even suggested that a new or expanded parking facility be built adjacent to newly rebuilt freeway ramps.[38] On the other hand, freeway removal, coupled with developmental opportunities in the former path of the freeway, meant there was much profit to be made on urban infill and densification in a centrally located part of the city that was relatively well served by public transit. The SFPD touted the development potential of Hayes Valley and stated that the eventual rebuilding of the Central Freeway "should be done in such a manner as best meet[s] the needs of adjacent neighborhoods."[39]

The SFPD, as proxy for the development class, was promoting Hayes Valley as an area well suited to dense, transit-oriented housing and invoking the emerging livability discourse. Yet it paradoxically called for doubling the number of parking spaces in the Performing Arts garage adjacent to the arts venues, signaling that generous automobile access to entertainment was still a priority for city planners, and it assumed abundant parking in the new housing developments as well.[40] The consideration of the Central Freeway required neoliberals to weigh these competing outcomes, and the decision to rebuild or remove the freeway was not as clearcut to them as it was to progressives and conservatives. Neoliberal ambiguity offered openings to progressives, exposed fissures in the political landscape, and further agitated the entire public planning process around the freeway.

The election of Willie Brown as mayor in 1995 summoned confusion and contradiction in regard to neoliberal discourses about the Central Freeway. Previously a state senator and major fundraiser in the California Democratic Party, Mayor Brown, who had strong ties to large-scale developers, initially committed to fixing transportation problems in San Francisco, particularly Muni. But he resisted such proposals as imposing new fees and an assessment district on downtown landowners, bowing to neoliberal opposition to taxes. During the row in 1996 over the temporary shutdown of the Central Freeway, Caltrans and pro-freeway advocates convinced Brown to expedite the rebuilding of the freeway rather than permanently shut it down. The new mayor, not wishing to be blamed if freeways collapsed in another earthquake, tacitly approved the proposal to remove the upper deck for safety reasons. Yet, as Caltrans wanted, he simultaneously endorsed the retrofitting of the lower deck in a way that expanded its width from two to four lanes.[41]

The CFCTF and others saw this as a backdoor attempt to achieve full rebuilding without proper public vetting because once the segment from Mission Street to Fell Street was retrofitted, it would be considerably harder to make a case for demolition of the freeway.[42] The chair of the CFCTF, a structural engineer wary of the freeway's durability, wrote an op-ed in the *San Francisco Examiner* stating that the task force unanimously opposed the Caltrans–Brown maneuvering, supported full freeway removal, and argued that the Caltrans scheme was really permanent.[43] Sensing the disappointment of both progressives and some neoliberals, including members of SPUR, Mayor Brown sent a letter to Caltrans asking that the entire Central Freeway be temporarily torn down from Fell to Mission Streets. But the letter also stated that the city's position rested in favor of an eventual, though undefined, replacement structure.[44]

Brown next sent a liaison to meet with ASTAC and subsequently asked Caltrans to reconsider a full-removal alternative in their environmental impact analysis. For advocates of total freeway removal, the politics of possibilities were fluctuating but gaining momentum. Caltrans had tried to use fear to compel a rapid rebuilding, but that strategy backfired, and now, with neoliberal ambivalence being expressed through Mayor Brown, removal was still an option. Vacillating yet again, Brown, fearing political backlash over traffic, agreed to allow Caltrans to tear down the top deck of the Central Freeway while retrofitting the lower deck. At a public hearing on June 5, 1996, advocates for full freeway removal pointed out the manipulative safety and traffic nightmare rhetoric and ridiculed Brown for having wavered indecisively, accusing him of a failure of leadership.[45]

Brown was ridiculed as well by pro-freeway advocates.[46] The Central Freeway Coalition urged that no demolition of the freeway occur until money for rebuilding was identified and an environmental report was conducted. The group's position was that the upper deck should be removed for safety reasons, but that the retrofitting of the lower deck should be done in a permanent manner, not just temporarily, as suggested in the agreement between Brown and Caltrans. They were worried that Brown would have parts of the freeway removed temporarily and then claim there was no money left for rebuilding.

The confusing, ambivalent positions on the freeway became more pronounced when Brown, after dithering multiple times, came to appreciate the idea of a surface boulevard north of Market Street rather than an elevated freeway. Pressed on by progressive planners who wished to remain anonymous, Brown directed the planning department to draw up render-ings of a hypothetical Parisian-style boulevard with new buildings on land that once lay beneath the freeway. Brown had the renderings displayed at his State of the City speech in 1997, and he loosely endorsed the concept. The development potential of the former freeway parcels had convinced the mayor that there was an economic benefit to freeway removal, and this suggested neoliberal compromise with an otherwise progressive idea.

The city next recruited the former director of the SFPD Allan Jacobs and his partner, Elizabeth MacDonald, who had researched boulevards in other cities, notably Paris and Barcelona.[47] The pair proposed a boulevard with six lanes, two of which were side lanes with on-street parking. The four inner lanes were divided by landscaped medians and separated from the outer parking lanes by more landscaped medians. Two wide side-walks rounded out the edges of the boulevard plan. With Mayor Brown's approval, a political consensus was emerging between progressives and neoliberal land developers that the freeway would be torn down north of Market Street. The consensus partly addressed progressives' broader agenda of challenging automobility and promoting livability. To neolib-eral developers, the land underneath the former freeway signaled oppor-tunity for profit.

There was no real, lasting, solidified coalition between progressives and neoliberals so much as the seedlings of an ad hoc agreement that the re-moval of a short segment of freeway benefited both neoliberal developers and progressives. Progressives knew that if they were to achieve freeway removal they had to have political allies beyond their normal bailiwick of environmentalists and sustainable transportation advocates. Therefore, by 1997 ASTAC was promoting freeway removal not simply as a tactic against automobility but also as an economic development tool that would benefit private developers. In sum, this was a tacit settlement between neoliber-als and progressives that shunted aside the conservative vision of a full freeway rebuild. The rapprochement would be tested in three rounds of ballot-box planning for the Central Freeway.

Dueling Ballots

In March 1997 the San Francisco Neighbors Association placed one thou-sand pro-freeway signs on major roads throughout the city. The signs proclaimed, "Open Central Freeway" and displayed a telephone number, which, when called, was answered by a service that asked for the caller's name and phone number. That spring and summer the association collected this information and organized a petition drive to put the question of rebuilding the freeway on the ballot. Joined by the Sunset Merchants Group, made up of white business owners, the association gathered over twenty-eight thousand signatures and qualified Proposition H to be on the ballot in November. The question was simple: "Shall the City authorize Caltrans to rebuild portions of the Central Freeway, and shall the City end the ban on construction of new above-ground Freeway ramps north of Fell Street?"[48]

The Yes on Prop H campaign was run by the Committee to Save the Central Freeway, and paid arguments in favor of the proposition included a range of conservative-leaning political organizations such as merchants' groups, the Coalition for San Francisco Neighborhoods, a conservative umbrella neighborhood organization, the Republican Party, building and construction trades unions, the association of realtors, and an array of local politicians with conservative positions vis-à-vis automobility. Freeway proponents used data from the environmental impact assessment of 1996 to argue that rebuilding the freeway was "safest for pedestrians and bicyclists," would be "least disruptive to public transportation," and would "end eight years of gridlock."[49] The logic was the same as that deployed decades earlier, that is, elevated freeways would minimize high-speed automobile interaction with surface streets and thereby improve conditions on them. The Prop H camp also noted that Los Angeles rebuilt its earthquake-damaged freeways in one year and that Oakland had already rebuilt the Cypress Freeway.

ASTAC fell into the lead in organizing against Prop H and created a political action committee called the Committee for Sensible Transportation Solutions, No on H. ASTAC built an extensive phone list too, and the organization used a phone tree to lobby against Prop H. A core group of ASTAC members did much of the groundwork and fundraising, soliciting citywide progressives and some neoliberals, including SPUR and the San Francisco Chamber of Commerce. The *San Francisco Chronicle* and the *San Francisco Examiner* recommended a no vote on H, calling the ballot box approach a folly, premature, sloppy, and expensive.[50] Mayor Brown wrote an op-ed with Supervisor Bierman arguing against it.[51] The city's Democratic Party opposed Prop H and put out a "No on H" mailer calling it a quick fix that was costly and unsafe and would lead to gridlock because it would take longer to build and thus prolong traffic conditions. The Alice B. Toklas LGBT Democratic Club, which counted key female politicians among its ranks, mailed a pamphlet calling the Prop H proposal expensive, disruptive, and unsafe. The Committee for Sensible Transportation

Solutions mailed a flier with excerpts from *Chronicle* and *Examiner* editorials opposing Prop H, highlighted that the Chamber of Commerce was opposed to Prop H, and called it a quick fix. The progressive–neoliberal rapprochement was epitomized in a campaign sign that read, "Chamber of Commerce and Sierra Club Agree: No on H, Costly, Unsafe, Gridlock." On the eve of the election it looked like Prop H would be defeated by a loose progressive and neoliberal political consensus.

On November 4, 1997, Prop H passed with 53 percent of voters in favor of rebuilding the Central Freeway. The passage of the proposition shocked not only the anti-freeway advocates and Hayes Valley residents but also the political establishment of the city. But in context it should not have been that surprising. It was an unexciting election year, with little enthusiasm in the political press. Progressives, beyond the sustainable transportation advocates and Hayes Valley organizers, were generally disorganized, and many were not attentive to the implications of Prop H. There was no major attraction on the ballot such as a high-profile mayor's race or national candidacy to draw more progressive voters.

An illustration of the political geography of all four of the freeway ballots, including Prop H in 1997 and the ballots of 1998 and 1999 (see below), is revealing (figure 4). Citywide, voter turnout in 1997 was very low, at 28 percent; in most of the more progressive inner precincts voter turnout ranged from around 20 to 25 percent, while on the west side it ranged above 25 percent to as high as 35 percent in the Sunset and almost 40 percent in the precincts of West of Twin Peaks.[52] These are the most conservative, pro-automobile precincts in the city. Prop H was defeated in the Western Addition, Cole Valley, the Haight-Ashbury, Lower Haight, Downtown, and the Mission, but the turnout was too low in the Victorian Belt to counter the conservative pro-freeway vote on the west side. All of the progressive precincts proximate to the freeway voted no, and immediately adjacent to the freeway the opposition ranged from 60 to 70 percent. These numbers were obviously too small compared to the voter turnout on the west side.

Prop H was about more than rebuilding the Central Freeway. It was the springboard for organizing the new, politically conservative Chinese American and other Asian constituencies that were asserting themselves in San Francisco.[53] By 1998, some 35 percent of the city was Asian, and 18 percent of San Francisco voters were Asian, the majority of that subgroup being Chinese. The most prominent Chinese American political figures, such as Leland Yee on the Board of Supervisors, championed Prop H. Chinese American political activists used this campaign as a launching pad

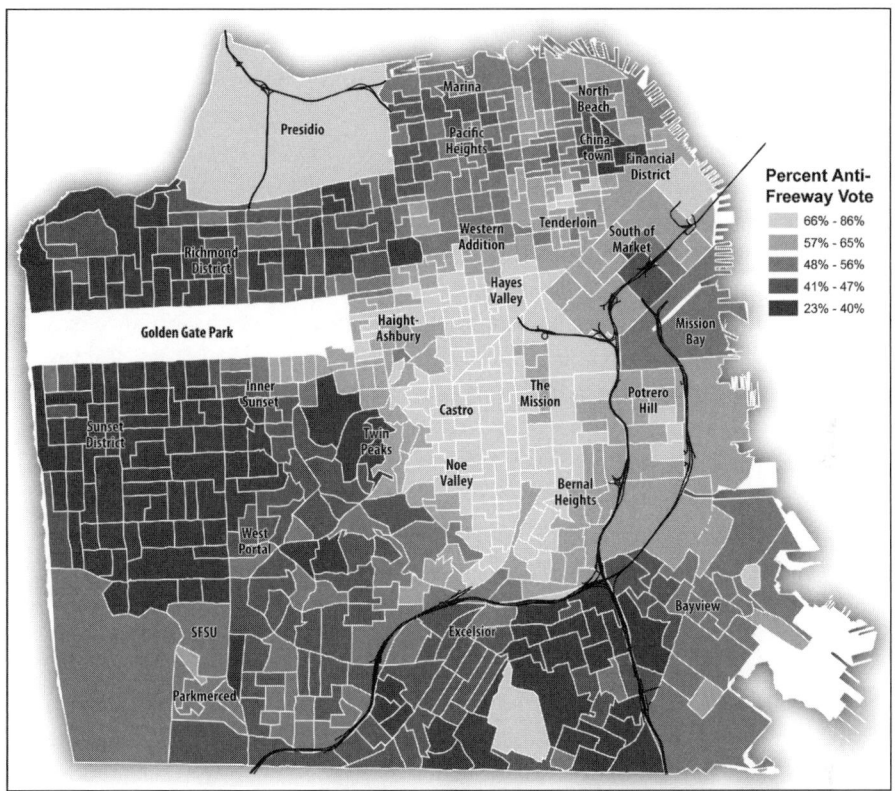

Percent Anti-Freeway Vote

- 66% - 86%
- 57% - 65%
- 48% - 56%
- 41% - 47%
- 23% - 40%

Figure 4. Geography of the Second Freeway Revolt. The map shows the combined votes for the four freeway ballots, using election results data from the San Francisco Department of Elections, precinct data files. Yes or no votes were translated into "pro-freeway" or "anti-freeway," respectively, for all four propositions. The propositions included Proposition H in 1997, Proposition E in 1998, and Propositions I and J in 1999. All votes were joined to their appropriate precinct in a geographic information system, anti-freeway votes were then added, and this figure was divided by the total number of votes to calculate the percentage of anti-freeway votes per precinct. These were then classed for the map as quintiles rounding to the nearest whole number. GIS Analysis and Cartography by Michael Webster.

for possible campaigns for the Board of Supervisors and sought citywide name recognition. They would continue to organize around the freeway question in two subsequent rounds of ballot-box planning because progressives were not ready to concede their goal of removing the freeway.

In early 1998 it looked as if progressive efforts to check the automobile were getting nowhere in San Francisco. Caltrans and freeway proponents moved quickly to get the rebuilding started. The state senator representing the west side quickly acquiesced to the Prop H victors and sought state funds to underwrite the rebuilding.[54] In another defeat for progressives, voters approved the building of a publicly funded parking garage in the middle of Golden Gate Park for the de Young Museum and the California Academy of Sciences. Just as in the previous Prop H vote, the precincts in the progressive Victorian belt opposed the garage and the outer neighborhoods supported it. The Victorian Belt neighborhoods were joined by citywide progressive organizations such as the San Francisco League of Conservation Voters, the San Francisco Bicycle Coalition, and San Francisco Tomorrow. Progressive neighborhood groups like the Haight-Ashbury Neighborhood Council and ASTAC also opposed the garage. But the garage had the widespread support of various groups, including the neoliberal establishment, and it revealed the weakness of the freeway removal coalition. SPUR, the Coalition for San Francisco Neighborhoods, labor unions, and even Congresswoman Nancy Pelosi supported the garage, along with the Republican Party and the Chamber of Commerce. Many of these groups and politicians had either stayed silent on or opposed Prop H, but a neoliberal–progressive alliance on mobility was not solid.

Activists in Hayes Valley were devastated when Prop H passed. A core group met early in 1998 and sought a strategy to confront the rebuilding of the freeway. They considered a second ballot but found it difficult to recruit support so soon after the defeat. Many supporters of removing the freeway felt that the battle was lost. But in view of the low voter turnout and a close election (47 percent voted to oppose the rebuilding) the core group in Hayes Valley felt there was a chance that a second ballot could bring better results. Supervisor Bierman, the veteran of the freeway revolts in the 1960s, encouraged activists not to lose hope and stimulated enthusiasm for a second ballot sponsored by progressives. This ballot would spell out and illustrate the idea of the surface boulevard first introduced by the SFPD and Mayor Brown in early 1997.

The activists received assistance from sympathetic insiders at the SFPD who helped craft the language of a second ballot that promoted the boulevard concept. A core group pushed forward by paying for early campaign materials out of their own pockets, used their phone tree from 1997, and called on allies to circulate petitions. They targeted movie theater lines and other spaces where crowds gathered. Momentum grew in the spring of 1998, and more progressives rejoined the effort.

The reinvigorated anti-freeway campaign formed into San Franciscans for a Better Freeway, and enough signatures were gathered to put the boulevard option on the ballot. Designated as Proposition E, it asked, "Shall the city repeal 1997's Proposition H and authorize Caltrans to replace the Central Freeway with an elevated structure to Market Street and a ground-level boulevard from Market along Octavia Street?"[55] The group redoubled their efforts from the previous year and established committees such as volunteer organizing, outreach and education, media and publicity, and fundraising. Using a strategy of phone banking, they believed that spending money on slick mailers was counterproductive because voters were sick of getting bombarded with that kind of propaganda. The group held house parties instead.

San Franciscans for a Better Freeway tightened their message with three to four simple points and designated a spokesperson to speak with media. Significantly, they focused on progressive precincts where voter turnout in November 1997 had been miserably low. The idea was to make sure that the progressive base voted en masse rather than making an effort to appeal to the entire citywide spectrum of voter ideologies. The group made a visible presence at local events in the Victorian Belt like the Castro Street Fair, Folsom Street Fair, the Latino Summer Fiesta in Mission, and the Jewish Festival. Learning from Prop H, the Prop E campaign was more media savvy and focused on the design of the boulevard, comparing it to Sunset Boulevard and Park Presidio Boulevard on the west side of the city. Comparing the proposed boulevard to the existing west-side boulevards was a tactic meant to suggest that all Hayes Valley was asking for was something the west side already had.

The result was that the anti-freeway campaign had a much broader coalition than in the previous year. It included all citywide environmental groups like the Sierra Club, the San Francisco Democratic Party, progressives on the Board of Supervisors and in the State Assembly, the city's gay rights organizations, including the Harvey Milk Club and the Alice B. Toklas Club, architecture and historic preservation organizations, housing advocates such as the San Francisco Tenants' Union, and, to counter the rising conservative Chinese American vote, the Chinese Progressive Association was recruited into the fold. Rounding out support for Prop E were most of the Victorian Belt neighborhood organizations, including North Beach, Telegraph Hill, and Russian Hill. As noted in the introduction, Lawrence Ferlinghetti also chimed in in favor of Prop E with his sermon on the poetry of the city.

Conversely, the west-side pro-freeway activists were less organized and less politically active leading up to the Prop E campaign, perhaps believing that the people had spoken and no one would take Prop E seriously after the vote in 1997. Prop H had been the first real flexing of conservative Chinese voter clout and was a symbolic victory to show that they could get something done, but further consolidation of this bloc had fallen short.

The west-side conservatives restarted the Save the Central Freeway organization, but they were less aggressive than before. The San Francisco Labor Council, the city's small Republican Party, and the *Richmond Review*
newspaper all opposed Prop E, consistent with the city's political alignment of conservative homeowners and construction trade unions.

Caltrans and the DPT, rather than west-side activists, led the thrust of
the publicity campaign against Prop E, circulating reports and pamphlets
that disputed the merits of a surface boulevard. Caltrans released a "Central Freeway Fact Sheet" in October 1998 to influence absentee voters, who
tended to vote early and more conservatively and who lived on the west
side. Caltrans argued that the costs of the boulevard were underestimat-
ed by its proponents and that the boulevard was poorly engineered and
designed.[56] The rebuilding of the freeway was actually cheaper, claimed
Caltrans, and the boulevard concept would take two years longer to build
than their alternative. Using data from the environmental impact assessment of 1996, Caltrans argued that the surface boulevard would create
more air pollution than the freeway-rebuilding alternative. Last, Caltrans
asserted that if Prop E passed, a new environmental assessment would be
required, adding further delay and cost. The DPT contended that the boulevard proposal would lead to more traffic and more pollution, impede
Muni, make driving riskier and walking and cycling more dangerous. The
chief of DPT openly opposed Prop E during the run-up to the election in
November 1998.[57]

Disputing the local highway lobby, the Board of Supervisors transportation agency, the SFCTA, again presented its version of the facts, lending
strength and legitimacy to the Prop E side and questioning the credibility
of Caltrans. The SFCTA pointed out that Caltrans was misrepresenting
the actual boulevard proposal by estimating the costs for a road that was
25 percent wider than the one Prop E was actually proposing. In reality,
Caltrans was estimating the cost of Prop E based on a very wide street with
traffic islands. Moreover, SFCTA reiterated that the Caltrans alternative
failed to acknowledge that the widening of the elevated freeway would
take the land parcels out of play, thus decreasing available revenue for the
project. The SFCTA disputed the claim that a new environmental assessment would be required for the boulevard alternative, reminding voters
that the assessment in 1996 had included a boulevard alternative in its
analysis.

Prop E won at the ballot box on November 3 by ten thousand votes,
receiving 54 percent of citywide votes in a much higher voter turnout (55
percent) than the previous year. The geography of the vote was almost

identical to the vote on Prop H. Consistent with San Francisco's progressive voting patterns, core Prop E votes were cast in the Victorian Belt neighborhoods and northeastern San Francisco. Bayview-Hunters Point, an African American neighborhood, also supported Prop E.[58] Large margins favoring Prop E were in the Western Addition (71 percent), the Mission (69 percent), the Lower Haight (76 percent), and the Upper Market area (70 percent). The core anti–Prop E areas were the Sunset (63 percent against) and Lake Merced, West of Twin Peaks, Visitacion Valley, Ingleside, Excelsior, Chinatown, Richmond, Sea Cliff, Marina, Pacific Heights, Presidio Heights, and Laurel Heights. Prop E, like Prop H, only in a more pronounced way, reflected the geography of a progressive Victorian Belt surrounded by a conservative C-shaped arc (see figure 4).

In December 1998 the Board of Supervisors, not wanting to lose its momentum, requested that Caltrans demolish the remaining Central Freeway and follow through on the commitment to local control by allowing the city to build the surface boulevard spelled out in Prop E. The board established a Central Freeway Project Office in the Department of Public Works (DPW) to develop and oversee the boulevard. DPW would be the lead agency for engineering and building the boulevard, and the SF-CTA, controlled by the board, not by the mayor, would be the fiscal agent and would develop a traffic management plan. Notably, control over the boulevard was not given to the DPT, whose traffic engineers opposed it. The Central Freeway Citizens' Advisory Committee was established to allow citizens' input into the boulevard project. The committee, appointed by the board, was made up of advocates from Hayes Valley and citywide groups that had supported freeway removal.

At the state level, a newly elected state senator representing the east side of San Francisco successfully passed legislation to formally exempt the boulevard from environmental review should there have been a legal challenge by Caltrans or some other pro-freeway organization.[59] The senator had previously served on the Board of Supervisors and supported freeway removal, and his legislation required that the state hand over the freeway parcels to the city and that the financing of the boulevard come from the sale of the parcels. By early 1999 the city had finally wrested control of the boulevard right of way from Caltrans. But the battle was not over.

As design issues were hammered out and the new citizens' advisory committee began to meet regularly, the pro-freeway faction reconnoitered and circulated petitions for yet another ballot initiative to rebuild the entire freeway. Once again the effort was led by the Chinese American San Francisco Neighbors Association. They warned anew that removing the freeway to south of Market "would cause a total traffic nightmare."[60] And once again they were successful in gathering enough signatures to qualify for the ballot in November. The Neighbors Association put Proposition J on the ballot, which repealed Prop E and required a full rebuilding of the freeway to Fell and Oak Streets. For good measure, the ballot language stated that a two-thirds vote would be needed to repeal Prop J.[61]

The summer saw a flurry of letters to the editor in the local papers and maneuvering by west-side politicians to halt the design and planning process of the boulevard as well as, in July 1999, a vote by the Board of Supervisors to approve the concept plan for the boulevard. Enraged at the momentum building toward freeway removal, local proponents of automobility held a Critical Car Mass starting at City Hall. An angry anti-bike member of the Inner Sunset Merchants Association called upon motorists to rally and clog up Polk Street (see chapter 5). Fewer than twenty-five cars showed up, but one of the people who appeared was Supervisor Yee. As in the Prop H campaign, the politics involved more than the freeway: for conservative Chinese Americans it was an opportunity to use the publicity surrounding the freeway issue as a path to higher office.

Now, progressive anti-freeway activists had a third ballot initiative to contend with. Exhausted from signature gathering, the progressive camp convinced four allies on the Board of Supervisors to place a counterinitiative on the ballot instead. That initiative, Proposition I, expanded the political tent for freeway removal even further, and there was now a fourth ballot! Prop I contained explicit provisions setting up the process for putting housing on the old freeway parcels in addition to reaffirming the boulevard idea. The Chamber of Commerce, frustrated with the antics of the rebuild camp, with ballot-box planning, and aware of the development potential, supported freeway replacement with a boulevard more aggressively than it had previously. Neoliberals and progressive factions revived their loose ad hoc coalition in spite of their deep differences on other transportation issues. Business-friendly, neoliberal-leaning progressives aligned through the San Francisco Environmental Organizing Committee, which formed around defending the boulevard concept and stopping Prop J and included members of SPUR and other development-oriented organizations.

The broader list of supporters of replacing the freeway with a boulevard and housing was impressive. Environmental organizations in support of I and against J included the Sierra Club, the Alliance for Golden Gate Park (which had opposed the garage in the park), the San Francisco Green Party, San Francisco League of Conservation Voters, San Francisco Tomorrow, and Urban Ecology. The more moderate San Francisco Beautiful also supported Prop I, as the boulevard came with landscaping and was, to this organization, an issue of broader aesthetics. Neighborhood organizations supporting the final vote on freeway removal and replacement with the boulevard included Alamo Square, Castro Area Planning Association, Duboce Triangle Neighborhood Association, the Haight-Ashbury Neighborhood Council, Mint Hill Neighborhood (which merged with the Hayes Valley Neighborhood Association [HVNA] shortly thereafter), North Beach Neighbors, North of Panhandle Neighborhood Association, Pacific Heights, Russian Hill, Sunset-Parkside Education and Action Committee, Telegraph Hill Dwellers, and, of course, Hayes Valley. Supporting merchants' organizations included the Haight-Divisadero and Hayes Valley Merchants Associations.

Political clubs that supported removal and replacement included the San Francisco Democratic Party, the Harvey Milk Club, the Richmond and Sunset Democratic Clubs, the Alice B. Toklas Club, and the Western Addition Political Action Coalition. Housing advocates included the Affordable Housing Alliance, the San Francisco Tenants' Union, the San Francisco Tenants' Network, and the Council of Community Housing Organizations. Women's organizations were recruited, including the League of Women Voters, the Democratic Women's Forum, and the San Francisco Organization for Women. Preservation groups included the National Trust for Historic Preservation, San Francisco Heritage Foundation, and a small group called Friends of 1800 Market Street, defending a historic building adjacent to the freeway on Market Street. Sustainable transportation groups supporting Prop I included the SFBC, Rescue Muni, and Walk San Francisco. Local politicians who backed Prop I included former mayor Agnos, State Senator John Burton, Assemblywoman Carole Migden, Supervisors Tom Ammiano, Bierman, Amos Brown, Leslie Katz, and Mark Leno, and the newly elected BART board member Tom Radulovich.

In sum, almost every identifiable progressive organization or influential progressive figure in the city was engaged. Moreover, 1999 was an election year that really mattered in broader progressive politics. Supervisor Ammiano, a stalwart gay rights advocate, was recruited by progressives to run as a write-in candidate against the neoliberal Brown and the conservative Jordan, the two front-runners in what had been an uninspiring mayor's race. Ammiano, representing the Mission District, was a relatively new member of the Board of Supervisors and was well to the left of Brown on housing and development issues.[62] His campaign tapped into the wider progressive movement, which had been in the doldrums but was now responding to the housing and gentrification pressures of the dot-com boom. Ammiano's candidacy also signaled a fusion with a politically dissatisfied younger generation of voters.

The tone of progressive advocacy for freeway removal included a concern about how to keep San Francisco from morphing into a Silicon Valley bedroom community. There was an active anti-gentrification movement, particularly in the Mission District. As housing prices skyrocketed and evictions of renters increased in the city, it was apparent to many progressives that much of the city's new wealth was linked to commuting by car to jobs in Silicon Valley. In extreme cases luxury cars parked in the Mission were targeted by vandals as symbols of gentrification. Tenants' rights and affordable housing advocates helped steer energy to Ammiano's brief campaign, gathering new low-income immigrant voters into the fold in the Tenderloin and South of Market. Ammiano spoke often about his support for removing the freeway, and a vote for Ammiano most likely meant a vote for Prop I.

In November 1999, Prop I won with 54 percent of the vote citywide, and Prop J failed, receiving 47 percent favorable votes. Although Ammiano's bid for mayor was defeated in a close runoff election a month later, San Francisco's second freeway revolt was over.

Freeway Removed

When progressive transportation and neighborhood activists suggested removing the Central Freeway many local officials laughed at them. They were told by Caltrans, local politicians, and the agencies that managed the city's streets that removing the freeway was impossible. The politics of possibilities about transportation futures were narrowly defined, and progressives were bumping up against the ideological supremacy of automobility. Yet activists in Hayes Valley would not accept this narrowly defined set of possibilities. They challenged the assumptions of a traffic nightmare and economic decline if the freeway was removed. They organized and built alliances citywide, engaged in a long political struggle, and remained persistent. Even their persistence did not guarantee victory, as they almost lost the struggle.

The advocates who managed the final campaign for freeway removal acknowledge that their victory was partly serendipitous. The great enthusiasm shown for a charismatic gay candidate for mayor who challenged neoliberals over the future of the city drew thousands of progressives to the polls, and the spirit of the progressives was high, despite their candidate's loss in the runoff for mayor a month later. Ironically, progressives, with neoliberal support, had beaten pro-freeway factions and established a political foundation for future possibilities to contest automobility. In 2000 that organizing momentum led to progressives' seizing a majority on the Board of Supervisors for the first time in San Francisco's history. Over the next decade this enabled a more robust discourse about mobility, including very explicit new challenges to automobility.

But whatever enthusiasm one might feel over these developments should be tempered. Although progressives have promoted freeway removal as part of a broader agenda of reducing car dependency, the necessary substitute investment in public transportation, bicycle infrastructure, and pedestrian improvements has lagged. The areas in the immediate vicinity of the new terminus of the freeway continue to have major traffic problems and associated safety and quality of life concerns. Parts of the neighborhood remain saturated with cars during peak periods. The arterial one-way Fell and Oak couplet and the Franklin and Gough one-way couplet still carry more than 150,000 cars through the neighborhood every day. Residents of the area, despite having lower rates of car ownership compared to other parts of San Francisco, are shouldering the burden of other people's automobility while, paradoxically, the cost of housing remains prohibitively expensive.

Further, the removal of freeways may be consistent with the progressive mobility vision, but it is complicated by the desires of neoliberals to profit from attractive new development opportunities and the broader gentrification and displacement that are occurring. After the freeway was removed, SFPD produced a land use plan called the Market and Octavia Better Neighborhoods Plan (MOBNP) for the area around the freeway.[63] The plan emulates many of the livability principles of dense, compact, mixed-use infill development that is walkable, bicycle friendly, transit oriented, and partly zoned to limit the amount of parking. Yet the plan, coupled with freeway removal, has contributed to an increase in land values in Hayes Valley, turning a once relatively affordable part of the city into an unaffordable one for many.[64]

A tacit and localized progressive–neoliberal détente over land use enables dense new housing development on former freeway parcels, but the neighborhood became inaccessible to many working-class people. This exposes rifts and remains a challenge to progressive organizing. The central location and livability of the neighborhood contribute to its desirability as a place to live, but ironically its proximity to the new rebuilt freeway segment just south of Market Street means there is tremendous pressure to build new housing that accommodates people commuting by car or private corporate commuter bus to Silicon Valley and other suburban job centers. New luxury infill housing is often marketed by realtors for both its walkability and easy access to the freeway, but it is also part of a transformation of many San Francisco neighborhoods into exclusive bedroom communities.[65]

CHAPTER 4

Between Walkability and Freeways

The Politics of Parking in San Francisco

In THE LATE 1990s, as the Central Freeway debate was finally settled, new housing construction accelerated in San Francisco, and the dot-com boom transformed South of Market, the Mission, and parts of Hayes Valley into hip, urbane alternatives to the low-density, homogenous office parks in Silicon Valley.[1] These neighborhoods were near the southbound freeways, and since most software and Internet jobs in Silicon Valley were accessible only by car, there was pressure for new housing with ample off-street parking. Real estate speculators sought investments in the core of the city on formerly industrial and warehousing spaces, on surface parking lots, and eventually on the former freeway parcels that the Central Freeway once spanned.

At the height of this real estate speculation activists in Hayes Valley organized with sustainable transportation advocates and, with the support of planning department staff, confronted the issue of parking. They feared that new housing with excessive off-street parking threatened the livability goals used to rationalize the removal of the freeway. In 1999 they objected to parking in a proposed 8-story, 126-unit upscale condominium building targeted at new tech workers. In calling the condo The Hayes, the developer exploited the neighborhood name for marketing purposes. The proposed building was a few blocks away from the boutique shops and restaurants on Hayes Street, the performing arts district, and the clubs in the Mission, but it was also a very quick drive by car to US 101 and south to Silicon Valley.

Situated as the building was between walkability and the freeway, the developer sought 176 off-street parking spaces for the 126 housing units. Hayes Valley activists called on their freeway-removal allies at SPUR, which was rethinking parking policies, as well as the SFBC to help them encourage the developer to reduce the parking. The activists also objected to an enormous garage entrance that abutted an important bicycle route through the city, which they hoped would one day become a bicycle boulevard with traffic-calming treatments that slow cars and privilege bicycles. They met with the developer, and, with the support of the SFDP, the small, informal group got the developer to voluntarily reduce the parking by 30 spaces.

Still, the HVNA was displeased with the amount of parking and asked the SFPD to further analyze the parking in the proposal.[2] The department argued that the traffic generated by the development would not have a significant impact relative to the existing background traffic volumes, which were already high, and the project was approved in 1999 with more parking than housing.[3] Meanwhile, a nearby funeral home was also the target of redevelopment, this time as transit-oriented affordable housing. The HVNA opposed the demolition of the funeral home because of its concerns about historical preservation and asked that the site instead be redeveloped through adaptive reuse. The city approved a 93-unit affordable housing project, and in spite of its being adjacent to a major transit node the development included a large underground parking garage. HVNA activists and their allies in sustainable transportation organizations were disappointed with these two developments and pushed for the city to reform off-street parking standards for new housing. After a decade of political struggle over the removal of the freeway, activists now embarked on what was to become another decade of struggle over parking. To San Francisco's livability advocates, parking mattered.

The Spaces of Parking

Parking should matter to the national livability movement as well, and parking reform must be a central part of how urban mobility is rethought.

Arguably, no aspect of the politics of mobility is more emotional than parking, and so it is understandable when livability advocates shy away from a confrontational parking debate. Limiting parking can stop or hinder a motorist from reaching destinations, and thus to a motorist a parking space is "one of the most precious and desirable objects of our time."[4]

Individual parking spaces may seem small and inconsequential, but the total space consumed by parking is massive. When access to and egress from parking spaces are included, the typical off-street parking space in North America ranges from 300 to 350 square feet—larger than most offices and bedrooms. In suburban areas, where landscaping is required for parking facilities, the typical amount of space per parking stall can reach 400 to 450 square feet, approaching the floor area of a small studio apartment. Throughout the United States the space allotted for off-street parking is far greater than the floor area of grocery stores and restaurants. Parking for 130 cars amounts to about an acre, and the aggregate of all nonresidential off-street parking is estimated to be equal in area to several New England states.[5]

If the world's population of 7 billion people had the same vehicle ownership rate as the citizens of the United States, there would be 5.8 billion vehicles on the planet.[6] Since the logic of automobility requires that each car have at least one parking space for the home and at least three or more off-street spaces at other destinations, the world would need at least 23.2 billion parking spaces, or 278 million square miles, an area larger than California and Nevada combined, to accommodate that many cars. From an ecological perspective, massive amounts of parking contribute to conversion of arable land to pavement, consume open space and forests, and cause increased flooding as paved areas accentuate stormwater runoff. Parking lots degrade water quality as runoff carries motor oil, grit, and worn tire pieces into local water supplies, and because pavement, being darker than land, absorbs more heat, parking has substantial heat island consequences, heightening the local impacts of global warming.[7]

In *The High Cost of Free Parking*, Donald Shoup outlines how parking policy reflects a vicious cycle that results in high VMT.[8] The derivation of conventional minimum parking requirements in the United States begins with the assumption that mobility means driving everywhere, for everything, all of the time. It is assumed that parking must be provided for every type of land use and function, and as a result zoning laws everywhere in the United States, even in Houston, which is known for its lax zoning laws, have rigid parking requirements, often in excess of what is realistically necessary. This oversupply of parking effectively brings the price of parking for an individual motorist to zero, thus contributing to the lower price of driving and to higher VMT.

Excessive parking requirements spread daily urban activities further apart, make peripheral land more attractive because it is cheaper to build acres of parking there, and hence induce sprawl, making it difficult to walk, bike, and use transit. Daily VMT increases, children cannot walk to school, shopping trips require greater travel distances, and commercial districts emerge as bleak, hostile spaces for pedestrians, cyclists, and transit users. Off-street parking policies and demand for driving are in a self-reinforcing feedback loop that results in low-density, automobile-dependent built environments and high VMT.

In more nuanced ways parking undermines the public realm and the broader goals of livability advocates. For example, the provision of off-street parking requires curb cuts and driveways, which result in a privatization of street space, especially noticeable in dense urban areas and in suburban, transit-oriented developments. The street space at the curb cut, which is public, cannot be used for anything else and thereby limits the possibilities for how urban space is used and who gets to use it. From an environmental perspective, curb cuts can result in the loss of street trees, and they degrade the pedestrian environment. From a populist angle, private off-street parking reduces publicly accessible on-street parking because curb cuts and driveways take away those spaces. Driveways are effectively a privatization of the commons. In San Francisco, with its small lot sizes of one to four housing units, many of the homes with garages have privatized the street space in front of them, though they pay no lease to the city for that space. Requiring parking in a dense, fine-grained urban environment can also ruin the *tout ensemble* of how buildings interact with streets, producing what might be called garagescapes instead of active, welcoming spaces.

Parking requirements can make it very challenging to introduce urban infill or the retrofitting of suburban areas into a walkable, transit-oriented form, and they can impede the development of neighborhood-serving commercial space such as small-scale walk-up shops. The SFPD estimates that about twenty-five hundred small parcels in neighborhood commercial areas can be retrofitted or redeveloped for small businesses, many with housing above.[9] Yet, if a minimum of one parking space per new residential unit is required and parking is required for retail, roughly thirty thousand linear feet of frontage for ground-floor retail would be lost citywide, amounting to fifteen hundred fewer small retail spaces. To put it bluntly, neighborhoods like Ferlinghetti's iconic North Beach, a major tourist draw in San Francisco and considered a gem of urbanism, simply could not be built today because parking policies require each housing unit and business to have parking. If North Beach were built today, up to one-third of the neighborhood's space would have to be devoted to parking.[10]

Parking requirements can reduce the amount of potential housing built at infill sites and also reduce affordability for tenants and buyers. A traditional apartment building with one hundred units would have to be two stories taller than usual if each unit has a parking space, but since San Francisco, like most cities, has strong height and bulk limitations the apartment building would likely have to remain low rise and have as much as 20–25 percent fewer housing units, thus reducing density.[11] Parking reduces the number of permitted units on a site because required parking and housing cannot be squeezed into the same site.

In San Francisco the provision of a parking space adds as much as 20 percent to the cost of each new housing unit, or anywhere from $100,000 to $180,000 depending on whether parking is above or below ground.[12] This means that funds for nonprofit or publicly funded affordable housing have to also be used for parking, and as a result fewer affordable units get constructed. In addition, parking increases the cost of market-rate housing. Units without parking sell for about 10–15 percent less than units with parking. One study of the relationship between parking and housing costs concluded that 24 percent more households (16,600 households) could afford to buy single-family housing in San Francisco if it had no parking, and 20 percent more households (26,800 households) could buy a condominium with no parking.[13] Seen from this approach, parking is part of broader conflicts over gentrification and defining whom the city is for.

Nationally the first zoning ordinances requiring off-street parking for housing developed in the 1930s, and San Francisco formally adopted off-street parking regulations in 1957. From the fifties onward the city mandated one off-street parking space per bedroom in all new housing, until, in 1975, the planning code was amended to provide one parking space per dwelling unit, usually stated as a ratio of 1:1. The 1:1 ratio is required in the vast majority of the city today, and, as noted, neighborhoods like North Beach and, indeed, most of the Victorian Belt could not be built today. Because of the 1:1 requirement, almost all housing built since the 1950s contains parking, but this formula also legalized and encouraged the insertion of parking into structures that originally did not have parking, such as the housing in Victorian Belt (this displaced countless ground-floor housing units, an important part of affordable housing).[14]

By 2010 San Francisco had an estimated 441,000 parking spaces in a city of 47.3 square miles, or 9,323 parking spaces per square mile, a number close to the density of registered cars and trucks in the city.[15] Assuming that each parking space is roughly 180 square feet—a low estimate based on the size of an average curbside space in San Francisco—then parking spaces in San Francisco equal roughly 79.4 million square feet, or 79,400 two-bedroom, 1,000-square-foot apartments. If one uses average U.S. standards of 335 square feet per space, San Francisco's almost 200,000 off-street spaces would equal the square footage of 67,000 two-bedroom apartments. These numbers are not negligible considering that San Francisco has an acute housing shortage and that at least 31,000 housing units should be built by 2014 in order for San Francisco to meet the state-mandated quota of regional housing needs.[16] The spaces of parking become even more mind-boggling considering that the long-range housing needs of the city must accommodate an estimated 90,000 new household units by 2035.[17] The issue has progressive mobility advocates asking, can the city truthfully absorb 90,000 more parking spaces?

Acknowledging the vast spaces and negative impacts of parking will be crucial to urban futures, especially since China and other developing nations are attempting to replicate the automobility found in the United States. The Congress for the New Urbanism, a central organization in the national livability movement, addresses parking reform in the *Smartcode*, a set of planning guidelines meant to encourage mixed-use compact development and minimize sprawl.[18] However, even the *Smartcode* allows parking to dictate land use intensity and density, and Shoup laments that "even at the fountainhead of New Urbanist thinking parking requirements dictate density, and cars rule the city."[19] The code recommends that in the highest-density central city developments each housing unit have one parking space and that office and retail developments have two or three parking spaces per one thousand square feet, respectively.[20] It further recommends more than one parking space per residential unit in mixed-use neighborhoods.

The *Smartcode* encourages less parking than is found in conventional sprawl developments, but in 2000–2010, with progressive advocacy and persistence, San Francisco pushed the envelope. In parts of downtown San Francisco and of the Victorian Belt, including Hayes Valley, the city has made it legal to build housing, offices, and shops without off-street parking. As called for in its transit-first policy, the city is gradually eliminating 1:1 parking minimums while establishing new parking caps (called parking maximums) that actually prohibit 1:1 parking. City planners, nudged by progressive advocates of sustainable mobility as well as by some neoliberal developers, recognize that conventional parking requirements are ultimately incongruent with livability. San Francisco's parking reform movement is yet another way in which the city is a pacesetter for the national livability movement.

The Market and Octavia Plan

In Hayes Valley the stakes over parking policy were obviously high. The neighborhood had twenty-two newly vacated parcels (amounting to seven acres) where the freeway once ran overhead, and further afield there were many more underutilized parcels, including surface parking lots, gasoline service stations, automobile dealerships, and a six-acre former college campus. Neighborhood residents acknowledged that infill development was on the horizon, especially since the city was mandated to sell the freeway parcels in order to pay for the new Octavia Boulevard. Not wishing to repeat the parcel-by-parcel skirmish exhibited in the debate over The Hayes, city planners, activists, and developers considered an areawide, consensus-based land use plan that would define the parameters of development, including heights, bulk, density, and parking.

Thus was born the Market and Octavia Better Neighborhoods Plan (MOBNP), which, as noted in chapter 3, was initiated in 1999 by the SFPD but not formally adopted by the city until 2008. Promoted by SPUR and the developer-funded Housing Action Coalition, the plan combined progressive visions of mobility with neoliberal ambitions for urban redevelopment. The premise of the plan was the restoration of the areas bifurcated by the Central Freeway and the establishment of zoning guidelines (such as heights, urban design, and permitted uses) for the redevelopment of the freeway parcels and the surrounding area. The plan was to retain existing housing and to minimize the traffic that might accompany new growth.

Now officially part of the city zoning code, the MOBNP is groundbreaking because it bluntly challenges automobility. It eliminates some (but not all) sections of the infamous one-way couplets and reduces the vehicular carrying capacity of the Z configuration by reintroducing the pedestrian crosswalks that were eliminated in the 1950s. The plan, coupled with freeway removal, slows the weaving movements of cars threading the Z configuration and heading to and from the regional freeway grid, and it calls for the city to study further removal of the Central Freeway, to Bryant Street, as originally proposed by progressive activists in the mid-1990s. The plan also calls for transforming alleys into pedestrianized green spaces and public plazas. The tenor of the MOBNP is thoroughly aligned with the national livability discourse, and it decidedly promotes the possibilities of car-free living. The plan envisions a place intimately connected to the city as a whole, a place where owning a private automobile is a choice, not a necessity, and the streets are active, friendly civic spaces.[21]

Further, the MOBNP not only replaces formerly automobile-oriented development with dense, urban infill but also seeks to "ensure some continued increment of car-free housing, similar to historic and existing patterns" by limiting the amount of new parking that infill development can provide for new residents and businesses.[22] It is with regard to parking that the MOBNP is truly innovative. With eventual full build-out over a twenty-year planning horizon, when implemented the MOBNP allows roughly six thousand new housing units, many of which must be accompanied by new ground-floor commercial activity.[23] Under the typical guidelines for residential off-street parking found in San Francisco, such housing would be required to have one off-street parking space for each new unit. These parking minimums, as codified in San Francisco's zoning code, mean that six thousand new parking spaces would be constructed under the conventional city zoning code. If the new housing in the MOBNP were built by mainstream national parking standards, more than ten thousand parking spaces would probably have to be constructed.[24]

But the MOBNP dispenses with conventional parking standards and eliminates parking minimums, while a range of maximums reduce the allowable ratios for parking to lower than 1:1. In the areas of the MOBNP closest to the downtown and surrounding the Van Ness Muni Metro Station, the permitted parking maximum is one space for every four residential units (0.25:1). In the mixed-use neighborhood commercial corridors along Market Street and other transit-served streets, the permitted parking maximum is one space per two residential units (0.5:1), and in the remainder of the MOBNP the maximum is one parking space for every three residential units (0.75:1).[25] Additionally, the MOBNP bans curb cuts for driveways on streets with transit service or identified as neighborhood-serving commercial corridors. With few exceptions, developers are prohibited from providing 1:1 parking for new housing as well as parking for new commercial or office development, although they continue in many instances to ask for exceptions.

The MOBNP reflects the core value of progressive advocates of sustainable transportation that government should regulate and limit automobility, in this case through limiting parking. In the early 2000s progressives promoted a vision of the city that privileged housing and public space over abundant parking, and progressives believed that city government should pursue that vision.[26] Progressive activists tapped their political allies on the Board of Supervisors and promoted the adoption of some of the most restrictive parking policies in the nation. Yet, as in the case of freeway removal, it was not easy to eliminate parking minimums and establish tighter caps. There was and still is a vitriolic debate about parking and a political backlash against limiting parking, further complicating San Francisco's politics of mobility. Furthermore, neoliberal ambiguity about parking, like that over the removal of the Central Freeway, lent an air of confusion that prolonged the debate.

Neoliberal Ambiguity about Parking

After two years of public meetings and visioning charrettes, the first draft of the MOBNP was presented in late 2002 and welcomed enthusiastically in Hayes Valley. However, the plan, like all development plans under California law, was required to undergo an environmental review, and this proved to be a lengthy process. In fact, it added almost three years to the deliberations, largely because of traffic impact analysis, which is a formidable challenge for progressive transportation policy (see chapter 5). The prolongation left Hayes Valley in limbo and uncertainty, even as the freeway was finally dismantled in early 2003.

In June 2005 San Francisco was host to a weeklong series of events centering on global environmental awareness and education and culminating in World Environment Day (WED), which is sponsored yearly by the United Nations Environment Program.[27] The purpose of the annual event is to encourage political attention to and instill a sense of social responsibility toward environmental issues, and in 2005 the theme was Green Cities: Plan for the Planet. An array of well-known architects, planners, politicians, and environmental activists converged on the city to discuss and debate the relationship between cities and the environment. Such luminaries as former vice president Al Gore and Governor Arnold Schwarzenegger spoke about global warming and lamented the absence of a sense of urgency about it in the U.S. government but celebrated the fact that localities like San Francisco exhibited inspiration and leadership. Yet the event, which occurred largely downtown and focused on the business elite, while mentioning transit and bicycles, privileged electric cars and alternative fuels more than alternatives to automobility and barely alluded to the idea of reconfiguring space in ways that reduced car space. Notably, parking was absent from the discussions.[28]

Progressive activists in Hayes Valley, meanwhile, joined by citywide sustainable transportation advocates and environmental groups, hosted their own event to acknowledge the removal of the Central Freeway and its replacement by what they called a human-scale boulevard, new housing, and new public spaces (that is, the then-proposed MOBNP). Their theme—reclaiming urban space from the automobile—pushed a little further than the mainstream discourse at WED. The activists, who were then lobbying the city to cap parking in new developments with the MOBNP, emphasized political action. Freeway removal and rethinking of automobility required the determination of an increasingly large core group that believed it was possible for San Francisco and the world to change for the better by reducing car ownership. Fittingly, the event was held in a new neighborhood park that was once a forlorn parking lot beneath the freeway. Anticipating the opening of the Octavia Boulevard later that summer, the activists invited local public officials such as the mayor and members of the Board of Supervisors to dedicate the park.

The politics of WED in Hayes Valley were awkward from the outset. The mayor, Gavin Newsom, had sought to upstage the mobility aspects of WED by highlighting the temporary art installation in the park known as the *Green Temple,* which his office had arranged to display at the Hayes Valley event. The tall, wooden *Green Temple,* placed in the center of the new park, was created by a well-known artist who made similar artworks for Burning Man, the annual hedonistic, hip, and, significantly, entrepreneurial do-it-yourself cultural event in the Black Rock Desert in Nevada. The event therefore drew aficionados of Burning Man who had little association with the neighborhood or freeway removal, although many of them shared an entrepreneurial, neoliberal ethos with the mayor. It also drew the media, and, while the Hayes Valley activists had promoted the event via a press release, it was evident that the media attention was directed toward the mayor and Burning Man, not toward the dogged persistence and in-the-trenches political activism that the hosts had sought to share with the public and with visiting dignitaries.

The event began with a smattering of neighborhood representatives and sustainable transportation advocates and one progressive from the Board of Supervisors, all of whom spoke mostly about the tireless effort and the gritty politics involved in getting the freeway removed and about the bureaucratic challenges facing the adoption of the MOBNP. Local politicians and city officials jockeyed for position as each one-upped the other in taking credit for the new park and for implementing the new mobility vision. The former supervisor and freeway revolt heroine Sue Bierman told a humorous, lighthearted story about the freeway revolt, describing her frequent stress-related nosebleeds in the final days of the Panhandle debate. Local restaurants handed out free coffee and pastries to the large crowd, a mixture of local activists, bureaucrats and planners, and fans of Burning Man.

Nowhere to be found during all of these activities, Mayor Newsom suddenly arrived in a large, black SUV, which was double-parked out of sight a block away. The mayor, appearing to have walked from nearby City Hall to Hayes Valley, walked briskly through the waiting crowd, sauntered to the microphone at the *Green Temple,* and remarked on how the new park represented a new sense of place and identity for Hayes Valley. He spoke glowingly of all the new economic development opportunity on the surrounding freeway parcels and commented on both the new boutiques lining Hayes Street and the vibrant walkability of the area. His most ebullient enthusiasm, however, was reserved for the potential of new-generation cars, and he expressed his keen interest in seeing San Francisco and the Bay Area emerge into a model for plug-in hybrid electric cars. In contrast to the previous hour's soliloquies, his zeal was directed at the profits of urban infill development coupled with a romance of green automobility. Revealingly, the mayor failed to mention the heated controversy over parking policy that was then under way. His aloof evasiveness reflected the underlying neoliberal ambivalence about parking.

The relationship between parking and neoliberalism is often contradictory. On the one hand, it seems self-evident that neoliberals would want to deregulate parking by eliminating minimums and allow developers the flexibility to build as they see fit. In a dense, transit-rich city, there are substantial reasons to redevelop without being burdened with parking provisions. This enables more housing provision per land unit and hypothetically more profit in that parking by itself does not bring a high rate of return. Indeed, many in the development community accept the reduction of parking minimums because it implies less government. And in San Francisco's downtown, some profitable new developments have been constructed with little or no parking (although, to be sure, there is market-rate parking available in nearby garages).

But neoliberal developers are less than enthusiastic about the more stringent maximums promoted by progressives, which cap the amount of parking that can be built. Many disdain government-imposed caps—that is, more government regulation—on allowable parking downtown and in inner neighborhoods. For example, as the MOBNP went before the San Francisco Planning Commission in April 2007, the mayor's appointees to

the commission, who constituted the majority on that body, voted to dilute the parking maximums in the original plan, giving developers more
parking allowances than progressive activists had wished for. Progressive
activists had to call on the Board of Supervisors, where they held a majority, to reinstate the tighter parking caps.

As the MOBNP plan was being vetted and as San Francisco was glow-
ing in a green aura from the WED spotlight, a handful of infill proposals
pushed forward by developers managed to gain approval despite having
parking ratios that exceeded the eventual caps in the plan. At one prominent site on Market Street and within view of the new Octavia Boulevard,
developers proposed an 8-story, 113-unit market-rate condominium complex with a parking ratio higher than what would have been allowed by the
MOBNP.[29] Initially the developer asked for the traditional citywide parking ratio of 1:1, but after pushback from HVNA activists and the SFPD the
developer requested a ratio of 0.8:1. The planning department, pressured
by HVNA to reduce the parking further, asked the developer to consider
0.5:1, which became the parking allowance eventually adopted for this
part of Market Street. Yet the Planning Commission, heavy with members
appointed by the mayor, approved the project at 0.8:1 in May 2006, two
years before the MOBNP was officially adopted by the city.[30]

In another very high profile debate, the sponsor of a proposed redevelopment of a six-acre college campus, closed because of seismicity concerns, pursued parking ratios that exceeded those in the MOBNP. The
debate over what is often referred to as 55 Laguna was probably the most
politically challenging development issue in the center of the city since
freeway removal, and it involved many more factors than parking, among
them historic preservation, community benefits, affordable housing, and
broader questions about using a public site for profit making. But parking
was always front and center in the debate.

When the campus, which featured historic buildings wrapped around
three large surface parking lots, was shuttered in 2003, the University of
California began to use the parking lots as remote commuter lots for its
other campuses. This offended nearby residents, who thought it was dis-
respectful of the university to think of their neighborhood as a satellite
parking area. During the early proposals to redevelop the campus, the
developer warned nearby residents that the university could, if it chose,
build a large parking garage without city approval, as long as it served the
educational mission of the university (in this case, providing parking for
students, faculty, and staff). This kind of talk implied a punishing outcome
that made the parking scheme advanced by the developer seem harm-

less in comparison. To the HVNA, such rhetoric—if the community does not accept the proposed parking for the redevelopment, then it will get a worse outcome—assumed an antagonistic posture.

In 2004 and 2005 two polarized extremes were put forward in the 55 Laguna parking debate. HVNA organized meetings with advocates of sustainable transportation from throughout the city to consider and lobby for a redevelopment with zero parking and promoted the idea of car-free development. Activists stressed that parking for this redevelopment, poised to include over four hundred new apartments, would overwhelm the streets leading to the new Octavia Boulevard and freeway, crippling transit service and further discouraging Muni ridership while negatively impacting the quality of service. They proposed that all new tenants to the project sign an agreement to commit to being car-free and that city car share, bicycle parking, and transit passes be included as part of the project.

At the other end of the spectrum, the developer proposed almost five hundred parking spaces in a two-level garage that would be buried beneath the campus. The developer blithely dismissed the car-free proposal, stating that the tenants would not be car free but would compete for scarce on-street parking. This tactic was meant to divide the neighborhood, isolating the car-free faction from members of the neighborhood who genuinely feared that if the development did not have a large amount of parking, residents would compete for on-street parking. The developer invoked conservative mantras such as "families with children need cars," thereby essentializing automobility, and claimed, without evidence, that lenders would not finance a development that was car free.

A series of community meetings held in the spring and summer of 2005 were well attended by neighborhood residents, citywide transportation and housing activists, and planners as well as by the development team. They brought the parking debate to a boil, and the proceedings became acrimonious. The developer hired a public relations firm that went door to door to target a list of people who lived in the neighborhood but who worked in Silicon Valley. Presuming that these residents commuted to Silicon Valley by car, the public relations firm suggested to them that HVNA and radical anti-car activists wanted to kick them out of the neighborhood, and at the very least make it impossible for future Silicon Valley commuters to live in the neighborhood.[31] This scare tactic led to demands by less politically engaged but vocal newer residents that the development must have parking.

A neoliberal–progressive fissure opened around parking ratios. Throughout 2006 and 2007 the HVNA and its progressive allies accepted that some parking would be built but insisted that the parking ratio reflect the ratios in the forthcoming MOBNP, which, as noted, would have held the parking to 0.5:1. Furthermore the HVNA suggested that residents of 55 Laguna be restricted from getting on-street parking permits, which are required to park in the neighborhood. The developer, pressured by the SFPD, also reduced the parking ratios down from 1:1 but pushed for a higher ratio than would have been allowed in the MOBNP. The rationale was that the large site was actually in two separate planning zones and should be allowed more parking.

In April 2008 the project was granted a parking ratio of 0.79:1 and, adding salt to the wound, the entitlement included 51 parking spaces for the university's School of Dentistry, which would remain on-site. Though the number of parking spaces was substantially lower than at the outset of development proposals, the project still contained 310 new spaces. HVNA did not appeal the decision, calculating that they could not get enough votes to overturn the decision and that the MOBNP had not been approved and was not yet binding on the site. Moreover, for political reasons activists sought to avoid a broader battle over affordable housing for gay seniors, which was an appendage to the project that was meant to make it more palatable to the city's progressives on the Board of Supervisors.[32]

These examples of neoliberal developers seeking to provide excess parking while progressives sought less parking undergird a bigger conflict over housing and gentrification. Neoliberals, at least in the purest sense of eliminating government interference in the market, favor regulations that allow more parking, at least one space per residential unit, because by adding parking to housing units they can increase the overall sales value of the unit if the market is targeted at wealthier households rather than at middle-class or low-income housing. The increased sales value lies in the fact that for-profit developers do not absorb the cost of parking provision. Rather, developers add luxury items to housing units that include parking and inflate the price in order to get a higher return.[33] Such stratagems attract more upscale demographics to the housing market.

Developers and realtors in San Francisco recognize that there is a reurbanizing class stratum interested in the consumption of livability. San Francisco attracts and incubates a new bourgeoisie and a petit bourgeoisie or creative class, including executives and management, self-employed consultants, engineers, and especially tech workers in biotech, software, and Internet social networking firms.[34] From a real estate angle, the most pronounced of these patterns of consumption in older cities like San Francisco has been reurbanization in the form of gentrification and historic preservation. Arts and music, bars, restaurants, a "café culture," museums, and other traditionally urban amenities are considered to be central to the lifestyle of the creative class.

Significantly, this segment of San Francisco's population has a profound mobility regime that, while centered on a lifestyle choice to live in a compact, walkable city, includes a car for commuting, recreation, and shopping as well as intensive air travel and frequent high-consumption holidays like driving to Tahoe for skiing. Neoliberal developers recognize this class's penchant for the good life and seek to provide parking while also "hiding the driveway" and what others have called "parking-in-the-back new urbanism."[35] That is, the new urban bourgeoisie seeks to minimize the negative aesthetics and more extreme externalities of automobility but not to meaningfully alter its primacy in everyday life. The irony is that as this stratum consumes the city as a spectacle or lifestyle choice, the very *tout ensemble* of the city is withered away one garage and one displacement of an affordable housing unit at a time. As suggested in the debate over 55 Laguna, the epitome of displacement and transformation is the so-called Silicon implants, who work in low-rise, sprawling office parks in the suburbs and solo-commute by car but who prefer to live in sophisticated San Francisco, particularly in places like Hayes Valley and the Victorian Belt. The daily reverse commute to Silicon Valley and other suburbs is clearly visible weekday mornings in the areas immediately adjacent to the rebuilt portion of the Central Freeway (as discussed in chapter 7, luxurious private corporate commuter buses have also been deployed by biotech and Internet companies).

Poised to construct thousands of new housing units in the downtown and in the inner neighborhoods surrounding the downtown, neoliberal developers seek to provide parking for their clientele, the new urban bourgeoisie, in order to maximize profit. For example, the San Francisco Chamber of Commerce argues that if the city wants to attract residents to the downtown, it must require all new development to have more parking.[36] The *San Francisco Business Times,* the leading media venue for neoliberal developers, is a champion of urban infill for the new urban bourgeoisie and states emphatically that progressives, through their policies of opposition to car ownership, are chasing families out of the city.[37]

Progressive parking policy dampens profit. With that understanding, development interests in San Francisco protested and have successfully diluted the new progressive parking standards outlined above. While the MOBNP was still under environmental review, in 2006 the Board of Supervisors adopted new standards that substantially reduce allowable parking for all new development in downtown San Francisco.[38] Like the MOBNP, the minimums were eliminated so that all new development in downtown San Francisco, including office and retail, can have zero parking. However, influential developers, landowners, and the Chamber of Commerce lobbied Mayor Newsom to veto the stronger parking caps passed by the progressive majority on the Board of Supervisors. The behind-the-scenes lobbying was revealed via a request for a sunshine meeting (that is, that what was discussed behind closed doors with the mayor be made public) from a progressive member of the Board of Supervisors who supported stronger parking regulations.[39] The rezoning of parts of downtown in order to cap parking became a high-profile public dispute between the neoliberal mayor and the politically progressive majority on the Board of Supervisors in 2005 and 2006. After the mayor's veto, progressives and neoliberals negotiated a set of weaker parking standards but continued the parking debate as the MOBNP was vetted.

Again, the neoliberal development class, through the mayor's proxies on the Planning Commission, sought to dilute progressive parking standards. After the environmental review for the MOBNP concluded in 2006, nine lengthy public hearings were held at the Planning Commission, which finally approved the plan, with conditions, in April 2007. In this version, much of the plan allowed 1:1 parking, and the parking maximums were weaker. Debates about parking as well as about the amount of affordable housing complicated final approval of the plan and added another year before it was officially adopted by the city. The Board of Supervisors approved the MOBNP in May 2008. The progressive majority on the Board of Supervisors reinstated the more progressive parking ratios. Taking advantage of its momentum, the city then adopted the Eastern Neighborhood Plan, a geographically more expansive rezoning of the Mission, Potrero Hill, South of Market and the deindustrializing of the central waterfront south of the downtown. This plan, too, eliminated parking minimums and had policies similar to those of MOBNP regarding parking maximums and limiting curb cuts.

Even after the MOBNP was adopted, the debate over parking ratios did not end. Built into all San Francisco zoning codes is the option for a conditional use permit to increase the amount of permitted parking in cases where a developer can supply evidence of the need for additional parking. In winter 2008–9, in an early test of the parking policies of the MOBNP, progressives lost an appeal of a conditional use permit for excess parking. The proposal, a five-story, thirty-six-unit building in the rapidly gentrifying Valencia Street corridor in the North Mission, was entitled to 0.5:1 parking. The developer sought a conditional use to increase the ratio to 0.75:1 but offered no compelling reasons for the increase except that the additional parking was needed to make the units more market-able (the developer wanted 1:1 parking, but the new MOBNP capped the maximum, even with a conditional use, to 0.75:1). When the Planning Commission, in a 4–3 vote, allowed the excess parking, activists led by HVNA and including the Duboce Triangle Neighborhood Association, Livable City, the Mission Anti-Displacement Coalition, the Aids Housing Alliance, the Sierra Club, and the SFBC as well as a progressive land use attorney appealed the decision before the Board of Supervisors. An appeal of a conditional use permit for parking requires a supermajority vote by the board to overturn the Planning Commission's decision. The appellants needed eight votes but mustered only seven, reflecting the political align-ment of the board at the time, which had a progressive majority but not a supermajority.[40]

At around the same time, progressives lobbied the Board of Supervi-sors and the Planning Commission to consider changing the zoning code to ban conditional uses for parking in the MOBNP. The SFPD, not wish-ing to limit its negotiating power with developers, convinced the board and the commission that the elimination of conditional use permits was not necessary because from that point forward the department would be more stringent in opposing conditional uses for excess parking. In-deed, in at least three large development projects debated in 2010 and 2011, the planning staff recommended against conditional uses for excess parking.[41]

Despite the dilution and the tenuous potential of allowing excess park-ing with conditional uses, San Francisco's new parking standards are, incrementally, a progressive change in parking policy compared to past parking policies. Transportation advocates point out that even the diluted standards are more progressive than those in the rest of the Bay Area, New York City, and even in new developments in London.[42] The standards continue to replace parking minimums with parking maximums, mean-ing that developers can choose not to provide parking. Significantly, the standards are below one parking space per housing unit, and curb cuts and garages on essential transit-oriented streets are restricted. A number of new developments have been proposed with zero parking or substan-tially less parking. A new performing arts venue called San Francisco Jazz was permitted in 2010 with zero parking, and a proposed condominium in the Mission included zero parking. In the MOBNP area, a handful of new development proposals have come forward without requests for excess parking, suggesting that the progressive politics of opposing conditional use permits has sunk in, at least in this part of the city and at least as of 2012.

The overall dilution of the new parking policies and the potential of neoliberal development interests to request further conditional use waivers to increase parking as they seek to accommodate the new urban bourgeoisie reflect the fact that parking is a politically negotiated process as much as a technical one. The process reveals the tension between progressives, who believe one can live in the city with less space for automobiles, and neoliberals, who believe that providing spaces for automobiles is necessary for increasing the profit in lucrative urban infill real estate. And yet even this politically negotiated settlement between progressives and neoliberals on the issue of parking has its detractors, and a considerable political backlash against any limits on parking remains a potent factor in San Francisco's politics of mobility.

Conservatives and Parking

Whereas progressives believe government should actively discourage parking and driving, and neoliberals theoretically believe the market should decide (but, as demonstrated, they oppose progressive parking caps), conservatives in San Francisco believe government should proactively require more parking. Conservatives maintain that parking is critical to preserve and promote a set of politically conservative social relations, including the status quo of car access to the downtown and throughout the city. This attitude is steeped in the normative vision that people still need cars and is rooted in the essentialization of automobility, the inevitableness in discourses about automobiles and parking. Two lines of conservative discourse about parking stand out in San Francisco: parking is needed for families, and parking is essential if small businesses are to survive.

The language of family values is deployed in debates about parking in San Francisco. For example, during the debates over parking reform in 2005–8, the supervisor representing the relatively conservative Marina and Pacific Heights argued that parking is an "important resource to families" and that as an advocate for families she believed more parking was needed.[43] This line of thought essentializes automobility, holding that families need cars to transport their children and run errands. Similarly, the Coalition for San Francisco Neighborhoods, a collection of conservative, mostly west-side neighborhood groups, states that "families with children cannot function without a car."[44]

Implicit in this rhetoric are certain conservative conceptualizations of family and responsibility (see chapter 2). The conservative politics of mobility addresses the day-to-day moralities involved in coordinating family life and social networks in an automobilized society. Using the family car is associated with caring for and loving one's family and friends.[45] Indeed, it shows a moral commitment to family, and feelings of protection, security, and safety are emphasized, giving parents a sense of empowerment. Such empowerment is especially evident among mothers who, despite the chauffeuring they do and the spatial expansion of their domestic duties, perceive they are afforded liberation by having access to a car. The highlighting of one's personal responsibility toward one's family results in the internalization of the necessity of driving and the need for parking.

Private consumption of the home by the family takes precedence over public consumption, and possessive individualism characterizes conservative discourses: the SUV and the minivan become an extension of the family living room. One need only look at the morning weekday queues of cars in front of schools throughout San Francisco to see the role motoring has in child rearing. But this possessive individualism through automobility translates into a lack of civic and social responsibility toward public space and notions of community. The transit system and the streets are perceived to be unsafe precisely because there is too much traffic. In San Francisco, the broader contemporary American political rhetoric concerning personal responsibility toward one's family can translate into lack of interest in collectively solving large-scale problems such as congestion, pollution, and the inequality that stems from automobility. Instead, it is supposedly responsible to move the family through the city by car—that is, to secede—and fill one's daily needs atomistically. Meanwhile, automobility enables one to circumvent, if not secede from, the perceived evils of the city, one of which is homelessness. This mode of thinking results in high demand for parking.

A second conservative thread in San Francisco's parking debates is promulgated by some small business owners in neighborhood commercial districts. For example, at a public hearing titled "Relationship between Parking, Neighborhood Business, and Families" speakers representing themselves as merchants or representatives of merchant organizations argued that small business in San Francisco required more parking in order to survive.[46] During the height of the parking reform debates in 2007, a leading proponent of more parking was the Council of District Merchants, which claimed to represent twenty business associations in San Francisco (fifty years earlier the council opposed the Western Freeway).

Their argument, made in a conservative might-makes-right tone, was that the majority owns cars and therefore the city should provide more parking. A representative of the downtown Union Square Business Association added that "city dwellers need parking."

Surprisingly, some gay merchants in neighborhoods like the Castro evoke conservative speech in arguing for more parking. For example, at a meeting of a working group on envisioning the future of the Upper Market–Castro section, merchants and small business owners lamented the lack of parking and argued that businesses in the Castro area were suffering because of parking problems.[47] The director of the business group for Upper Market insisted on a parking garage somewhere in the area to enable more motorized retail from beyond the neighborhood. The president of the merchants' association also chimed in for more parking.

The progressive majority on the Board of Supervisors notwithstanding, conservatives have played a substantial role in shaping the course of parking reform in the city. In the early 2000s, as progressives and neoliberals promoted parking reform, albeit for very different reasons, a conservative backlash rose to defeat a citywide parking reform effort, limiting reform to the eastern side of the city. Briefly, in 2003–4 the SFPD drafted a revised *Housing Element,* which is required by the State of California as part of the city's general plan.[48] *Housing Elements* must show where cities plan to enable the construction of low- and moderate-income housing, in this case based on forecasts of future employment and population trends as calculated by the Association of Bay Area Governments (ABAG), a regional entity assigned with measuring and predicting regional housing needs and then allocating that regional need to cities and counties.

In the early 2000s ABAG recognized that between 1988 and 1998 very little housing was built in the city relative to the rest of the Bay Area and that there was, at a minimum, a 30,000-unit shortage in the city. Moreover, ABAG warned that what had been produced during the dot-com boom was high-end housing that was unaffordable to low- and moderate-income brackets. The regional agency proposed that San Francisco needed to use zoning to enable the production of up to 3,000 housing units annually to keep pace with the existing shortfall, including demand for affordable housing. ABAG further proposed that the city enable upward of 70,000 new units to keep up with future demand. The SFPD responded to the housing shortage by proposing the less ambitious production of 20,000 new housing units over a five-year period between 2004 and 2009 (when the next *Housing Element* update was required). The plan was to rezone corridors that contained high-capacity transit, allowing modestly higher heights and density, and, significantly, reducing parking require-ments. The plan also called for legalizing secondary units, which are often small apartments on the ground floor of a single-family unit of housing. To lessen competition for on-street parking, progressives on the Board of Supervisors proposed that secondary units be legalized within two blocks of transit lines and that on-street parking permits be forbidden to tenants of secondary units. The secondary unit proposal suggested that 150 afford-able housing units could be added throughout the city annually, but that this required relaxing off-street parking ratios.

The entire *Housing Element* was contested by conservative neighbor-hood activists led by the Coalition for San Francisco Neighborhoods, who corralled activists to speak out at Planning Commission hearings and who eventually met with the mayor to demand that the *Housing Element* be stripped of the parking reform and density proposals. Heeding the conser-vative backlash, the mayor and the majority on the Planning Commission, which, as noted, he appointed, diluted the *Housing Element* and erased language aimed at reforming parking and encouraging densification in transit corridors. The *Housing Element* was adopted in 2004 without park-ing reform. Progressives, rather than appeal to the Board of Supervisors, regrouped and began to focus on the area-specific plans for downtown and the MOBNP, for which there was less conservative opposition.

Yet the conservative backlash continued, and conservatives next ral-lied around a ballot measure in 2007 that mandated parking for all new development in San Francisco.[49] The ballot measure, popularly known as the Parking for Neighborhoods Initiative and officially as Prop H, was backed by the Council of District Merchants Associations, a coalition of small business owners; the signature-gathering campaign was funded by the billionaire founder of the Gap, Don Fisher, and the chief executive offi-cer of Webcor Construction, Andy Ball. Now deceased, Fisher was widely known as a conservative in San Francisco, one who had strong opinions about parking and homelessness and a deep hostility toward the city's pro-gressive politics. Webcor builds garages, and the company's involvement reflects the neoliberal opposition to parking restrictions (although other developers opposed the ballot because it *required* parking, indicating the division and ambivalence of neoliberals).

Prop H would have amended the San Francisco planning code to re-quire more parking and nullify the recent and anticipated gains made by progressives.[50] The proposed initiative would have required considerably more parking for new offices, retail, and housing in the downtown, and it abolished maximums, replacing them with required minimums. This meant that developers had to provide parking, whereas under progressive reform parking was an option but not a requirement. The initiative would have frozen all remaining citywide parking to the pre-reform standards, thereby preempting years of efforts by progressives, planners, and neighborhood activists to reduce the impacts of parking in the inner-ring neighborhoods. It would have also eroded the quality of transit stops, bike lanes, and neighborhood commercial streets throughout the city because it allowed the placement of garages and curb cuts to take priority over these spaces.

Progressives naturally cringed at the initiative, but some neoliberals sought to thwart it as well.[51] Led by SPUR, neoliberals recognized that the exchange value of the city was at stake with this measure. While neoliberal developers may have liked the requirement for residential parking in new high-rise condominiums, a blanket approach that imposed more government regulation was threatening ideologically as well as financially. The proposed increases in required parking would have actually dampened office and retail development in the downtown because the street capacity there would not have been able to handle the increase in cars, thus creating a diseconomy. Under the reformist policies, over two thousand parking spaces could be added downtown in the next twenty years (but recall that currently developers can opt not to provide parking). The proposed initiative would have led to an increase of over eight thousand spaces, bringing the total required parking downtown, for offices only, to twelve thousand new spaces. This would have translated into upward of twelve thousand more cars entering an already saturated street network, not to mention overwhelming the congested freeway and bridge network leading into the downtown. The diseconomy would ultimately shunt more office and retail outward, aggravating sprawl and decreasing the exchange value of the downtown. The proposed parking standards for residential development, which would increase parking by some 300–400 percent, would have also decreased the amount of housing that could be constructed downtown, further reducing exchange value and exacerbating regional sprawl. Again, the neoliberal stance on parking is that government should not impose a requirement or a cap on parking.

Recognizing this, and despite their nuanced differences regarding parking caps, a coalition of progressives and neoliberals organized to defeat the ballot initiative. The coalition was successful when, in November 2007, Prop H was defeated by 67 percent of voters (voter turnout was low at around 36 percent). Critical to progressives' and neoliberals' success was a strategy of using a phone-banking campaign, fliers, and mailers to link Prop H to global warming, the excesses of fossil fuel consumption as exemplified by the Hummer SUV (which was pictured in anti-Prop H mailings and posters), and to the ideology of President George W. Bush. Joining the local to the global helped rally rank-and-file environmentalists and other progressives. Also critical to the progressive victory was the campaign's contrasting of Prop H to another ballot initiative, Proposition A, which prescribed fixes to the city's ailing transit service.[52] Notably, Prop A had language directly concerning transit workers' relations with management and drew the support of several prominent unions, including the Service Employees International Union and the local transit workers' union. Thus an alliance of environment and labor ultimately defeated Prop H (while simultaneously passing Prop A).[53] The end result, however, was and still is simply a holding of the line, as the campaign exhausted the coalition's financial resources (it spent nearly $400,000 dollars on both Prop A and H).

The defeat of Prop H did not stop conservatives from protesting parking reform. During the multiple public hearings on the MOBNP, begun at the Planning Commission in September 2006 and lasting through 2008, reduced parking ratios came under fire from conservatives. The major opponent of the MOBNP was the Coalition for San Francisco Neighborhoods, which, invoking the previous *Housing Element* debate and Prop H discourse, continued to use family values and small merchants' arguments to warn that if the MOBNP was adopted it would be followed by a rezoning and reduction in parking citywide. In 2010 and 2011, when San Francisco's *Housing Element* was once again being revised, conservatives rallied and pressured the city to leave the west side of the city out of potential increases in density, parking reform, and other housing-related measures. As the city expects to add upward of ninety thousand new housing units in the next two decades, little to no housing will accrue to the west side, with the exception of a development adjacent to San Francisco State University.

Moreover, conservative arguments continued to be deployed in debates over allowing conditional uses for excess parking after the plan was adopted. In 2011 several conservative members of the Planning Commission argued that a new development in the MOBNP needed parking because families needed parking. One commissioner said, "This is a higher end, higher quality project for more mature people, who will not be hopping on a bike."[54] Conservative opposition to a proposed development with zero parking in the Mission invoked a discourse about families needing cars but went further and suggested that transit was not attractive because it was ridden by crime and filth.[55] When progressives protested the parking ratios for a large new Target store in the downtown, the Planning Commission acquiesced to the developer and to conservative arguments that families needed a car to shop at the store. The project was approved with an excess of ninety-seven parking spaces beyond that which was allowed by right, despite being immediately adjacent to the city's signature transit street and near several large public parking garages.

Parking Matters

Rethinking automobility in cities requires a rethinking of parking, and the reform of parking is one of the most radically important elements of contesting the spaces of automobility. Between 2000 and 2010 progressives in San Francisco were able to reform parking, but the city's progressive parking reforms are tenuous at best and are constantly tested. The rapprochement between progressives and neoliberals over removal of the Central Freeway survived when it came to parking reform, but only to a point. Neoliberals support eliminating minimums but dispute caps.

Conservatives, by contrast, believe government should require ample parking, and their antagonism to parking reform dampened progressive enthusiasm for citywide approaches to parking. This limited the geography of parking reform to the eastern side of the city, specifically to the downtown, the Market and Octavia area, and neighborhoods just south of downtown. Aside from some large-scale projects conditionally approved with excess parking, in 2011, as financing for housing started to rebound, conditional use requests for garage inserts into older, one- to three-unit Victorians proliferated in the eastern part of the city, accompanied by rhetoric about families needing cars and about the need for a garage insert to enable grocery shopping by car. But, more critically, the insertion of parking makes the resale value of older homes more profitable.

There are some people with a stake in parking policy who are less vocal and less engaged. Certainly the presumed average motorist who opts to not be politically engaged still has an effect on the politics of parking. The battle over Prop H occurred in an off-year election with roughly 36 percent voter turnout (the incumbent mayor ran unchallenged, and no other high-profile issues were on the ballot). Many apolitical or disengaged motorists might have voted for Prop H had there been a dynamic electoral contest. Moreover, San Francisco's large minority and immigrant communities—many working-class Asians, blacks, and Latinos—are less involved in the local politics of mobility but nevertheless do have a stake in parking policies. This no doubt aggravates tensions within progressive ranks, as some demand less parking while populists might demand more parking for the working class. This is exhibited in debates over metering of curbside parking, which is part of a strategy to finance Muni (see chapter 6).

One of the main barriers facing the implementation of progressive parking policies is that many progressives themselves may feel constrained under a stricter parking regime. They likely find it quite difficult to envision how one might easily obtain everything one needs without a car, given that existing urban form is constructed along a dimension that measures driving distance rather than bussing or walking distance. Progressives are working on a radical restructuring of urban form, and San Francisco is already a dense, compact city in parts, but change will not happen quickly. If large numbers of people are to be convinced that parking is not necessary, they will have to see it to believe it. Many people I have talked with, for example, including some progressives, seek out classic old European cities for vacationing precisely because of their walkability and ample transit but are unable to envision a similar alternative in the city they call home.

What the parking debate illustrates is that progressive politics vis-à-vis parking and San Francisco's broader politics of mobility are really at the cutting edge relative to much of the United States. Throughout much of the United States the spaces of the car are not challenged. Instead, mobility debates are dominated by deliberations on how to replace gasoline with ethanol and how to reduce the negative environmental impacts of automobility with green hybrid or hydrogen-powered cars. Transit, walking, and bicycling are increasingly popular in localized discourses from Atlanta to Seattle, but they often are promoted in ways that do not substantially challenge the physical space of the automobile. On parking, San Francisco is poised to be the place where seeing is believing.

CHAPTER 5

"We Are Not Blocking Traffic, We Are Traffic!"

The Politics of Bicycle Space in San Francisco

Bicycle space—an interconnected, coordinated, multifaceted set of bicycle lanes, paths, parking racks, and accompanying laws and regulations to protect and promote cycling—has been extremely difficult to implement in the United States, even in San Francisco.[1] Detractors often object to bicycle space because they claim bicycling is childish or not a legitimate form of transportation, or that Americans will simply never replace driving with bicycling because it is too hot, too cold, too rainy, or too hilly or because most places are too far to get to by bicycle. Despite what seem like insurmountable arguments in opposition, the San Francisco Bicycle Coalition (SFBC) has twelve thousand members, is a formidable force in electoral politics, and has been at the leading edge of redefining the politics of possibilities for an urban space that is not dominated by automobiles.[2] The local political establishment, from the mayor and the Board of Supervisors to city department heads, has committed itself to a goal of dramatically increasing the mode share in cycling for all trips within the city. This goal is the result of determined and passionate advocates in San Francisco who have successfully promoted bicycling, and their story offers lessons for advocates around the nation.

Why Bicycling?

Bicycling makes up a tiny share of daily travel in the United States: 1–2 percent of all trips.[3] But in the face of increased gasoline prices and congestion, more public awareness of the relationship between global warming and driving, and interest in physical activity, bicycling has experienced a small boom in many cities since 2000. Chicago, Minneapolis, New York, Pittsburgh, Portland, Seattle, Washington, D.C., and many smaller university cities like Boulder and Madison have seen increases in utilitarian bicycling.[4] In 2010 an estimated 3.5 to 6 percent of all trips in San Francisco were made by bicycle, 9.3 percent of adults used bicycles daily as their main mode of transportation, and 16 percent of adults rode a bicycle at least twice a week.[5] This amounts to roughly 128,000 bicycle trips made within San Francisco each day, of which 66 percent are for utilitarian purposes such as shopping and commuting, not for recreation. Bicycling surged in San Francisco during the period 2005–10, rising 71 percent citywide, and on some streets in the Victorian Belt more than 15 percent of trips are by bicycle.[6] On weekday mornings bicycles outnumber cars on segments of Market Street near Van Ness. In parts of Hayes Valley, the Mission, and Upper Market areas almost 10 percent of commuting is by bicycle.[7]

In San Francisco and throughout the United States, bicycling is well suited to be a substitute for many short-range automobile trips and has enormous potential to contribute to reductions in VMT. Nationally, some 72 percent of all trips shorter than three miles in length are by car, a spatial range that an average cyclist can cover easily.[8] In the Bay Area, 67 percent of all trips are less than five miles long, and for an average adult five miles amounts to a thirty-minute bicycle ride.[9] The bicycle can be practical for running many errands, especially in compact cities but also in conventional, lower-density suburbs. Bicycling is compatible with rapid transit, particularly for the "last mile" segments, and there are opportunities to integrate bicycle parking at major transit nodes rather than expensive, land-intensive car parking. Bicycles do not require costly, long-term capital investment or operating funds like those of transit and can be deployed quickly. In many respects bicycling is among the most equitable forms of urban transportation because it is affordable and accessible to almost everyone.[10]

If the many advantages of bicycling are to be realized, space must be allotted to it, and that includes bike lanes and paths that are separated from car traffic and that are direct routes to where people need and desire to go; it includes as well comprehensive traffic calming along bicycle routes, modification of conventional street intersections to allow so-called bike boxes with advanced stop lines for cyclists far ahead of stopped cars, special bike lanes for turning, turn restrictions for cars, extra green traffic signal phases for bikes, the retiming of traffic signals to reflect bicycle speeds (known as green waves), and ample, secure, covered, high-capacity bicycle parking, especially at major transit hubs and major activity centers.

Beyond these physical reconfigurations of urban space, a true bicycle system must embrace education that reinforces bicyclists' rights to road space, and bicycle education must be incorporated into traditional driver's education. The legal system must also change, bringing more enforcement against motorists for dangerous infractions such as speeding, red light running, reckless and aggressive behavior, parking in bicycle lanes, and cellphone use while driving. Motorists must be made legally responsible and persuaded to drive more defensively if bicycling is to become a viable practical component of urban transportation.

On the basis of evidence from Europe, systematic bicycle space makes bicycling attractive and safe for less agile males and for women, children, and even the elderly.[11] In northwest Europe women bicycle as often as men, and the rates of bicycling are similar across all ages and distributed evenly across all income groups. In Austria, Denmark, Germany, Sweden, and Switzerland, bicycling accounts for between 10 percent and 15 percent of all daily trips, while in the Netherlands, 27 percent of all trips are by bicycle. In cities the rate of bicycling is much higher; for example, in Copenhagen bicycling amounts to 35 percent of daily commuting trips. Moreover, the barriers of topography and climate to bicycling are often overstated.[12] Bicycle facilities can be made to circumvent steep grades or integrated with lifts in extreme cases, and some of the cities with the highest rates of cycling, such as Amsterdam and Copenhagen, are often cold and wet.

In the United States the main barrier to the production of bicycle space is lack of political will. There is no strong national bicycle policy with dedicated funding programs as there is for automobiles. While there is a national Alliance for Bicycling and Walking as well as a League of American Cyclists, most successful advocacy for bicycling has been a largely local, fragmented, and isolated effort. Therefore, the patterns in the few cities that have established the political will to promote bicycling and that have seen meaningful increases in bicycling are instructive. In San Francisco dedicated, persistent political activism has sprung bicycling's mode share upward, and the SFBC has lobbied for the production of bicycle space and shaped local political discourse about bicycling. The city's transit-first policy includes bicycling, and politicians and planners subscribe to a future bicycle mode split of 20 percent of all trips within the city, approaching the urban cycling patterns of northwestern Europe. San Francisco has a large, vibrant political movement advocating the redefinition of the possibilities regarding bicycle space. Yet it is by no means easy to reconfigure the city's streets, and many of the same themes that appeared in the debates about freeway removal and parking permeate the discussions of bicycle space.

Critical Mass and San Francisco's Bicycle Movement

Utilitarian cycling was virtually nonexistent in the United States when, in 1971, a small group of environmentalists, neighborhood advocates, and bicycle enthusiasts formed the SFBC. They lobbied the city to install bike lanes on a very limited number of streets, and got bicycles to be part of the city's master plan for transportation, which was revised that year.[13] The SFBC successfully lobbied for bicycle access to the Golden Gate Bridge, which was a boon to recreational cycling, as well as for bicycle access to BART. Although bicycling at the time failed to take hold the way it did in the early 2000s, these successes laid a foundation for future bicycling. Throughout the seventies and eighties recreational cycling remained popular in the Bay Area, but utilitarian cycling lagged, the SFBC remained small, and by the 1980s the coalition was inactive.

In 1990 there was no effective bicycle advocacy organization in San Francisco, but a handful of cyclists were able to convince the city to establish a Bicycle Advisory Committee, made up of citizens appointed by elected officials. The advisory committee advocated that the city establish bicycle planning positions within the transportation department, and eventually such a position was created. On the twentieth anniversary of Earth Day, in 1990, some bicyclists organized by riding through San Francisco to Golden Gate Park, the city's signature open space, where an environmental rally was held. This event was aimed at stirring interest in resuscitating a nonprofit bicycle advocacy organization.[14]

Through the early and mid-1990s, despite a growing and vocal SFBC, San Francisco's transportation planners and politicians were reluctant to aggressively and systematically pursue bicycling, instead instituting a "low-hanging fruit" policy of striping bike lanes only where they would not delay car traffic. Bike lanes were placed on streets with very low vehicular volumes and very wide rights of way, often leaving out the very places bicyclists wished to be, such as neighborhood commercial corridors and downtown. When a bike lane approached a busy intersection or street segment with moderate or high car traffic, bike lanes were dropped owing to concerns that they would delay automobiles. While often expressed as unbiased scientific engineering, the use of intersection level of service (hereafter LOS, pronounced *ell, oh, ess*), a traffic engineering metric that assesses the delay motorists experience at street intersections, made the production of bicycle space challenging.[15] One of the most widely used tools of traffic analysis in the United States, LOS, in simplified terms, considers the actual time it takes for a vehicle to move through an intersection compared to the theoretical optimum time it would take if there were no interference from other vehicles or impediments. The optimal conditions for "good" LOS are twelve-foot-wide travel lanes at level grade with no curb parking on approaches, no pedestrians or bicycles, no buses stopping in lanes, and only passenger cars in the vehicle mix.[16] Delay is described by a six-letter grading scale, or ranges, which is similar to a school report card. LOS *A, B,* and *C* indicate reasonable traffic flow but with steadily increasing delay, while LOS *D,* which means a thirty-five-second delay, is considered a point at which an intersection is approaching capacity and should be expanded or modified to avoid "bad" LOS *E* or *F* conditions, *F* being an extreme delay, that is, one of eighty seconds or more.

In San Francisco, as almost everywhere in California, LOS *D* at peak travel times is considered a threshold of significance in environmental review. In other words, when reallocation of street space for a bicycle lane is predicted to increase motorists' delay to more than thirty-five seconds (LOS *D*), a lengthy, expensive traffic analysis is required. If the results of that analysis show that the bicycle lane contributes to pushing an intersection to LOS *D* or worse, this is a seriously negative environmental impact that should be avoided, mitigated, or accepted with overriding considerations but with distinct justification. In built-out cities like San Francisco, adherence to LOS conflicts with other spatial planning goals, such as the transit-first policy, which states that decisions about the city's streets should prioritize buses and light rail, and the city's bicycle plan, which calls for bike lanes and other facilities to replace automobile lanes on many streets. In the 1990s, when there was no transparent discussion of public policy, intersection LOS was dictating where bicycle lanes could and could not be deployed. Some bicycle lanes would simply end, and bicyclists would be left to suddenly fend for themselves in the traffic. San Francisco bicycle advocates jokingly referred to bicycle lanes that suddenly disappeared because of LOS as S.O.L. lanes (shit outta luck lanes).[17]

Moreover, when bike lanes were striped, they were placed within the dangerous so-called door zone of parked cars; the city was reluctant to make them wider because that would require removing or narrowing car travel lanes. The city's priority was to optimize LOS for cars, with the result that very few improvements were made for cycling and few people cycled in the city. It was a lonely and sometimes daunting existence for San Francisco cyclists in the 1990s, a situation in which many contemporary bicycle advocates around the nation find themselves today.

Frustration over the lack of political will to create bicycle space led bicyclists to improvise their own spaces. These were the spaces of Critical Mass bicycle rides, which, since 1992, occur on the last Friday of every month in downtown San Francisco. The name Critical Mass is, as the term implies, a critical mass of cyclists that, once reached, can recapture urban space from the automobile, enabling the mass to progress through city streets unimpeded and to block intersections in a way that makes most motorists resigned to simply wait for it to pass. The name of this appropriation of space was inspired by *Return of the Scorcher,* an independent documentary film that included a narrative observing hundreds of cyclists bunching at an intersection in China and pushing their way into traffic.[18] Bicyclists waited until they had critical mass to push into the stream of cross traffic, and the phrase was borrowed by the local activists who organized the monthly ride.

As a direct-action protest, Critical Mass was incidentally influenced by the radical Earth First protests against logging in Northern California's redwood forests during the early 1990s, demonstrations in which individual protesters attempted to physically impede logging operations.[19] The protests in 1991 against the Gulf War also had a part in inspiring Critical Mass. In January 1991 the Federal Building in the Civic Center area of San Francisco was shut down by six thousand protesters, and one thousand protesters blocked traffic on Van Ness Avenue. On the afternoon of January 15, 1991, two thousand protesters, including four hundred on bicycles, proceeded down Market Street, then to an on-ramp to the Bay Bridge, where they disrupted traffic for two hours. For the first time in history the Bay Bridge was shut down by a protest. Bicycling was a symbol of San Francisco's demonstrations against the Gulf War, representing the antithesis of the car culture and oil-induced warfare.

The first Critical Mass was held on the last Friday in September 1992 and included 48 cyclists who rode from the Ferry Building up the length of Market Street to Valencia and then to a local bar in the Mission. Originally titled the Commute Clot, an early flier called automobiles death

monsters but also stated that the event was sponsored by the SFBC (in recent years the SFBC has distanced itself from Critical Mass). The first ride
was covered by a local weekly paper, and the next month between 85 and
150 cyclists appeared, depending on who counted. In the early years activists from the SFBC promoted Critical Mass by putting fliers on bicycles
parked around the city, and by 1993 hundreds of people were participating
monthly. Police began following and trying to tame Critical Mass, and the
first arrests occurred in April 1993. Organizers of the rides began to shift
the emphasis of Critical Mass away from a direct-action protest against
cars to a celebration of bicycling and the liberation of street space and
berated participants who taunted motorists and the police. The cofounder
Chris Carlsson called it "bicycling's defiant celebration."[20]

By 1994 Critical Mass had more than five hundred participants, especially on warm summer days and was drawing young, professional workers who worked in the support of the postindustrial, high-tech economy,
including programmers, office managerial and support staff, accountants
as well as nonprofit employees, artists, and students. Most subscribed to
progressive values.[21] They were frustrated with the increased isolation engendered by the accelerated pace of daily life and the transient nature of
jobs and housing. Many bicycled to their jobs in downtown San Francisco in solitary fear and felt assaulted by the brutality of streets devoted to
high-speed car movement. Most participants were experienced, utilitarian cyclists, but the rides helped them become aware of the possibilities
of safe, car-free bicycle space. Critical Mass helped reframe the questions
about urban sustainability and pushed the debate about street space in a
more progressive direction. Many participants said the ride allowed them
to reclaim connectivity to community and showed them the possibilities of a humane city.[22] They felt that the bicycle—a swift, graceful, quiet,
low-energy form of transport that takes up little space yet offers a social,
connected form of movement—was ideal for the sustainable city of the future. Critical Mass participants found that bicycling could make streets a
place, not simply a conduit for movement but a space for social interaction
where meaning and identity could be produced, and it empowered a new
sense of possibilities for urban living. According to one early participant,
"When you realize it can be different, you feel empowered and you see
where we can go."[23]

Through the early and mid-1990s the monthly rides, although growing,
were largely innocuous and drew little media criticism; police crackdowns
were rare and isolated, although incidents between motorists and cyclists

occurred from time to time. In 1996 the *San Francisco Chronicle* used an image of Critical Mass in a commercial promotion of "authentic" San Francisco that included a dissident, yet celebratory, character.[24] It seemed that Critical Mass had become a legitimate part of San Francisco. Participation expanded into the thousands on spring and summer evenings, and the annual Halloween ride became a masquerading spectacle. Then in June of 1997 the sedan carrying Mayor Willie Brown was delayed by a passing Critical Mass. Infuriated, the mayor directed the police to crack down on the ride, not by prohibiting it but by controlling the route and tone of the event.[25] Over the next month a great deal of media attention focused on Critical Mass and the broader conditions of bicycling in the city. More than five thousand cyclists appeared at the ride the next month, and a showdown with police ended in a melee in which over two hundred arrests were made and images of police violently subduing cyclists were broadcast. Every arrest was dismissed in court, but Critical Mass was now a story of national interest.

Even faced with the negative attention of some media outlets, the SFBC grew in numbers. In the month after the melee, almost three hundred new members joined, and bicycling was now front and center in a local politics increasingly concerned about congestion, removal of the Central Freeway, and the state of the public transit system in the city. Critical Mass made national headlines, including *Time,* the cover of *USA Today,* and *The NewsHour with Jim Lehrer* on PBS.[26] The progressive *San Francisco Bay Guardian* selected Critical Mass as a Local Hero in its annual "Best of the Bay" edition. The *San Francisco Chronicle* called bicycle advocacy "the hottest political movement in the country today." Critical Masses eventually spread to New York City, Chicago, Portland, Vancouver, and even Rome. The transportation scholar Martin Wachs opined that Critical Mass demonstrated that San Francisco's bicycling movement was powerful enough to warrant public expenditures on cycling.[27] He pointed out that complementing Critical Mass was a well-organized outfit of advocates who appeared at every public meeting, flooded local newspapers with letters to the editor, and successfully gained support from leading environmental organizations and progressive politicians.

After the melee, Brown, pinpointing the SFBC as the organizer of Critical Mass, asked the leadership of the SFBC, "What do you want?"[28] The SFBC, now in the spotlight and growing in numbers because of Critical Mass, asked for eight specific bike lane projects to be advanced, most of which would require removing car space to make bicycle space. All of these projects was delineated in the city's existing bicycle plan but not implemented because of concerns about LOS, that is, delay to cars. The mayor directed the traffic department to hold hearings around the city in 1997–98, and bicycle advocacy flourished, even as the contentious ballot initiatives over the Central Freeway were under way. Hundreds of cyclists attended these meetings, and the SFBC took the more pronounced position that the city needed to move beyond its low-hanging-fruit approach.

Although the SFBC was at pains to differentiate itself from Critical Mass, the fallout strengthened the SFBC, which had seventeen hundred members by 1998 and was gaining progressive allies on the Board of Supervisors. Some key streets were made more welcoming to cyclists. For example, the city approved a so-called road diet and bicycle lanes for Valencia Street and a level route through the Mission District. Advocates had lobbied for those improvements for almost a decade to no avail, mainly because of opposition from merchants and motorists. Now the city felt it had to do something because of the political upwelling after the Critical Mass melee.

When bicycle lanes were added to Valencia Street in 1999, bicycling increased by 144 percent.[29] The success of the Valencia Street project further emboldened bicycle activists and proved that with adequate infrastructure more people would choose to bicycle. It eventually came to be supported by shopowners after the fact, and today Valencia is a thriving retail and entertainment corridor. By 2000, 16 percent of all trips on the street were by bicycle. A long-awaited resurfacing and widening of bike lanes to address the door zone safety hazard was completed in 2010.

Success, however, exposed the raw truth about the limited road space in San Francisco and about the concerns over car drivers' LOS, and the transportation agency stalled on most bicycle lane proposals for fear they would inconvenience too many motorists. Of the eight bicycle lane projects Mayor Brown promised to consider, only two were implemented and a third partially implemented. While Critical Mass continued with rides of several hundred participants in winter months and several thousand in the summer, the SFBC responded to the unwillingness of city planners and engineers to reconfigure streets with open, aggressive political campaigning in city elections.[30] In the early 2000s the SFBC had almost every local elected official worried about alienating the bicycle vote, and very few of them spoke against the notion of bicycling, although ambiguity about how to implement bicycle space was widespread among many politicians.

The Backlash against Bicycle Space

As in the debates over freeway removal and parking, the bicycling issue experienced a backlash, and it featured a decidedly conservative, essentializing discourse. Angry that the city had backed off its enforcement against Critical Mass, in 1999 a west-side businessman (who had cosponsored the third ballot initiative to rebuild the Central Freeway) called for a Critical Mass for Cars to circle City Hall. The objective was to show that "the car was king," but the immediate outrage was a new bicycle lane on Polk Street, which fronted City Hall and which was opposed by merchants on the street. The Polk Street lane was one of the eight that the mayor had promised to consider in response to the Critical Mass melee in 1997, and one of the three actually striped. Hoping that between five hundred and a thousand motorists would show up, Critical Car Mass sputtered when fewer than a dozen vehicles appeared, even as two supervisors participated. Yet it did get considerable press and empathy as it fed into the political debate over the removal of the Central Freeway.[31] That same year, when the city proposed the aforementioned Valencia Street bike lanes in the Mission, Bill Maher, a member of the DPT, which oversaw bicycle planning at the time, said, "There will be bike lanes on Valencia over my dead body."[32]

As San Francisco's planning and transportation departments were directed by politicians to work with the SFBC on bicycle planning, conservative opposition to the bicycle plan germinated. In the background, the morning news anchor on AM talk radio station KGO engaged in a year-long diatribe against bicyclists in 2003 and 2004.[33] He lamented that bicyclists wearing spandex regularly blocked his way on local roads and that radical environmentalists thought they were better than everyone else and were really out just to make people feel bad about driving. The commentator was especially incensed by the language of progressive bicycle advocates, who linked global warming, oil wars, and a myriad other environmental and social problems to automobility and implicitly suggested that motorists needed to exhibit more social responsibility by choosing not to drive.

The leadership of the SFBC—the group now had almost five thousand members—grew more aggressive in their advocacy for adopting a revised bicycle plan but also more frustrated with the city's skittish behavior and lack of clarity regarding LOS, environmental review, and how these considerations might complicate the plan. Bicycle advocates took two parallel tracks. First, they lobbied the city to quickly adopt the revised bicycle plan and to declare an exemption from the required environmental review of the plan. Second, they asked the Board of Supervisors to direct city staff to conduct a review of LOS and make recommendations on how to reform or replace it. The directive resulted in a report in late 2003 that stated that San Francisco's use of LOS was in direct contradiction to the city's official transit-first policies.[34] This contention led to an effort to propose discontinuing the use of LOS in environmental review for bicycle projects and to the consideration of other metrics more in line with livability policies (see below).

As a revised bicycle plan was circulating for public review, conservative opposition mounted. Complicating matters, the city, using a state community planning grant, contracted the SFBC to conduct public outreach for the plan. A collection of west-side neighborhood organizations, rallied by the Coalition for San Francisco Neighborhoods, grew very hostile toward both the city planning process and the SFBC. In one acrimonious meeting, west-side activists threatened to gather ten thousand signatures to oppose the bicycle plan.[35] They protested what they called the proliferation of bike lanes in the city and complained that the SFBC was too influential and too powerful. The angry group associated the bicycle plan with what one opponent called stealth planning issues of infill development, increased density, and the increasing of transit to the west side and grouped the bicycle plan with the controversial *Housing Element,* whose transit and parking components were diluted by conservatives (see chapter 4).

One vocal opponent of the bicycle plan, implying that freeway removal and parking reform were synonymous with bicycling, singled out activists in Hayes Valley, stating that "Hayes Valley was a cancer creeping to the west side." The leadership of the Coalition for San Francisco Neighborhoods complained that bicycle space would take away parking and car travel lanes and that bicycles blocked traffic. Finally, the attendees insisted that the plan should be slowed down because it needed an elaborate environmental impact report that would reveal that bike lanes caused substantial delay for cars.

The SFBC was worried about the backlash but even more so about the plan, which, threatened by conservative maneuvering, was languishing and would be delayed even further by an environmental review. The revisions of the plan had begun in the late 1990s and were to have been adopted by 2002, but it was now 2005. The plan was also based largely on a previous plan that many activists felt lacked ambition because it was limited to only twenty bicycle projects around the city; the activists contended that bicyclists had compromised enough by not demanding more.

Within the ranks of the SFBC there was impatience, a growing sense that the city should have already implemented the twenty bike projects and that a more visionary planning process should be under way. The SFBC was wary of the political makeup of the city and wanted to accelerate the approval of the plan while there was a progressive majority on the Board of Supervisors.

In June 2005, as the city celebrated its green image during the events of World Environment Day, the bicycle plan moved toward final approval by the Board of Supervisors. Now seriously weakened because of concerns over LOS and the possibility of litigation against the plan, the document on the table, the *San Francisco Bike Plan Policy Framework*, embodied only a broad-brush, confusing policy. The plan received a "General Rule Exemption" for environmental review, was unanimously adopted by the Board of Supervisors, and signed by Mayor Newsom. All the supervisors, recognizing that the plan was very modest and not impacting the streets in their respective districts in a major way, ignored the protests of conservative activists. Not versed in the nuances of LOS or the broader environmental review process, the board assumed that bicycles were environmentally benign and did not suspect litigation on environmental grounds would be successful. Shortly after adopting the plan, the city moved ahead on several of the bike lanes proposed in the plan, including new lanes on Market Street, which quickly raised opposition from merchants troubled by the removal of on-street parking. Within a month an opponent of bicycling filed an appeal with the Superior Court of California, which hears cases involving environmental review.

The appellant was self-identified as the Coalition for Adequate Review (CAR) and the Coalition of Ninety-Nine Percent, suggesting it represented the 99 percent of San Francisco travelers who presumably did not bicycle. The lone appellant was known in the bicycle advocacy community as a disgruntled conservative gadfly who detested the SFBC and who had often blogged angrily about Critical Mass, berating almost every politician in the city, whether progressive, neoliberal, or conservative. His attorney had nothing but contempt for a bicycling and traffic-calming project on her street and claimed the city was empowering bicyclists to take over the streets. Before they filed suit, the appellant and his attorney alike routinely spoke against the bicycle plan at public meetings (they also spoke out against MOBPN), but neither was taken seriously by the political establishment at the time.[36]

In 2006 the California Superior Court, however, agreed with the pair of litigants that an adequate environmental review, including LOS, had not been undertaken. The court compared the bike plan to a clear-cutting strategy in logging, alluding to the fact that timber companies often propose to cut clusters of trees in isolation to minimize environmental harm but cumulatively end up logging an entire forest. In the case of the bicycle plan, each bicycle lane might seem benign, but cumulatively the plan could cause extensive delay to motorists, thereby having a potentially grave environmental impact on existing automobile traffic conditions. San Francisco's bicycle plan was enjoined against "any signs, pavement markings, or making any other change to any street, traffic signal, building, sidewalk, or other land use or other physical feature in San Francisco to implement the plan or any part of it."[37]

The court ruled that San Francisco had to conduct an environmental study that included LOS analysis of every intersection impacted by the bicycle plan. The legal ruling was against not bicycle space per se, but implementation without detailed analysis of traffic impacts. The injunction resulted in officials' extreme caution and reluctance to redefine the possibilities of street space, beyond just bicycle lanes, because intersection LOS was arbitrating space for transit, for pedestrians, and for infill development plans such as MOBPN, which in fact was also delayed because of complicated, expensive LOS analysis. One local politician concluded that the fear surrounding LOS made "San Francisco a city that had perfected inaction."[38] The inaction and dampening of possibilities was propagated in some measure by the conservative ideology arguably embedded in LOS.

One of the enduring legacies of LOS is that traffic engineers and decision makers believe that, as an analytical tool, its methods can be separated from ideology. Transportation historians have shown that this veil of depoliticized objectivity spans the breadth of traffic engineering.[39] Engineers developed esoteric techniques overlaid with years of field observation and experience and composed a set of professional standards, including a systematic rating system for proposed roadways.[40] But the claim of expertise operating in the absence of politics and ideology was actually deeply biased. The box of tools used by traffic engineers was designed to reflect motorists' desires and perceived need for traffic relief. The statistical approach, based on empirical observation, favored and enhanced the expansion of automobility and especially bigger, wider, faster roads. When, in 1963, the federally funded Highway Capacity Committee adopted an early iteration of LOS methodology, one insider said, "God created the heavens, the earth, and five levels of service."[41]

LOS is wrapped in the critical infrastructure of the production and circulation of automobiles and undergirds a historically contingent form of capitalism centered on automobility. The objective of using LOS is to measure how to reduce circulation time for automobiles, thereby increasing speeds and spatial range and hence quicker accumulation for businesses centered on automobility. Good LOS preserves the incumbency and exchange value of the system of automobility, which is a fixed capital investment threatened by congestion, rising fuel prices, and the entire concept of livability, if implemented. The system of automobility requires metrics like LOS to maintain its functionality as a system, but so does the individual motorist, who has sunk costs in a car, insurance, garage, perhaps a home easily accessible by car, and a retail system structured by the car. To ignore, eliminate, or reform LOS in a way that privileges other modes will bluntly devalue the spaces of the car.

The broad gamut of livability includes an emphasis on reducing VMT at the metropolitan scale through densification and reconfiguring of urban form around transit. Incorporating the themes of livability, California's SB 375, the Sustainable Communities and Climate Protection Act, explicitly calls for reducing VMT by redirecting residential growth to compact urban centers, places like the Market and Octavia area in San Francisco and in the areas around BART stations in suburbs. The bill, whose passage was the result of a political alignment between neoliberal developers and progressives in the statewide environmental movement (see chapter 1), gives incentives to builders of compact infill developments and discourages sprawl. Progressives envision SB 375 as achieving spatial planning goals that address climate change and the environment, while neoliberals envision the bill as a streamlining of the production of highly profitable infill development. One incentive for infill is a waiver for environmental review of traffic, including LOS, but only if the locality actually accepts that not using LOS is reasonable. That is a political decision that, particularly in suburbs, has implications for conservative objectives of minimizing delay for motorists and maintaining high carrying capacity of local roads. In the Bay Area, as the regional plan for addressing climate change advances, the LOS around compact development nodes will be intertwined with motorists' concern about delay on streets in those areas.

Yet localities use LOS not just to minimize delay but to accommodate subtly the conservative vision of using government to actively preserve automobility as a set of social relations. Assuming an inevitability of automobility, LOS is steeped in the conservative vision that people need cars and will continue to need them—that is, in the essentialization of automobility. For example, as the regional planning agencies in the Bay Area seek to promote compact development, there is a conservative suburban backlash, such as in Contra Costa County, to the east of San Francisco. There, a discourse about families needing to transport their children to school and to run errands, while controlling their children's environment within the car, was promulgated in 2011 and 2012 at public meetings envisioning a smart-growth retrofit of areas around BART stations.[42] Implicit in this discourse was the notion that good LOS enables a family to move their cars swiftly and conveniently while seceding from spaces that might harm children (the attendees at the meeting in 2011 berated the city of San Francisco as a place uninhabitable by families because of crime, traffic, and high-density apartment buildings).

The walkable, dense (and perhaps diverse and democratic) urban street is too cluttered and congested. In its place must be streets engineered for the free movement of vehicles that enables people to escape to an environment of health, family life, and enjoyment of nature. Fast-moving streets with good LOS serve a conservative utopia free of noise, pollution, other drivers' through traffic, and crime. Since it is allegedly responsible to move the family through the city by car, to secede, and to achieve daily needs atomistically, good LOS is an enabler of high-speed secession from the spaces of the city. When proposals are made to remove a traffic lane near transit stations so that a bicycle lane can be installed, LOS will be the technical (and presumably dispassionate and objective) metric informing conservative resistance to change.

The politics of mobility in the city of San Francisco are less conservative than in some far-flung suburban areas in the East Bay, but the litigation against the bicycle plan, which invoked similar conservative discourses, was a major setback for bicycling in the city, and it fostered a sense of confusion and cautious inaction among the city's political leaders. It tempered the momentum for change—exactly what the litigant and the conservatives wanted.

For example, a popular route for bicyclists known as the Wiggle because it circumvents steep hills via multiple jogs onto different streets includes a dangerous three-block stretch along the high-speed Oak and Fell couplet. Advocates and city planners proposed creating fully separated "cycletracks" on the Oak and Fell portion of the Wiggle, but that requires removing curbside parking spaces. Rather than remove the parking, the city could reduce the travel lanes on Oak and Fell by one and shift the parking lane outward, creating a parking buffer for the cycletrack. But this is not an option because the city would be required to do an LOS analysis, taking more time and resources and, most important, supposedly proving that bicycle space would delay cars.

To avoid this trajectory, the city decided to move forward by proposing to remove the parking. Yet this enraged some residents on the segment, who objected to losing curbside parking. Appeasing them, the mayor and the SFMTA delayed the installation of the cycletrack along this major cycling route.[43] The city tried to find seventy parking spaces to placate motorists before making the improvement to bicycle space. In this case, bicycling is stuck between two unpopular choices: travel lane removal or parking removal. Given the city's nine thousand plus cars per square mile, coupled with an official city policy goal of 20 percent of all trips by bicycle, there will be more conundrums like this unless the city truly rethinks how it systematically analyzes streets.[44]

Apart from bicycling, the litigation made local politicians less enthusiastic about removing car space to provide exclusive bus lanes or other methods of improving transit. In 2012 two major bus rapid-transit projects were undergoing lengthy, expensive traffic analysis in anticipation of opposition to the reconfiguring of streets to enhance bus speeds. The studies have taken more than five years to complete and have cost millions of dollars. In another instance, planners decided that instead of removing a travel lane to create an exclusive bus lane on one block of Haight Street in Hayes Valley they would remove curbside parking. A travel lane could have been removed, but this would have required an extended, costly LOS analysis, and the city decided it was easier to expedite the project by removing the parking. Since the bus lane proposal included removal of several bus stops, the city "found" an equivalent number of replacement parking spaces to defuse the opposition.[45]

While dampening the politics of possibilities, the setback over litigation and LOS nevertheless inspired advocates to propose changes that deprioritize motorists' LOS and prioritize metrics favoring transit, bicycling, and walking. Bicycle advocates initiated their own investigation of the planning process and found that LOS was not part of a rigid state law. Nowhere did the law require automobile LOS to trump the needs of other street users or compel the city even to apply LOS in its studies. California does not mandate that delay be analyzed by localities as part of environmental review.[46] Localities must provide substantial evidence regarding what types of environmental analysis tools they use, but they do not have to use LOS as a metric. San Francisco quietly adopted LOS in the 1970s, as did most jurisdictions around the state and nation, without public input or discussion. The adoption was largely instigated by the State of California Office of Planning and Research, which provided guidelines to localities about how to conduct environmental review in the 1970s. Those guidelines virtually codified that delay at intersections was a significant environmental impact that must be analyzed and minimized. Motorists' perception of comfort, in sum, was a central environmental concern. Since then, few had ever publicly questioned that LOS should be part of the environmental review process, that is, until bicycle advocates bumped into it.[47]

San Francisco, in short, can discontinue using LOS because state environmental law allows local governments to define the metrics of analysis for the environmental impacts of traffic.[48] Instead of dictating a one-size-fits-all approach, the state authorizes local governments to adopt by "ordinance, resolution, rule or regulation" their own "objectives, criteria, and procedures for the evaluation of projects."[49] Furthermore the San Francisco Administrative Code delegates the defining of environmental impacts to the SFPD staff. Historically, the SFPD opted to use the LOS metric promoted by the federal government's *Highway Capacity Manual* and by way of state advice and did not create its own location-specific metric. Exasperated by all of this, the SFBC pressed its allies on the Board of Supervisors to direct city staff to rethink LOS.

The Politics of Reforming LOS

Though not yet adopted as of 2012, proposals to replace LOS with a new metric have been introduced.[50] One proposal is to replace LOS with an alternative metric called auto trip generation (ATG), coupled with a schedule of impact fees on all new projects that produce additional car trips (hereafter called ATG+1). The ATG+1 proposal would change the environmental review process to evaluate any new development, such as housing or retail, in terms of the number of car trips it generates rather than of the delay it causes at intersections. A mitigation fee linked to every car trip produced would go into a citywide fund for all approved transportation plans, that is, for such projects as bicycle lanes, bus rapid transit, and improvements to the existing street system. Critically, ATG+1 would not penalize bicycle lanes or transit-only lanes because they would not generate car trips.[51] ATG+1 could, however, encourage new developments to have less parking because parking is considered a major generator of car trips. In an iteration of the proposal from 2012, discounts might be granted for developments that reduce parking below maximum allowances.

The proposal to replace LOS with ATG+1 leapfrogs the national discussion about reforming LOS, which proposes amending how streets are analyzed but preserves automobile LOS as part of the analysis. Complementing the national livability movement, a national "complete streets" movement has emerged in recent years with the aim of rethinking traffic engineering and automobility in the United States.[52] The complete streets concept includes providing wider sidewalks and bicycle lanes, improving transit stops with seating and aesthetic accoutrements, minimizing curb cuts and driveways, reducing turning radii at intersections, introducing bulb-outs and raised crosswalks, and including street trees, street furniture, and pervious surfaces for managing stormwater runoff.

A counterweight to the metric of automobile LOS, complete streets advocates urge the deployment of multimodal LOS metrics, such as measuring the quality of the pedestrian environment (sidewalk width, connectivity, curb cuts) and the transit system (frequency, crowding, service hours, dwell times).[53] Continuing to use the six-letter grade schematic, the new multimodal approach allows planners to quantify the interaction between modes that share the same street and to test trade-offs against one another. Multimodal analysis lets the planner model the reallocation of lanes on a cross-sectional profile of the street to compare varying configurations and how they impact different modes.

The new multimodal LOS metrics will not revolutionize urban transportation planning. Whether to hold out hope that agencies adopting multimodal LOS standards will reform their use of automobile level of service standards is debatable given the impetus in traffic engineering to focus primarily on moving cars, not to mention the conservative discourses found in many localities throughout the nation. Some agencies may decide that in some circumstances lower automobile LOS is acceptable in order to reach a satisfactory LOS for bicyclists, pedestrians, or transit. Places like Seattle, Washington, and Charlotte have exhibited this possibility by relaxing, though not eliminating, automobile LOS in specific locations. Yet multimodal LOS does not explicitly call for the other modes to trump automobility in the decision-making process. New multimodal LOS may allow trade-offs to be analyzed, but ultimately the decision of which mode trumps is political. If moving of cars is still the local priority, then the other multimodal LOS metrics will just be interesting data points.

San Francisco's ATG+1 proposal pushes the envelope further than a multimodal LOS approach and is consistent with the city's progressive ideology. Rather than a predict-and-provide approach, which characterizes the way conventional LOS is used, progressives believe, as an executive director of a nonprofit organization put it, "We can choose how much traffic we have." Unlike conventional traffic engineers, advocates of sustainable transportation in San Francisco are decidedly nonpositivist. They believe that simple empirical observation of car movements and extrapolation into the future are insufficient in an era of complexity and diversity. Yet between 2003 and 2012, during most of which period there was a progressive majority on the Board of Supervisors and a considerable time lapse after the city acknowledged that conventional LOS was problematic, the city had yet to replace LOS with ATG+1 or any similar metric.

There are several reasons change had not happened by 2012 despite progressive efforts. First, bureaucratic stagnation, lack of interdepartmental coordination, competing objectives, bureaucratic fiefdoms, and inconsistent priorities have been substantial barriers. For example, old-guard traffic engineers, tenured through civil service and with allies in political decision-making positions, believe their mission is to move cars swiftly and efficiently, and they therefore cling to LOS. Some simply do not want to be publicly shamed for defending the use of LOS. Other traffic engineers defend LOS because it is also an indicator of transit delay. That is, intersections with poor LOS are going to impact buses, a problem, however, that would be remedied by exclusive bus lanes and other transit priorities that are often themselves thwarted by LOS. Still other transportation planners, empathetic to the desires of progressives, believe there is no legally defensible evidence to replace LOS because of a thirty-year precedent in existing environmental decisions (despite the procedural openings described above). Rounding out the bureaucratic inertia is an accusation that a culture of indolence rules within the transportation planning bureaucracy. As one anonymous interviewee put it, "It is not that other metrics aren't available, it's that planners and consultants are lazy and want to minimize their work."

A second criticism levied at the process has been that the deliberate purpose of abolishing LOS and replacing it is not owned or championed aggressively by a specific local political figure. Although there has been some push from one or two members of the Board of Supervisors, it has largely been symbolic, largely panders to bicyclists, and is not binding. Sympathetic politicians exist, but the complex details surrounding transportation and land use are not well understood by politicians, and the fear of litigation now runs deep. Politicians frequently defer to transportation planning staff and consultants, who are stuck in the bureaucratic passivity described above. The ultimate decision makers are left directionless.

Most significant, although there was a progressive majority on the

Board of Supervisors between 2000 and 2010 as well as progressive planners employed in the agencies that oversee land use and transportation, sustainable transportation advocates and the broader progressive movement in San Francisco were not able to muster their political capital to effect change quickly. What may tip the political momentum toward a rethinking of LOS is the neoliberal developer class, which is cognizant of the role mobility has in maintaining the exchange value of the city and also envisions bicycling and transit as part of the broader commodification of livability. Sympathetic to the regional sustainability goals of reducing VMT through urban infill and compact development, neoliberal developers are poised for a livability development boom in the city.

An indication of the developer industry's support for abolishing LOS is the position of SPUR, the prominent think tank made up of developers, attorneys, architects, and planners as well as an assortment of transportation industry experts. The official position of SPUR vis-à-vis LOS is that it needs to be rethought.[54] SPUR's members and the broader development industry have long been frustrated with the burden of environmental review and particularly of LOS analysis. As the city enables upward of ninety thousand new housing units in the next several decades, LOS will complicate planning. If developers are to maximize profits it behooves them to support the abandonment of LOS or else face an environmental review process that is lengthy, uncertain, and expensive. For example, the environmental review of MOBNP took almost four years and was delayed largely because of LOS, thus putting on hold a handful of infill projects as well. Neoliberal developers also have an interest in avoiding adoption of multimodal LOS because they will be billed for the extensive studies made of each mode. They will have to fund expensive traffic studies, as they have always had to do, but in addition studies of pedestrian LOS, bicycle LOS, and transit LOS, all of which were not part of environmental analysis in 2012.

Yet simply replacing LOS with ATG+1 is not a move neoliberals will endorse unless it is made on their terms, and in 2012 a variation on the ATG+1 proposal was put forth by the city, partly on behalf of developers. This proposal dispensed with using LOS in environmental review, but instead of examining ATG it considers the impact of development on the motorized transportation system as a whole, proposing a new, citywide transportation sustainability fee. This omnibus Transportation Sustainability Program would estimate development in the city over the next twenty years—presumably the ninety thousand housing units suggested by ABAG—and conduct a nexus study and environmental review of projected development and transportation projects. Ironically, the Transportation Sustainability Program also requires an environmental review, but it is not clear if it must include analysis of LOS.[55]

A critical juncture in the abolishing of LOS and replacing it with ATG+1 or the omnibus transportation impact fee will be the debate about the amount of the impact fee. If neoliberals believe the proposed fee is too high, they could abandon support for LOS reform or at least attempt to block adoption. The new metric is also intertwined with parking policy, and while developers might be induced to reduce parking in order to avoid fees, they are also compelled to provide more parking because of the profits derived from it (see chapter 4). If the fee is too low relative to the profits made in parking provision, then it will not discourage more parking. If progressives believe the fee is too low, the already tenuous progressive-neoliberal détente on LOS reform could become frayed. Already there is worry that a fee on each car trip could be construed as anti-car and that many motorists will oppose the measure.

Neoliberals see the issue through the lens of how much the ATG+1 or transportation impact fee reduces their profits. That potential drawback was aggravated by the global real estate financial crises of 2008–12, which resulted in limited new housing construction in the city. Neoliberal developers who accepted exactions and impact fees during economic boom years before 2008 turned hostile to more fees in 2009 and remained so into 2012. In fact, they successfully lobbied for fee deferral on the city's other impact fees, including the community improvement fee for the Market and Octavia area.

Despite the lack of finality, there is much to be gleaned from how San Francisco's debate about LOS is unfolding, and it is probably safe to anticipate that some sort of change in how streets are analyzed and configured is forthcoming. San Francisco is on the vanguard of a new politics of street space. If progressive advocates, bolstered by neoliberal reurbanization of capital, are successful in abolishing LOS in environmental review, it will be a precedent that leapfrogs the more incremental multimodal LOS approach proposed nationally by the complete streets movement. SB 375 shows there is statewide recognition that LOS impedes strategies of reducing VMT through compact growth, and attempts have been made to revise the environmental review process pertaining to traffic analysis. Most profound, however, is that despite the injunction and complicated setbacks and delays regarding how streets are analyzed, bicycling boomed in San Francisco. But with that boom came a new bicycle politics.

Sunday Streets and the Moderate Politics of Bicycle Space

Notwithstanding the sideshow over the rethinking of LOS and the discouraging impact of the injunction, bicycling expanded in San Francisco by 71 percent, and by 2012, as noted, the SFBC had grown to twelve thousand members. Not a single bike lane was constructed between 2006 and 2010, suggesting that bike space, while important, is not the only reason for bicycling. Ideology matters too. Specifically, a progressive mobility ethos, stressing that social responsibility requires less driving and more attention to how one lives and behaves, has contributed to increased rates of bicycling. Complementing this is people's desire to be physically active and health conscious. Yet bicycling has also come to be seen as a key part of economic development in neoliberal, entrepreneurial discourses. In sum, a successful city is one that has a youthful, fit, creative class that bicycles. This neoliberal discourse about bicycling has influenced the politics of the SFBC.

While not necessarily abandoning its core progressive values, such as seeking to promote a more equitable and environmentally sound city, bicycle advocacy in San Francisco underwent an ideological shift between 2000 and 2012. Significantly, the SFBC further distanced itself from Critical Mass, especially the more radical, confrontational aspects of the rides, while also carefully crafting a mainstream, often neoliberal political discourse and invoking a family values message that countered the conservative framing of mobility and families.

The original agenda of the SFBC, closely aligned to the Critical Masses of the 1990s, had its roots in a broad criticism of automobility, but the new SFBC took pains to stress that the majority of its membership owned cars and yet chose to bicycle. The SFBC of the nineties was characterized by a leadership that offered progressive critiques of the geography of capitalism and of a lifestyle centered on unfettered hyperconsumption, the incessant speeding up of everyday life, competition rather than cooperation, and possessive individualism rather than collective action: in others words, a critique of neoliberalism and conservatism.

In 2012 the new SFBC was sponsored by large corporate foundations whose wealth came from capitalist investments, and this included a who's who of San Francisco and Silicon Valley businesses and entrepreneurs. Among them, Google, Microsoft, Pacific Gas and Electric, an array of private transportation, urban planning, and architectural consultants, real estate firms, attorneys, and individual donors connected to software and social networking firms. The organization maintained a very large volunteer base as well, one that provided some sixteen thousand hours of free work, and 26 percent of its income came from the fees of its thousands of progressively inclined individual members.[56] Moreover, the staff of the SFBC maintained core progressive values even if these were not front and center in the organization's public promotional materials and talking points. In addition, despite the large corporate and foundation financing, the SFBC relied very heavily on in-kind support from hundreds of independent small businesses such as restaurants, bicycle dealers, bars and cafes, and other small-scale retailers.

The progressive–neoliberal hybridization was pronounced at the fortieth anniversary fundraiser for the SFBC, held in June 2011. The event, known as the Golden Wheel Awards, took place in the Green Room of the stately War Memorial Building, which has a large, elegant veranda overlooking City Hall and suggestively symbolizes the new power of the twelve-thousand-member organization. After cocktails and hors d'oeuvres, the executive director of the SFBC opened the awards ceremony by observing that "a room full of stars" was attending the gala, acknowledging such key donors as the Hellman Foundation (heirs to Wells Fargo Bank) and well-heeled law, tech, and engineering firms. The director then congratulated the Union Square Business Improvement Association, which, ironically, had historically opposed parking reform and freeway removal yet was now promoting a pedestrianization project on Powell Street in the heart of the city's premier shopping district. The project, while improving conditions for pedestrians, was also an improvement that brought more value to property owners. Notable public officials in attendance included a spectrum of progressive and neoliberal members of the Board of Supervisors (missing were conservatives), the directors and pivotal staff of the city's planning and transportation departments, the city attorney and city assessor, who was campaigning for mayor, and the keynote speaker, San Francisco's interim mayor, who had replaced Mayor Newsom in early 2011 when he was elected as lieutenant governor of California.[57]

The new mayor, who came from the city bureaucracy and had previously never held elected office, was suspected of stealthily running for reelection despite promising he would not seek office but rather remain satisfied as a place-holder for the next mayor. In his remarks to the room of three hundred SFBC supporters, he stated that he was planning to boast about San Francisco's bicycle agenda at the U.S. Conference of Mayors later that month. He also remarked that, Critical Mass and the antagonistic injunction aside, the "SFBC brought fun back into streets," meaning that a more conciliatory tone characterized the SFBC. More important, the mayor promised to advocate acceptance of the coalition's new signature plan, called Connecting the City, which proposed fully separated cycletracks, even on portions of controversial high traffic volume streets like Fell and Oak.

This progressive–neoliberal rapprochement around bicycling was mutually beneficial in that progressives were realizing possibilities of comprehensive bicycle space, while neoliberals were recognizing that bicycling, as part of the broader livability agenda, was a profitable economic development strategy. Somewhat more cynical, the *San Francisco Bay Guardian* declared the end of the progressive era in San Francisco politics because of the loss of a progressive majority on the Board of Supervisors in 2010, and the paper lamented that many self-identified progressives had gravitated to neoliberal discourses about the city's development.[58] The backdrop of the awards ceremony was a heated election campaign in which a handful of candidates were straddling the progressive–neoliberal divide and jockeying to get SFBC's endorsement, but also in the air was a national neoliberal discourse about livability as an economic development strategy. Truly entrepreneurial cities were cities that encouraged bike lanes, as enunciated by the new neoliberal mayor of Chicago, Rahm Emanuel, and as practiced by Mayor Michael Bloomberg in New York City. In San Francisco, as neoliberals demanded tax breaks to keep the social networking firm Twitter from moving to the suburbs, bicycling was promoted as vital in keeping creative class companies in the city.

Bicycle advocates, too, were tactically deploying conservative rhetoric promoting bicycling. Invoking a family values discourse, the director of the SFBC concluded the anniversary ceremony in 2011 with a promotional film about the Connecting the City campaign that outlined how eight-year-old children and eighty-year-old grandparents would be safe and comfortable using cycletracks, making it possible for families to bicycle through the city on one hundred miles of fully separated bikeways by 2020. Finally, she stressed that San Francisco was at a tipping point for bicycling, with 33 percent of respondents to a recent poll expressing a desire to bike daily if true bicycle space was in place for them to do so. The SFBC, steeped in progressive history, had a new Connecting the City campaign financed by neoliberal capital that was invoking conservative discourses and, in the words of the SFBC executive director, enabling more San Franciscans to "imagine the possibilities." Like Critical Mass a decade before, the SFBC was building political support for the removal of car space in order to have safe cycling and walking spaces in the city. Yet rather than couch its message in an adversarial tone, the emphasis was now on the safety of children and parents and on providing more equitable access to open space.

The most pronounced manifestation of this new politics was SFBC's involvement with the city's Sunday Streets program, promoted as a family-oriented event that temporarily opens long segments of streets exclusively to bicyclists, walkers, and other nonmotorized users while banning automobiles. Sunday Streets began in 2008 while the bicycle plan was still under injunction and borrowed from the Cyclovia concept first introduced in Bogotá, Colombia, and now found in several other Latin American cities and in New York City, where it is called Summer Streets. The idea of holding a Cyclovia event in San Francisco came from the SFBC in 2008. After visiting a similar event in Portland, the SFBC worked closely with the city and with physical fitness, health, and urbanist organizations to hold a Sunday Streets event in September 2008.[59] Unlike Critical Mass participants, the advocates took a more mainstream, less confrontational approach but promoted the same ends—to provide a car-free space for safe bicycling and, in this case, walking, jogging, and skating.

Supporters framed Sunday Streets to appeal to a broader segment of the political establishment, one that went beyond simply sustainable transportation activists. For example, the concept was put forward as supplying much-needed open space in neighborhoods lacking adequate parks and recreation, such as Chinatown, the Mission District, and the low-income Bayview neighborhood in the southeastern sector of the city. The target audience of the initial Sunday Streets was a hypothetical young mother with two children who had difficulty juggling her children's recreation needs. She could not let her kids play in front of the house because of automobiles, but then she had to lug them across town to Golden Gate Park to find safe recreational opportunities. The idea of bringing the parks to underserved neighborhoods had a very strong social justice angle. Families with children have indeed packed Sunday Streets events. In June 2010 twenty-five thousand people were estimated to have enjoyed the Sunday Street event in the Mission District. Large numbers of children wandered the length of the open roadways. These are children rarely seen on bicycles or walking in the city on a normal day because their parents are afraid and chauffeur them in cars or on public transit. A huge latent demand for bicycling has been discovered via Sunday Streets.

While Sunday Streets did not explicitly engage the sustainable transportation vision of ending automobile hegemony, immediately after the first event organizers got numerous emails and phone calls suggesting that many people became more excited about bicycling because of the event.

Attendees pointed out that they had forgotten how easy it was to ride a bicycle, and that riding a bicycle for distances of three to five miles was easier than they thought. Children were also nagging their parents to bicycle more. As one organizer put it, Sunday Streets showed that "people aren't afraid of bicycling or walking for transportation, rather, they are afraid of car traffic."[60] Sunday Streets expanded residents' politics of possibilities, and more people realized that car traffic is a profound mental barrier to bicycling in a city that is otherwise generally easy to bicycle in.

From 2009 through 2012 Sunday Streets led to a cautious optimism among officials and advocates about rethinking San Francisco's streets. For example, it reignited a decades-long debate about banning cars on San Francisco's signature thoroughfare, Market Street. Not to be outdone by Mayor Newsom, who claimed to have come up with the idea for Sunday Streets, his progressive rivals on the Board of Supervisors called for a study to reduce car traffic on Market Street.[61] Instead of a total ban, the city took an innovative approach and experimented with forcing diversions for private automobiles at key points along the thoroughfare. The pilot project, initiated in early 2010 and modified incrementally, included the use of impact-cushioning soft-hit posts to create a barrier between a generously wide and now green-painted bike lane and motorized lanes.

In May 2010 the city released preliminary results that suggested two hundred fewer private cars were using Market Street during rush hour.[62] The interim study showed that transit travel times decreased by almost one minute and that bicyclists and taxi drivers liked the forced right turn of private cars. The results have been positive, and in 2011 the diversion was made permanent, although the signage and sandbagged barrier, as opposed to a permanent physical structure, remain in place. The incremental rather than the comprehensive approach was cautious, but it changed the order of implementation. Instead of making a design proposal and then spending years studying it, the approach now is to make modest changes and study the impacts as they unfold in real time. As a trade-off, the SFBC and other advocates backed off their bolder vision of a completely car-free Market Street. In 2011 Twitter signed a lease for office space directly on the new green bike lane.

Connecting the City

In the early 1990s there were few bike lanes, few cyclists, and little enthusiasm for bicycle space among San Francisco politicians. Critical Mass challenged the status quo and inspired thousands of mostly youthful progressive residents to take up bicycling and to get engaged in the political process. By 2005 the SFBC was five thousand strong, but a conservative backlash culminated in a punitive injunction restricting the production of bicycle space for almost five years. Not daunted, thousands more San Franciscans took up bicycling even though there was inadequate bicycle space, showing that ideology and values matter as much as infrastructure. Yet this could go only so far, and absent adequate bicycle space young children, families, and less adventurous adults would not cycle. The SFBC shifted away from an anti-car politics represented by Critical Mass and toward an ideological détente with neoliberals, while also embracing some conservative discourses about families. In August 2010 the injunction on the city's bike plan was lifted after the city was found to be in full compliance with court-required environmental reviews of traffic and parking issues.[63] The city moved forward on thirty-five bicycle projects, adding thirty-four new miles to the existing forty-five miles of bicycle lanes, and by mid-2011 had completed half of the projects on an accelerated schedule.

On many mornings more cyclists than automobiles can be seen on Market Street, and bicycling is rapidly increasing: its mode share is projected to reach 10 percent of all trips citywide in the next few years. A resolution by the Board of Supervisors promotes a 20 percent mode share by bicyclists by 2020. Inspired by the success on Market Street, the city is experimenting with innovative temporary street closures, diversions, and the creation of "parklets" in some curbside parking spaces (also endorsed by neoliberals because they enhance the value of adjacent properties). The SFBC began the Connecting the City campaign, advocating that one hundred miles of fully separated cycletracks be built, resembling the type of infrastructure found in northwest European cities like Copenhagen. Their immediate goal is a set of strategic east–west and north–south bicycle trunk routes crossing the city.

These results are largely due to the persistent promotion of well-informed, passionate, and at times savvy advocates. They all began with visions, and by organizing around that vision they fostered a politics of possibilities for urban space that is not dominated by automobiles. The grass-roots efforts to enhance bicycling pushed the envelope for residents and for the city. However, the SFBC has clearly moderated its politics, and it remains to be seen if it has been co-opted instead. While still an important part of the broader progressive politics of the city, bicycling is only part of the formula for a progressive mobility vision.

CHAPTER 6

Transit First?
The Politics of Financing Muni

Relative to the rest of the United States, San Francisco has a good reputation for public transit use. While nationally 5.1 percent of workers commute by public transportation, the San Francisco–Oakland metropolitan area has the highest transit share of commuting (15.5 percent) of any metropolitan area outside of New York City.[1] It is among the few metro areas, followed in descending order by Washington, Boston, and Chicago, with a transit commute share above 10 percent. Portland, which also has a reputation for green transport modes, lags behind even Los Angeles, with about 6 percent of workers using transit.[2] Moreover, the city of San Francisco has a considerably higher transit ridership than the rest of the Bay Area, with 31 percent of all commute trips within the city by public transit, compared to 9.4 percent of commuters to other Bay Area employment nodes and a paltry 4 percent in greater San Jose.[3]

San Francisco's transit ridership reflects the fact that public transit is the keystone for making compact development viable. Every weekday morning 88,000 people use Muni to access the 343-acre downtown core, one of the densest concentrations of office space in the country.[4] The overall mode share for transit to downtown San Francisco from all over the region ranges between 64 percent and 70 percent of all trips. In some of the large office buildings, 72 percent of commuters use public transportation. In the wider, 2.5-square-mile area, half of workers—170,000—take public transportation, more than those who drive alone.[5] Transit is what makes density work.

If the Bay Area, arguably a national leader on policies to address climate change, is to reduce per capita driving by 10 to 15 percent while adding two million people and 900,000 housing units by 2035, the region must expand transit capacity.[6] What's more, 70 percent of new growth (1.4 million people, 630,000 homes, and hundreds of thousands of jobs) is planned to be concentrated in relatively small geographic areas within existing urban and suburban nodes, known as priority development areas. Without adequate transit capacity this will be a dysfunctional embarrassment to livability, as it will mean continued heavy reliance on cars.

Yet despite the obvious need there are few details about how the Bay Area transit armature will expand or how transit will be funded in ways that substantially reduce car dependency.[7] The best-case scenario presented by regional planners is that 80 percent of future travel will be in cars.[8] The Bay Area's twenty-eight transit agencies, each with its own funding and organizational structure, schedules, and politics, are fragmented, and there is little coordinated visioning between the systems for expansion, although a new universal fare card has been introduced.

Contrary to the Bay Area, San Francisco has planners and sustainable transportation advocates who have begun to imagine what kind of transit system is needed to substantially reduce driving, reduce emissions, and allow livable infill. This transit-first policy is potentially an inspiring benchmark for other cities to aspire to. However, the major impediment to achieving transit first is money. In 2011 the city had identified only 10 percent of the $167 million needed for a modest set of transit-first proposals and still needed to conduct a $1 million, two-year environmental impact report. Two separate, long-planned transit projects, bus rapid-transit lines on Van Ness Avenue and Geary Boulevard, also languished in prolonged environmental review, as LOS impacts on automobiles were studied and hostility was expressed toward removal of car space, making such lines politically volatile. In short, a politics of possibilities for a stable, expanding transit-first program—one that truly reduces automobility—is difficult to realize. But what would a city like San Francisco need to do to make meaningful transit improvements?

What "Transit First" Might Look Like

Geographically limited to the forty-seven square miles of the city, San Francisco's Muni, used roughly by 700,000 passengers boarding 1,050 buses and trains daily, is the Bay Area's largest transit system and seventh largest in the United States. More than half of Muni's fleet is composed of electric trains and trolley buses running on overhead wires, the electricity being generated at the city-owned Hetch Hetchy hydroelectric facility in the Sierra Nevada Mountains; the balance of the fleet is composed of conventional diesel and hybrid-diesel electric buses. Muni is one of the greenest transportation systems in the United States. Compared to the city's 350,000 registered automobiles, which, together with visiting cars, produce 33 percent of GHG emissions in San Francisco, Muni produces just 1.5 percent of the city's total emissions.[9] If Muni were expanded to carry 920,000 passengers per day, per capita GHG emissions in San Francisco could be reduced by 30 percent, even if the population in the city increased.[10] These potential reductions are noteworthy when compared to Bay Area targets of less than 12 percent per capita.[11]

Recognizing Muni's promise for reducing emissions, a majority of San Francisco voters approved Proposition A in November 2007 and directed the SFMTA to show how driving could be reduced and transit ridership increased.[12] Aligning with state emissions reduction targets of 80 percent below 1990 levels by 2050, the new policy included aggressive short-term incremental yardsticks for the city's transportation system: 20 percent below 1990 levels by 2012, 25 percent by 2017, 40 percent by 2025, and 50 percent by 2035.[13] These targets are ambitious, and the city failed to reach the goal for 2012, but, while there is no penalty if the city fails to reach targets, the directive has shaped dialogue about reducing automobility through expanding transit. San Francisco already has the advantage of relatively high transit ridership, but in terms of truly reducing automobility Muni has a long way to go. Yet planners have mapped out how the city might achieve more.

If San Francisco is to reduce GHG emissions to 50 percent below 1990 levels by 2035, driving must be reduced from 62 percent to 30 percent of all daily trips in the city.[14] Concomitantly, transit must increase from 17 percent to 30 percent of all daily trips by 2035. These figures reflect the abovementioned 30–30–40 split the SFMTA envisions for mode shares in the city, and while a substantial part of the reduction in automobility would come from land use changes that promote bicycling and walking (roughly 20 percent mode split for each), expansion of transit is obligatory.

To meet the ambitious reductions in emissions and driving, San Francisco will need to do two things: radically reconfigure streets to privilege transit and dramatically expand the number of transit vehicles.

A transit-first policy includes prioritizing transit over automobiles through the deployment of exclusive bus lanes, the removal of lanes and curbside parking available to cars, signal prioritization for buses at intersections, restrictions on turns for automobiles, bus stop improvements, including bus stop bulb-outs and amenities, proof-of-payment schemes, which eliminate fare collection by the operators, new low-floor, multi-floor, quick-boarding buses, and other infrastructure that expedites the movement of public transit.[15] Much as in the case of bicycle space (see chapter 5), San Francisco must create a transit space in the city, including a comprehensive grid of transit-first streets overlaid upon the city's existing transportation armature. Transit space must exclude car-oriented land uses like drive-in fast food restaurants, garages and curb cuts, surface parking lots, filling stations, and car washes. Other requisites include relatively low fares, deeply discounted monthly and annual transit passes, and user-friendly route maps and directional signage, scheduling, and high frequency, reliable service at all hours of the day and late into the night. Furthermore, although a matter beyond the scope of San Francisco city politics, a meaningful transit-first system would include seamless connections to an equally comprehensive regional transit system, such as to BART, to the regional ferries, and to Caltrain, the commuter rail system serving the Peninsula, as well as coordinated links to other local transit operations.

Transit first is a modest, pragmatic approach to making the existing transit system work more efficiently, and it reflects that, at least for now in San Francisco, more dramatic infrastructures such as new subways to the south or west side are politically infeasible. On paper, San Francisco has had transit-first guidelines since 1974, partly as a remedy to the canceling of the freeways in the 1960s and partly because voters rejected subways in 1966. But since then very little street space has been reconfigured for transit, and the city was frozen in a mobility stalemate. In 1999, in an atmosphere of high-profile debates over removal of the Central Freeway and bicycle politics, transit first was codified as part of the city's charter but remained elusive because for the most part the city's streets lacked transit-first treatments. In 2006 the transit-first policy was reaffirmed with the Transit Effectiveness Project (TEP, pronounced *tee, ee, pee*), which asserted a goal of enabling anyone in San Francisco to contemplate living in the city without a car.[16] The TEP was the first comprehensive analysis of the transit system since the late 1970s and one of the most thorough in the nation, and in 2011 a more detailed package of transit-first treatments drawing from the TEP was presented.

In addition to transit-first policies on city streets, more buses and trains are needed. SFMTA planners suggest that to decrease emissions to 50 percent of 1990 levels the capacity of Muni might need to be doubled by 2035, from the ability to carry 700,000 daily passengers to 1.4 million passengers.[17] The highest daily ridership Muni ever had was 970,000 passengers immediately after the Second World War, and the most aggressive plan the city has considered in recent years was a variation of the TEP, called *TEP Enhanced,* which included a scenario to accommodate 920,000 daily passengers by 2015 with only a 25 percent expansion of service.[18] Expanding capacity is expensive. In a detailed analysis of what it would cost, in 2008 dollars, if Muni were to increase daily ridership by 78 percent (from 700,000 to 1.25 million trips daily), the city would need $888 million to acquire 283 new buses, 30 new streetcars, and 138 new light-rail vehicles for the Muni Metro, and 420 new operators would have to be hired, with an annual operations and maintenance budget of $139 million.[19] New storage and maintenance facilities would be needed because existing facilities are jampacked, and at current procurement rates it would take at least ten years to achieve this expansion.

In a separate analysis, planners advise that Muni would need between $1 billion and $1.7 billion above routine maintenance and replacements to reduce emissions by 50 percent of 1990 levels by 2035.[20] This includes only vehicle procurement and related infrastructure such as overhead wires for electrical trolley buses. If transit-first ideas like exclusive bus lanes on complete streets were included, an additional $410 to $450 million would be needed.[21] It is not known what the operating costs would be, but by doubling capacity, hundreds of millions of additional dollars will be needed annually to operate transit (in 2011 SFMTA's operations cost $780 million annually). A less ambitious but quicker package of transit-first infrastructure, the *TEP Implementation Plan,* was proposed in 2011 at a cost of $167 million but expanding the amount of transit service only between 5 and 10 percent, depending on the extent to which the plan is implemented; it excluded new vehicles and operations costs.[22]

Regardless of the scenario, San Francisco transit planners are developing a map of what needs to be done in terms of physical infrastructure to substantially reduce driving. Yet, with the exception of a 1.7-mile, $1.6-billion downtown subway extension project that is years from completion, instead of financing transit expansion the city of San Francisco has cut

Muni service and doubled fares since 2000. In 2009 Muni raised fares by 33 percent, the largest single increase in a century, while reducing frequency and eliminating routes.[23] In early 2010 Muni made even deeper cuts, eliminating roughly 10 percent of all existing service hours, and obviously has not been able to expand capacity. Muni estimates that simply keeping up with existing service and deferred maintenance requires $455 million annually, and it costs just under $200 million to compensate the 2,200 operators.[24]

Muni is not the only transit system beleaguered by financial misfortune. The seven largest transit systems in the United States need at least $50 billion just to be up to code on safety and maintenance, and all transit systems need a total of $78 billion.[25] In 2009, 90 percent of the nation's transit systems had implemented or proposed fare increases or service cuts, and the vast majority had cuts in state and local funding.[26] The Bay Area's twenty-eight transit agencies need an estimated $1 billion a year in addition to what is already available simply for upkeep of the systems, and few are thinking beyond that present reality.[27] Both Oakland's and San Jose's transit service was reduced by 8 percent, fares were raised, and each system imposed layoffs, deferred maintenance, hiring freezes, and furloughs in 2009 and 2010.[28]

What's more, the State of California withdrew large amounts of operating funds for Muni and other transit agencies in order to backfill the state's financial problems. Between 2007 and 2010 the state withheld $180 million from Muni for operations, while Bay Area transit agencies lost $700 million, and $4 billion was cut from transit statewide.[29] Meanwhile, the subsequent bailouts of the automobile industry by the Obama administration included financial incentives to entice people to buy new cars, but there was no federal funding either for transit operations or to help people purchase transit passes. Consequently, transit agencies all around the United States continued to cut service and raise fares to meet their budget shortfalls. By 2011 at least 150 transit systems had cut service and raised fares.[30]

Ironically, these severe cuts to transit came at a time when transit systems around the nation, including Muni, were reporting record ridership. In 2008 the Bay Area saw the highest ridership in decades, at 500 million passengers, as gasoline reached $4.50 per gallon. Both Muni and BART were unable to adequately transport commuters at peak times, and in San Francisco anecdotal evidence suggests many transit riders switched to bicycling and informal carpooling or back to solo driving because of the persistent overcrowding. Today, Muni is filled to capacity when commuters stream into the downtown. Mainline bus routes and light-rail lines are saturated, and in neighborhoods like Hayes Valley waiting passengers regularly find that buses are already filled by the time they reach their neighborhood. This transit crowding is especially problematic given that new infill plans such as MOBNP were adopted with the understanding that there will be more transit capacity to absorb thousands of new residents. The suggestion of adding 90,000 housing units in San Francisco, mostly in the eastern half, is workable only if transit capacity is expanded.

The Politics of Muni Finance

The question of how to properly finance Muni is one of the most vexing and complicated aspects of San Francisco's politics of mobility. Part of the problem stems from a long history of insufficient federal and state support for transit. Historically, the federal government has limited funds to transit infrastructure and vehicles and provided minimal operating funds for a short time in the 1980s only to retreat by the 1990s. Federal policy toward transit has devolved largely to cities and states. California's Proposition 13, which since 1978 has limited local governments' ability to raise taxes, has restricted state and local support of transit as well. Prop 13 capped local residential and commercial property tax rates to 1975 levels and restricted tax increases by requiring a two-thirds majority in the state legislature for all increases, reducing public funding for local and state programs from parks and schools to transportation. It also mandated a two-thirds voter approval for special local taxes for transit.

Ideologically, Prop 13 represented an antigovernment ethos among a sizable number of mostly white suburban voters in California that was interlinked with conservative discourses about social welfare for immigrants and the working poor, term limits on elected officials, opposition to new affirmative action programs in the public sector, and broad disenchantment with the racial and class shifts in the state, especially in the public schools.[31] It also reflected an ideological shift from a belief in the merits of large public works, such as transit, water, and universities, to distrust in government public works and the broader public realm. Hence it was not just a suburban-based conservative backlash but also a new neoliberal thrust toward privatization, minimizing government regulation, and maximizing profit on private property. The geographer Richard Walker identified Prop 13 as the bridgehead to neoliberalism in the United States, and particularly in California.[32]

Consistent with its progressive spirit, San Francisco was one of the only counties in California in which a majority of voters opposed Prop 13. But the statewide approval of the proposition was a blunt and frustrating reality for San Francisco progressives. Their city may have a simple majority of voters empathetic to such progressive values as raising taxes to underwrite transit expansion, but not a two-thirds majority. For example, in the early 1980s progressives advocated for a transit assessment district (TAD), an annual property assessment on downtown commercial land that would provide revenue for Muni operations, and for a transit impact development fee (TIDF) on all new downtown office developments, which would pay for new buses and trains.[33] The logic of progressives was that downtown land was incredibly valuable because of the access provided by Muni. Taxes and fees on property owners were a fair exchange for the value supplied by society at large. However, progressives could not muster enough support either to sway the Board of Supervisors or to put a transit tax on the ballot and were outmaneuvered by downtown landowners.

Recognizing that some amount of revenue was reasonable, business elites, including SPUR, developed a preemptive lower TIDF and shifted attention away from the annual TAD. In 1981 a TIDF for new offices only (retail was exempt) was adopted, and progressive momentum was diminished. Making the situation even more discouraging, the city's largest real estate mogul, Walter Shorenstein, sued the city, asserting that the TIDF violated Prop 13 because it was a new tax that needed voter approval.[34] While the litigation ultimately failed, it became apparent that even a minor fee increase on property owners would require tremendous political capital, and no formidable, sustained transit advocacy organization materialized in the 1980s to promote Muni finance. Instead Muni lurched through the 1980s.[35]

By the early 1990s Muni fares had risen to eighty-five cents, the quality of service was eroding, and the federal government reduced operating subsidies for public transit, which had peaked in the early 1980s but then declined during the Reagan, Bush, and Clinton years and were finally eliminated in 1997. In 1994 a coalition of citywide progressives collected signatures to place a downtown TAD on the ballot, titled Proposition O, "Downtown Transit Assessment District Preparation."[36] Progressives proposed that the city create a two-square-mile TAD on commercial office property, excluding retail and hotel properties, and suggested that downtown office property owners collectively pay $54 million annually to offset the impact on commuters using Muni to access downtown. Prop O mandated only that the city study, not adopt, the proposal, so it needed only a simple majority rather than two-thirds. The final decision for imposing the assessment would still lie with the Muni governing board, appointed by the mayor, and Prop O was, in effect, an advisory proposition.

Prop O had widespread support. It was backed by seven members of the Board of Supervisors, the newly resuscitated SFBC, teachers' and trade unions, social service providers, disability and senior advocates, environmental groups, affordable housing and tenants' rights groups, and Muni's operators' union. Despite the broad progressive coalition that endorsed the TAD, it was defeated by 55 percent to 45 percent via an aggressive campaign led by the Chamber of Commerce.[37] Among the opponents were a combination of downtown real estate interests, such as the Shorenstein Company and the Building Owners and Management Association (BOMA), and the San Francisco Republican Party, the Republican mayor Frank Jordan, two conservative members of the Board of Supervisors (who had fought against freeway removal in the 1990s), the Golden Gate Restaurant Association, and an assortment of smaller business associations that argued that the tax would be passed on to tenants.[38] During the campaign the opposition portrayed Muni as being ridden by crime, filthy, strewn with graffiti, unsafe, and unreliable and further argued that before businesses were taxed Muni needed to reform its operations and management. SPUR, while acknowledging that Muni needed additional revenues, nevertheless sided with the opposition, stating that Prop O was a blank check for the city to simply drop its subsidy from the general fund and shift it to social services while saddling businesses with more taxes. SPUR may have advocated for progressive transit-first policies on city streets, but at its core, when it came to finance, SPUR was neoliberal about transit financing.[39]

Prop O was the last progressive attempt to create a TAD, but by 1998 widespread public anger at Muni's poor reliability and quality of service exploded, especially among a new gentrifying cadre of white urban professionals who relied on it for commuting downtown.[40] Muni's on-time performance hovered around 50 percent, but the flashpoint was the infamous so-called Muni meltdown, when the operations of the Muni Metro light rail began breaking down repeatedly because of problems with new but defective automatic train control computers. Thousands of commuters were stranded underground, sometimes for hours at a time.[41] The surface system fared no better: it was swamped with automobile traffic as the dot-com boom drew new people with cars into the city, many of whom were commuting by car to Silicon Valley. Frustration with transit was accompanied by the backdrop of citywide debates over the removal of the

Central Freeway and the rancor over Critical Mass and the bicycle movement. Political reform of Muni was therefore timely, and the mayor, the
Board of Supervisors, and an array of business, environment, and neighborhood groups plotted a reform package. Yet this time the reform had a
decidedly neoliberal tone rather than a progressive one.

With a coherent progressive transit advocacy virtually absent in the city,
a new transit advocacy organization, Rescue Muni, engaged in a neoliberal discourse to reform the railway. Established in 1996 by a small group
of technocratic transit enthusiasts and downtown professionals who regularly used transit for commuting, Rescue Muni was thrust into a central
role of promoting transit first but also directed much of its political ire at
Muni's management and labor unions, stressing that both parties were un-
responsive to passengers.[42] Affiliated with SPUR, Rescue Muni promoted
a set of largely neoliberal reforms, tempered by some progressive input,
that went to the ballot as Proposition E in 1999. The politically expedient issue was to resolve the immediate breakdowns in Muni and keep the
downtown functioning and lucrative, but, with the exception of diverting general fund money collected from existing parking fees to Muni, the
initiative decisively did not include new net revenues. This meant it did
not need the two-thirds threshold, but also that substantive, long-lasting
transit-first policies would remain elusive.

The centerpiece of Prop E—what attracted widespread public endorsement despite the frustrations with Muni's reliability—was a mandated
on-time performance of 85 percent (similar to that of commercial air-
lines). The neoliberal discourse promoted by Rescue Muni, SPUR, and
downtown land interests emphasized that worker absenteeism, rude
drivers, overtime pay for drivers, and generous work rules, which restricted the agency from hiring part-time drivers, were to blame for the
dismal performance of Muni. Prop E directed Muni to create new work
rules and pay scales based on performance of the system, making Muni
more businesslike.

A second goal of Prop E was to create the SFMTA, folding the city's
disparate transit, parking, and traffic engineering agencies into a single
transportation agency. This move reflected good governance and efficiency policies promoted by some progressives and neoliberals, but especially
by SPUR and the Chamber of Commerce. It placed decisions about street
space in the same agency as Muni, and to progressives the merging of the
various departments meant that the allocation of street space could be
more closely coordinated with transit space. It made transit first an official part of the city charter and folded bicycling into the transit-first pol-

icy, thus garnering the support of the SFBC. The language in Prop E also mandated that the new board overseeing Muni diligently seek funding for transit, including expanding parking revenues to help finance Muni and avoiding burdensome fare hikes, which disproportionately impact lower-income riders.

Tellingly, Prop E delineated that a portion of the city's existing general fund go to Muni, meaning the city would need to shift priorities, such as social services or libraries, in order to meet this new obligation, and, as mentioned, it did not include any explicit new funding sources, such as a TAD or TIF.[43] These schemes effectively pitted one progressive program against another and aggravated the divide between progressives focused on sustainable mobility and those concerned with access for the poor and working class.

In November 1999 Prop E was approved by 61 percent of voters, with widespread promotion by the San Francisco Chamber of Commerce, BOMA, SPUR, Rescue Muni, and even the San Francisco Republican Party. To be sure, Prop E got part of the progressive vote because it was on the same ballot as the Central Freeway, and advocates for freeway removal, neighborhood groups, and environmentalists endorsed Prop E because the establishment of performance measures and reliability was part of the progressive mobility platform. It was supported by Supervisor Tom Ammiano, the progressive write-in candidate for mayor in 1999. Labor unions did not object to Prop E because the ballot language, despite its rhetoric about disciplining labor, was vague, open-ended, and easily circumvented. Some progressives did oppose Prop E but could not marshal the detailed attention needed to shape or defeat it, and many were cornered because, like the Central Freeway removal and Octavia Boulevard, it offered the best immediate compromise for reforming Muni at a time of crisis.

A legacy of Prop E was the creation of the seven-member SFMTA board, which was appointed by the mayor. The board was an additional bulwark against progressive reforms as long as the mayor's office reflected neoliberal values. The budget for Muni was set by the SFMTA board, and when the budget was sent to the Board of Supervisors for approval, it could only reject the budget with a two-thirds veto but could not modify it. This was critical because in 2000 and 2002 progressives swept the elections for Board of Supervisors and held a slim majority until January 2011. While the progressive majority on the board supported transit-first policies, the neoliberal political establishment, with the mayor as proxy, was loath to diligently seek new sources of revenue for Muni and instead leaned toward raising fares coupled with minor increases on some public parking.

The SFMTA board of directors could, for example, place a TAD on the ballot without the mayor's direct involvement but did not. The SFMTA board could also reallocate street space to prioritize transit, but did not. Transit first remained largely advisory, and between 2000 and 2010 very few transit-first policies were implemented. The twin reality of no new funding and no substantive transit-first deployments has stifled progressive transit advocacy, putting progressives mostly in a defensive posture to stave off cuts and fare increases. It has also aggravated the already volatile local politics of mobility because it has meant progressives look to pricing automobiles and parking. This put progressives directly at odds with car drivers and also magnified the schisms between sustainable transport advocates and advocates for the working poor and immigrants.

Progressive Muni Politics

Organizing against fare increases and service cuts dominated progressive Muni politics between 2000 and 2010. Responding to neoliberal and conservative charges that Muni fares were too low and provided only about 24 percent of Muni's total operating revenue, progressives countered that Muni's low fare was something to be proud of and that low fares showed compassion for the working class and a true transit-first priority. Moreover, progressives argued that because of San Francisco's extremely high cost of living—it has some of the highest rents in the nation—fare increases created a disproportionately higher burden on the financially strapped working class and poor, who were also largely transit dependent and could not afford to live close enough to their workplaces to walk or bicycle.

Additionally, while fares amounted to just over $182 million of Muni's operating revenue in 2011, if SFMTA's subdepartments (such as planning, parking, and administrative management) are separated out, the total wage and benefits package for Muni's two thousand operators costs about $195 million, a 94 percent farebox recovery ratio.[44] Muni certainly needs more than operators; it needs planners, managers, and equipment, but so do automobiles, and, progressives argue, few are demanding that automobile drivers pay the total sum of the system of automobility that makes driving possible. Last, progressives argued that Muni had a lower level of service compared to peer cities like New York and Chicago, which had higher fares in the early 2000s but also frequent all-night service and extensive subway and elevated systems that covered a much greater area.

Nevertheless, in 2003 Muni fares rose from $1.00 to $1.25 to stave off a $60-million operating shortfall, and the discounted monthly fast pass increased from $35 a month to $45.[45] This being the first Muni fare increase since 1992, progressives protested largely from a reactive, disorganized posture. Livable City demanded that parking prices and fees on downtown real estate transactions be used to balance the budget rather than fare increases (there was a minor real estate boom in the city that could have feasibly brought in more revenue for Muni). A disjointed and ineffective protest for "transit justice" called for boycotts of Muni and for fare evasion on the day the fare increase went into effect, but the action had no lasting outcome. For its part, Muni line workers agreed to a 7.5 percent pay cut, and drivers dropped some paid vacation days.[46] The SFMTA board, largely reflecting the neoliberal mayor who had appointed the seven members, opted for fare increases, and the majority on the Board of Supervisors, despite some dissent, acquiesced (as spelled out in Proposition E, the board could not modify an SFMTA budget, only vote it up or down).

The next year SFMTA reported a $40-million budget shortfall and proposed decreasing service and cutting certain routes. Met with widespread progressive protest, that year's budget proposal was rejected by the progressive-majority Board of Supervisors by means of progressive advocacy, but the structural problems were not resolved, and middle-management positions went unfilled.[47] Pushing debt off into the future, SFMTA in 2005 reported another $57-million shortfall.[48]

Despite the progressive majority on the Board of Supervisors, in 2005, for the first time since the 1980s, Muni service was cut and fares were raised simultaneously. The SFMTA proposed five comparative budget scenarios, including one with a draconian cut in weekend and evening bus service and another with a doubling of fares to $2.50 per ride.[49] A so-called spread-the-burden scenario, preferred by organizations like SPUR and featuring modest parking meter increases, a 25-cent fare hike, and a 7 percent systemwide service cut, was also promoted. Obviously no scenario proposed a TAD, but in deference to progressive advocacy, especially from Livable City, and in reaction to prodding by progressives on the Board of Supervisors, the SFMTA did present a scheme for patching the entire shortfall by pricing automobility: an across-the-board increase in parking charges, raising many citations to $100 minimum, raising all parking meters to $2.50 per hour, and increasing towing fees and parking rates at publicly owned garages.

Progressive supporters of sustainable transportation, drawing from Livable City, the SFBC, the Green Party, and Sierra Club, lobbied for this comprehensive parking pricing reform.[50] Their argument was that automobility was underpriced and inequitably subsidized, while transit, which provided greater public good, was being unwisely cut. While these advocates were not able to stop the fare increases and deferred maintenance, their activism generated much discussion about how automobility was underpriced at a time when parking was a contentious issue in neighborhood planning (see chapter 4). They pointed out a number of flaws in the city's public parking policy, flaws which they argued contradicted transit-first policies. These efforts were not wasted, as their ideas would be considered by the city in coming years.

For example, Livable City pointed out that the city was derelict in collecting the existing parking tax on revenue collected by private commercial parking garages, which, they argued, cost the city millions annually. Advocates said the city should have raised the parking garage tax by 10 percent, which prompted the SFMTA to calculate that under Livable City's proposal the city would raise $21 million annually, of which $8.6 million would be allotted to Muni (parking tax revenues were split between the general fund and Muni until 2007). By broaching the parking tax, advocates revealed a funding formula: increased revenue from a parking tax had to be balanced with a 50 percent reduction in equivalent general fund transfers to SFMTA. If Muni got $8.6 million for a 10 percent tax increase, the city would reduce its general fund allocation to Muni by $4.3 million. The discussion of the parking tax eventually led to reforms of parking tax collection, which was bundled into Prop. A in 2007 and allotted all parking tax increases directly to Muni.

The discussion of parking reform encompassed a rethinking of on-street, curbside parking, although the reforms promoted by Livable City and other advocates were much slower to manifest. For example, a local transportation consultant estimated that the worth of an average curbside parking space in San Francisco was $1,000 per year (including the cost of maintenance) and that in the aggregate the city, by charging a basic market rate for each space, could theoretically collect $320 million annually—far more than Muni's recurring budget shortfall and a potential source of funding for the types of expansion Muni needed to undergo in order to reduce GHGs.[51] This back-of-the-envelope calculation was not part of SFMTA's funding scenarios either in 2005 or anytime since, but it did influence advocacy for reforming metered parking and nudged the broader discussion about how much automobiles were being subsidized while curbside parking also preempted other uses of public space, such as wider sidewalks, bike lanes, transit lanes, and green space.

Over the long term, the budget deliberations of 2005 forced the city to reexamine on-street metered parking, and sustainable transportation advocates, joined by SPUR on this narrow issue, lobbied for increases of curbside parking prices to reflect market rates and be indexed to inflation. Emphasizing downtown parking and invoking neoliberal philosophy, they argued that even the increase in hourly metered parking rates from $2.00 to $2.50 was a deep subsidy, since off-street garages in the financial district charged between $7.50 and $10 per hour. The city was basically providing a 75 percent discount on what the market rate should be for 2,700 downtown parking meters.[52] They also pointed out that in 2005 New York charged $4 per hour and Chicago $3 per hour for downtown curbside parking.[53] Progressive emphasis on curbside parking subsidy eventually led to debates on expanding the hours of metered parking into evenings and weekends (metered parking covered only daytime hours), augmenting the geography of metered parking beyond the downtown and limited neighborhood commercial zones, and enforcing expired meters and other parking violations more aggressively.

Not surprisingly, the proposals for increased parking charges were met with loud protests by conservative merchant and neighborhood groups and by some neoliberals who characterized them as off-target because they priced driving in order to underwrite what neoliberals considered bloated labor agreements at Muni (to be sure, SPUR endorsed parking pricing). But the increased parking charges met with objections and ambivalence by some progressives also. While opposing fare hikes, they contended that rather than place Muni's operating shortfall on the backs of motorists, downtown businesses should pay taxes. Moreover, progressives representing working-class organizations remained either silent on or tacitly opposed to many of the increased parking charges because, they said, increased parking charges also disproportionately impacted the poor and working class as well as families with children and cars. On this front, a new ad hoc Coalition for Transit Justice, an informal group with no designated leader, tapped into tenants' rights and social service organizations like Mission Agenda and the Tenderloin-based SRO Families Unite. Dozens of Asian and Latino immigrants were organized to speak against fare increases. Yet these protests did not emphasize a comprehensive rethinking of automobility and parking costs.[54] Rather, progressive social service providers and community organizers argued that Muni was a public service as well as a social service and that provision of social services transcended concerns over cost and efficiency.

Increased fares and service cuts faced off against higher parking rates at a heated public hearing of the Board of Supervisors, but progressives were unable to assemble the necessary two-thirds majority needed to block the rise in fares and the reduced service.[55] Only four of the seven progressives on the board were willing to veto the fare increase by substituting deeper parking reforms, and the remaining three, wary of the backlash on parking, joined the neoliberal–conservative balance of the board and voted to spread the pain. While spreading the pain was more palatable than a fare increase or service cuts alone, the lack of enthusiasm among social justice advocates for parking reform meant there was no unified, politically potent effort to target automobility in this round of the Muni debates. The city's politics of mobility instead settled on the spread-the-burden scenario with a 25-cent fare hike to $1.50, a 7 percent reduction in service, some minor increases in parking costs, and delayed maintenance and deferred hiring of Muni workers.

Progressive discourse about pricing automobility in order to provide revenue for transit and other livability initiatives ultimately gained traction. It led not only to securing increased parking tax revenue for Muni in Proposition A in 2007, but also to increased rates for curbside parking permits in neighborhoods in 2010. As was the case with Prop 13 and other statewide measures, however, San Francisco's desire to raise the cost of on-street parking permits is hamstrung by a state regulation that allows revenue from residential parking permits to go only toward paying for the management of such a system, and surplus revenue cannot be raised for other purposes. It also led to a neoliberal high-tech pilot project involving curbside metered parking, called SF Park, which promised to generate more revenue through optimizing how parking was managed and implemented variable pricing in select neighborhood commercial districts.[56] By 2012, SF Park was installed in seven commercial districts in the city and had won national acclaim. In addition, the city was prepared to extend metering to Sundays and later in the evenings, although that plan still had many detractors.[57] Beyond parking, progressive discourse over Muni financing, limited from considering the option of a TAD, has contributed to efforts to create new vehicle license fees and to introduce congestion pricing (which, like parking, invokes neoliberal approaches), two other politically charged but important items to consider in the politics of Muni.

Transit agencies like Muni depended indirectly on revenues the state collected by charging a fee for every new car purchased in the state. Established in 1948, the state vehicle license fee (VLF) was appraised at 2 percent of a car's value, and much of the revenue went toward operating the Department of Motor Vehicles, which administers licensing, and to the California Highway Patrol, which policed state highways. In 1998, during the tenure of Governor Pete Wilson, the VLF was reduced to 0.65 percent. As California entered a budget crisis in the early 2000s, Governor Grey Davis reestablished the 2 percent fee to offset the budget crisis. Sensing a conservative voter flashpoint, Republicans made the VLF a centerpiece of their recall campaign of Davis in 2003.[58] Upon taking office after the recall, Governor Arnold Schwarzenegger repealed the fee, reducing it again to 0.65 percent of a car's value. The state immediately lost $4 billion in annual revenue, and, to offset this loss, Schwarzenegger tapped gasoline sales tax revenues, a portion of which went to state support of transit operations, and roughly $60 million was withdrawn from San Francisco annually.[59]

In 2005, paralleling Muni's service cuts and fare hike and as pricing automobility was being elevated in local politics, representatives from San Francisco proposed that voters in counties or metropolitan regions should be allowed to self-impose VLFs to underwrite local transportation. This proposal needed enabling legislation through the California legislature, where Republicans, led by Schwarzenegger, vetoed the efforts repeatedly. In subsequent years regional environmental and transportation advocacy organizations promoted VLF for counties and for the entire Bay Area but were also repeatedly rebuffed. Finally, in 2009 enabling legislation passed, and in 2010 Bay Area voters were allowed to decide on VLFs at the ballot box. However, the state enabling legislation capped fees at $10, meaning very little real revenue would be raised. In San Francisco the modest $10 VLF was approved by voters in November 2010, but none of the revenue could be applied to Muni operations. Raising just $5 million annually, the low fee was to be targeted at small-scale, nimble street improvements that prioritize minor changes for transit first and bicycles. The trifling fee does not meet real needs and it will not radically change or improve Muni. Yet the passage of the fee reaffirmed that San Francisco was willing to consider fees and taxes on automobiles to help address transportation.

Congestion pricing, that is, tolling automobiles in specific congested parts of the city, such as the downtown, was also proposed by progressives as a way to raise revenue for Muni. First implemented in Singapore in 1975 and later in London in 2003, congestion pricing in San Francisco would be deployed by creating an electronic toll cordon around the downtown or other parts of the city and then charging a fee for each vehicle that enters the cordon. Many transportation policy experts, economists, and environmentalists point out that congestion pricing has great potential for providing funds for transit, but that even if no revenues were used for transit, people would still be discouraged from driving, which would create more transit patronage and also clear congested streets of automobiles, allowing transit to move faster.[60] Though no cordon-based congestion pricing scheme has yet to be deployed in the United States, the political left in London, Oslo, and Stockholm supports tolls since the revenue is used to build transit and improve the city for all, not simply for motorists.[61]

With that support in mind, progressive members of the Board of Supervisors in 2007 directed transportation planners to conduct a study of the feasibility and potential impacts of congestion pricing and authorized the city to apply for federal grants to expand the study to the entire city, including the creation of a congestion cordon on the city's southern border with suburban San Mateo County.[62] In 2010 the study suggested that with a $6.00 peak period charge to drive in the northeastern part of the city, $60 to $80 million could be raised annually, but, most significant, Muni service could be sped up by 20 to 25 percent in the most congested part of the city.[63]

However attractive these funds and transit improvements may be, congestion charging still had several politically difficult hurdles to overcome. As in the case of VLFs, the implementation of congestion pricing will require state enabling legislation because state law prohibits localities from charging for the use of public streets. The city will need to create a toll collection authority that can borrow in advance of implementation in order to construct the cordon as well as provide revenue for transit improvements in advance of the congestion charge. Moreover, congestion charging will require an environmental review, not under way as of April 2012. Locally, congestion charging elicited political opposition from conservatives, who oppose more encumbrances to automobility and from suburban politicians, who have vowed to block the charge through state legislation; the San Francisco Chronicle, the Chamber of Commerce, and downtown retailers scoffed at the idea.[64] A hint of the politics of congestion pricing comes from the debate in New York City, where in 2007 the neoliberal mayor and progressive sustainable transport activists promoted an $8.00 congestion charge for Manhattan but were defeated by an ad hoc coalition of conservatives and moderate progressives residing outside of the city, in suburbs, and in upstate New York.[65]

Progressives in San Francisco express a nuanced acceptance of congestion pricing. For sustainable transportation advocates the discussion of pricing has merit because it leads to a more rational discussion about the subsidies to automobility and would lead to substantial revenue for public transit as well as to reductions in GHGs and other environmental and livability benefits. The proposed congestion charge on the northeastern part of the city would reduce car trips by 12 percent in the quadrant and reduce citywide GHGs by 5 percent.[66] If implemented correctly, it could remove many cars from downtown streets, allowing Muni to speed up, and thus result in efficiencies for the system that might translate into cost savings or expanded capacity. However, as in the case of parking pricing, advocates for low-income workers express concern that congestion pricing might have a regressive side. To their mind, the wealthy will still drive into the congestion charging zone, which will have less traffic, while low-income motorists are priced out. The challenge for unifying progressives will be to highlight the potential stable funding for Muni, which benefits the working class and a broader segment of society. And because TADs and TIDFs may remain elusive, congestion pricing, coupled with parking pricing, offers a tangible source of future funding for Muni.

Pricing aside, the organizing of progressive transit advocacy in San Francisco remains a challenge. In 2007 sustainable transportation advocates rallied environmentalists, labor unions, community organizers, and even SPUR in opposing Prop H (the pro-parking ballot initiative) and supporting Prop A (the counter, pro-transit, GHG-reduction ballot initiative). Yet following the success at the ballot box, a progressive Transit-Not-Traffic coalition failed to promote a cohesive progressive transit vision, and by spring of 2008 the coalition had all but fizzled into a loose e-mail list. Progressive transit activism reemerged in late 2008, but, again, in a reactive posture as SFMTA reported that state and federal funds were cut and that a decline in parking revenue and sales tax—related to the fact that fewer visitors were driving to the city—meant that the system would face another round of cuts.[67] In 2009 Muni had a $129-million shortfall (over two years rather than one, as budget accounting practices changed), and, as protests of disparate social justice and progressive organizations remained disjointed, more service cuts were made, fares were raised once again, employees were laid off, and vacancies went unfilled.

A new San Francisco Transit Riders Union (SFTRU), established by the former director of the SFBC and a handful of dedicated transit professionals and advocates, mobilized against cuts and had limited success in dampening their severity. SFTRU coordinated with progressive Asian and Latino community organizations and sought to develop a technocratic transit-first vision that expanded to social equity—in essence, combining sustainable transportation and social justice into a comprehensive transit vision.[68] The SFTRU has persisted by adopting a logo and holding regular, albeit modestly attended, monthly meetings, but it has fallen short on raising funds to employ full-time staff to better organize diverse riders into a political force.

Meanwhile, the SFMTA staff, in studying how the city's transportation sector should reduce GHGs, proposed an array of progressive new funding ideas, including an annual automobile mitigation impact fee of $50 to $150 per car, which would raise $24–$72 million annually, and an off-street commercial parking fee of $100–$300 per stall, which would raise between $6 million and $17 million annually.[69] Some of these ideas could be linked to the possibility of LOS reform, as part of implementation of the Transportation Sustainability Program proposal (see chapter 5). The 2012 proposal for the Transportation Sustainability Program collects $630 million (in 2010 dollars) from new commercial and residential development over a twenty-year horizon.[70] Most of this onetime fee would be directed at transit capacity and not operations but would amount to $31.5 million more than is currently available annually.

Over the long term, SFMTA staff were considering an annual transit utility fee on single-family homes (ranging from $60 to $180 per home) with variations for apartments, which would raise $26–$74 million per year; they also were revisiting the idea of a TAD by suggesting a citywide parcel tax of $100–$200 per property as well as the immediate expansion of parking pricing, implementation of congestion pricing, and aggressive defense of the transit-first policy on city streets. Because of the legacy of Prop 13, many of these taxes and fees would require a supermajority in local elections, and it remained to be seen if an organization like the SFTRU would be able to take the lead in advocating these measures.

To progressives, the debates over how to finance Muni are a struggle for the heart and soul of San Francisco's progressive legacy. That legacy includes advocacy for low fares, high-quality service accessible to all incomes, age groups, and races, transit-first policies that discourage automobile use, and peace with organized labor, coupled with taxes on wealthy commercial property owners. This is the progressive transit agenda in San Francisco, yet, as neoliberal discourses have all but removed TADs from the menu of options to stabilize and expand Muni, and a new transit impact fee has yet to be established, a unified progressive politics of transit is complicated. The alternative has been to look to other revenues that can be relatively regressive, thereby undermining a cohesive progressive vision of transit finance. Over the decade 2000–2010 the progressive search for alternatives to TADs and TIDFs exposed fissures and made a unified progressive front difficult to achieve.

The challenge for progressives is to overcome this schism and create a cohesive progressive transit vision and a unifying politics through which to advocate it. Nonprofit organizations like Livable City and the SFTRU have made headway but have not rallied a groundswell of advocacy mirroring the twelve-thousand-member bicycle coalition or the smaller but persistent advocacy for off-street parking reform among livability advocates. While ambitious expansion of transit is preferred by most progressives, the undertaking in the next decade will likely include only the modest, $167-million *TEP Implementation Plan* proposed in 2011. But for that implementation the city has identified only $16 million in available funding, mostly from local (and regressive) sales taxes, and so new funding sources must be found. While the *TEP* plan is under environmental review the city has time to identify more funds, and progressives will need to produce a comprehensive platform to secure this $167 million while making sure implementation is equitable. In the meantime, progressive advocacy has been complicated by both a neoliberal and a conservative politics of transit.

CHAPTER 7

Disciplining Muni

Revanchism and the Gentrification of Transit

REVANCHISM IS THE RECOVERY of lost territory or status. Used in critical geography, the term refers to the neoliberal and conservative undoing of the redistributive social policies established in the New Deal and through the 1960s.[1] In this sense revanchism means a return to the original liberalism of nineteenth-century capitalism unfettered by regulation and progressive policies and enabling markets to dominate the organization and allocation of urban space.[2] With respect to livability, revanchism includes the strategies of disciplining certain aspects of the city, making the city "safe" for gentrification through such policies as removing the homeless and displacing social services. Revanchism includes the defunding of affordable public housing and education and the disciplining of public sector workers, while offering tax incentives to corporations, privatizing education, and subsidizing (with public funds) upscale housing and urban amenities through redevelopment schemes.

In San Francisco's politics of mobility there are salient revanchist discourses about Muni that have significant bearing on how livability might unfold. To neoliberals and conservatives, Muni is not a collective, egalitarian social good, but a system that must be reclaimed from unruly lower-class riders and antagonistic unionized bus drivers and made safe, efficient, more businesslike, and welcoming for law-abiding middle- and upper-class residents who use transit primarily for commuting or who seek to live in a reclaimed, super-gentrified city.[3] Revanchism includes the reclaiming of the discourse over how Muni is funded, directing it away from taxing elites to spreading the cost burden onto lower classes, and it includes appropriating the progressive elements of transit-first policies and using them to achieve neoliberal and conservative visions of transit. Many nuanced, subtle, yet poignant revanchist policies are being implemented, proposed, and vetted, and this can be confusing for a progressive politics of mobility. These revanchist transit policies must be laid bare if a truly progressive politics of mobility is to be achieved in San Francisco and if San Francisco is to be a national and global bellwether for reducing automobility in an egalitarian manner.

Financing Revanchism: Spreading the Burden while Concentrating Wealth

One of the most enduring legacies of Muni politics has been the devitalizing of local consideration of a downtown TAD and its erasure from the menu of possibilities. Neoliberals have literally recaptured the discourse of how transit can be financed. This political achievement is most impressive when one considers the role transit has had in making downtown San Francisco functional and profitable. Downtown San Francisco, as noted earlier, covers 343 acres and contains 70 million square feet of office space and 125,000 office workers, one of the densest concentrations of office space in North America; as of 2011 upward of 8 million more square feet of office and commercial space were in the construction pipeline.[4] The adjacent Civic Center, parts of South of Market, and Mission Bay contain millions of additional square feet of office space. Moreover, 9 million square feet of retail space and 20,000 hotel rooms, adding 25,000 and 11,000 workers, respectively, make the downtown core the Bay Area's premier retail and hospitality concentration. If one expands the definition of downtown to include a larger, 2.5-square-mile area, an estimated 341,000 workers are brought into the fold.

Given such a dense concentration of activity, automobility has passed its threshold in downtown San Francisco. Having 35,000 off-street parking spaces (roughly 102 spaces per acre) and only 500 spaces approved since 2008, the downtown cannot add more parking or else the already congested streets would be overwhelmed. No new freeway lanes will be built, and I-280 south of the downtown may one day be removed.[5] San Francisco's historical limitations on automobility make the city relatively livable and competitive compared to other American cities, and that livability is a key part of what enhances the exchange value of downtown real estate. In 2011 and 2012 several social network firms chose to expand or relocate to downtown San Francisco rather than to suburbs because their employees desired an urban lifestyle and could use public transportation to get to work. The downtown area has experienced the largest residential growth in the city, new developments adding upward of 20,000 new residents between 2000 and 2009. Many of the new residents have higher education and higher incomes than people in the rest of the city, but, significantly, 59 percent of households are car-free, up from 55 percent in 2000.[6]

Yet between 1981 and 2010 San Francisco raised only $142 million from the downtown TIDF, at $4.8 million annually, while the annual operating budget for Muni rose to $780 million.[7] Muni needs $167 million just to make the very modest capacity improvements called for in the *TEP Implementation* proposal of 2011, much of which will benefit the rapid network serving downtown, and this does not include operating costs.[8] To be sure, downtown landowners pay property taxes and real estate transfer taxes, a small portion of which, as part of the city's general fund, has been allotted to Muni annually, but as the costs to operate transit have increased, those tax rates and the shares provided to Muni have not.

In 2008 Mayor Newsom convened a blue ribbon panel of local officials and transit experts to address Muni financing. The panel discussed fare increases, parking pricing, and congestion pricing at length, but the idea of a TAD or a new TIDF was dismissed, as it had been by elites for decades.[9] Instead, the dominant approach, as exhibited in both the budget debates of 2005 (see chapter 6) and subsequent budget negotiations, was to spread the burden through an array of complicated funding mechanisms ranging from local sales taxes, transfers from the general fund, increased fares, modest parking pricing, and reliance on state and federal funds, however unpredictable these were.

In San Francisco and elsewhere in the United States one of the cornerstones of spreading the burden for transit funding is a one-half-cent local sales tax (locally referred to as Prop K), first approved by voters in 1989 and renewed in 2003. Prop K is the single most important source of funding for transportation infrastructure in the city, raising $70 to $80 million in sales tax revenue annually for capital projects such as street repairs, acquisition of buses, and extensions of light rail.[10] It is estimated that by 2033 Prop K will raise $2.5 billion (in 2003 dollars), which could leverage an estimated $10 billion from state and federal matching sources.[11] When voters renewed the sales tax they mandated that 65 percent of all revenues be directed toward transit infrastructure, including transit-first projects, but the sales tax decidedly cannot be used to underwrite regular Muni operations.[12] Innocuous on the surface, the use of a sales tax to spread the burden is part of a subtle revanchist approach to financing Muni.

Sales taxes are regressive. Based on taxes as a share of household income, low-income households pay a disproportionately higher portion of their income in sales taxes relative to wealthier people. One national study of sales taxes concluded that poor households paid eight times more of their income in sales taxes than wealthier households, and middle-class households paid four times more than wealthier households.[13] Transportation sales taxes also shift the burden from more frequent and intense users of transportation, who tend to be wealthier, to lower-income users, who use transportation with less frequency and intensity.[14] In general, lower-income households travel shorter distances and with less frequency than higher-income households. Nevertheless, the emphasis on regressive sales taxes has drawn attention away from taxing elites.

Local transportation sales taxes, which have proliferated throughout the United States, also embody neoliberal and conservative discourses regarding devolution of federal and state funding, especially germane at a time when progressives believe that national leadership is needed on issues like climate change, peak oil, and rethinking the configuration of cities. Local transportation sales taxes evoke a conservative self-help, personal responsibility discourse that presumes localities, like individuals, should pull themselves up by their bootstraps and not rely on national government to finance transportation. Through devolution, a truly far-reaching progressive national-scale transportation policy is thwarted. It dampens the possibilities for large, visionary, transformative change, makes regional coordination more difficult, and constitutes a frugal financial base that can do little but provide funds for very limited improvements.

Typical of most local transportation sales taxes in California and the nation, Prop K bundled road, transit, bicycle, and pedestrian projects into one omnibus package in order to maximize political support and to reach the two-thirds voter threshold required to levy taxes. Bundling of projects attracts more votes but also makes local sales taxes appear to transcend ideology since they often elicit endorsements from cross sections of business groups, labor unions, environmentalists, and often leadership in both Democratic and Republican parties. In San Francisco, Prop K received 75 percent voter approval, and progressives, neoliberals, and even some conservatives endorsed the measure, suggesting it transcended ideology.

Despite concerns about regressive taxes, equity, and devolution, paradoxically it was progressives who helped promote San Francisco's transportation sales tax renewal in November 2003. This is not unusual, as around the nation progressive transportation advocates find themselves supporting regressive sales taxes. As elsewhere in the United States, progressives' support of the sales tax renewal in San Francisco was tactical and politically expedient. It stemmed from the broader stalemate over TADs and TIDFs, but it also reflected the fact that progressives had difficulty in leveraging adequate transit funds from the regional transportation agency, which distributed state and federal funds to Bay Area cities and which was at the time largely biased toward road building and rail transit extensions in the suburbs.[15] A city-based sales tax enabled San Francisco to build projects that progressives desired but otherwise could not fund. Justifying renewal of a regressive tax, progressives used a pragmatic, nonideological tone of "keep[ing] the city moving," and "somebody can always come up with reasons why we shouldn't do something."[16]

The progressive majority on the Board of Supervisors placed the renewal on the ballot and appointed key leaders of the sustainable transportation movement to the committee that drafted the expenditure plan for the sales tax, including the SFBC, Walk San Francisco, and Livable City. Progressive voters, engaged in a lively, emotionally charged mayor's election that year, also approved the renewal.[17] The outspokenly leftist *San Francisco Bay Guardian* even endorsed the sales tax renewal while apologetically acknowledging it was regressive.[18] Advocates promoted the tax renewal as a step toward living without a car, as it directed 65 percent of revenues to transit, and the majority of the remaining funding was targeted at livability projects such as bicycles, pedestrian improvements, and traffic calming. A smaller portion was dedicated to street maintenance and traffic signals, but, unlike most suburban transportation sales taxes, Prop K did not include expansion of roadway capacity, with the exception of rebuilding the roadway that connects to the Golden Gate Bridge.[19]

The renewal dovetailed with progressive-neoliberal rapprochements in that leaders in the sustainable transportation advocacy movement coordinated the expenditure plan with SPUR and the San Francisco Chamber of Commerce, and the director of Livable City chaired the committee drafting the tax renewal measure. The Chamber of Commerce, referring to progressives, stated, "We don't always agree [with them], but on this we do," and the chamber paid for ballot arguments for Livable City and Walk San Francisco as well as for some progressive supervisors and labor organizations.[20] Yet, despite this rapprochement, a close look at the bundling of projects exposes revanchism in the spread-the-burden approach.

When an array of projects are bundled, crucial projects identified in expenditure plans can privilege very specific geographies that benefit neoliberal and conservative visions of transportation while undermining progressive visions. For example, Prop K allocates $124 million to the controversial Central Subway project, a 1.7-mile, $1.6 billion light-rail extension from Mission Bay to Chinatown (figure 5). Long planned as an extension of the existing Third Street Light Rail line, the Central Subway is characterized by some of its supporters as a step toward transit justice because it links lower-income communities in Chinatown to the Bayview and Visitacion Valley in southeastern San Francisco.[21] By all accounts these transit-dependent communities do need improved service, and upward of 70 percent of households in the proposed subway corridor do not have automobiles. To that end, social service and tenants advocacy organizations like the politically influential Chinatown Community Development Center have aggressively promoted the subway.[22] Yet the subway has divided progressives, and sustainable transportation advocates have levied ample criticism at the project.

Critics of the subway have argued that for far less money Stockton Street, overhead of the subway alignment, could be made into a transit-first street and bus service dramatically improved in the corridor by adding capacity and improving bus travel times.[23] Progressives contend further that the balance of the billion dollars dedicated to the subway could be spread into citywide transit-first proposals such as the *TEP Implementation Plan* or the kinds of capacity expansion discussed in the *2011 Climate Action Plan*.[24] For example, in May 2011 the Bay Area chapter of Sierra Club argued against the Central Subway and asked that the remaining allocation of funds for the subway be directed to other transit needs in the city, including the Stockton corridor.[25] In a more muted approach, Livable City promotes transit first on Stockton Street but excludes promotion of the Central Subway in its agenda, despite otherwise positive endorsements of Caltrain electrification, the Transbay Terminal, and High Speed Rail, all large-scale rail projects.

An ad hoc coalition called Save Muni claimed that SFMTA will not be able to maintain the existing bus system because, given fiscal instability, the subway will sap funds. They point out that limited Prop K funds, if used to finance the subway, will not be used for other transit-first needs.[26] Critics warn that although the federal government has promised almost

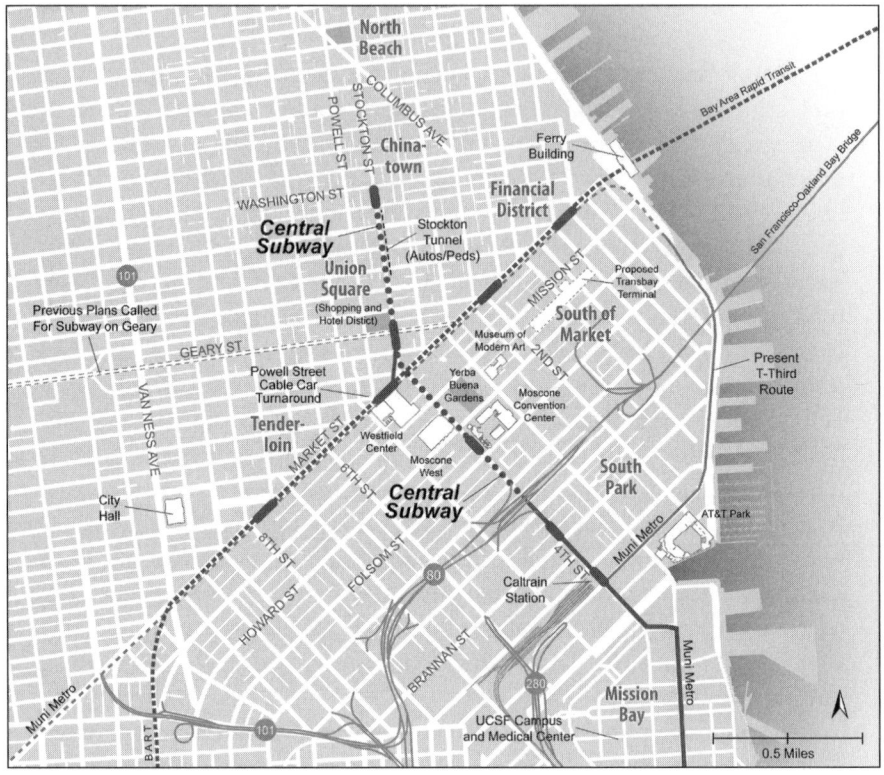

Figure 5. The proposed Central Subway corridor, showing major attractions and greater downtown San Francisco. Cartography by Michael Webster.

$950 million, federal funding is unstable, and San Francisco will be liable if there are cost overruns, which would invariably mean sapping more Prop K funds. In 2011 a civil grand jury report on the subway pointed out that Muni had not identified operation funds for the subway and that seismic and hydrologic concerns made it extremely risky and costly (it requires expensive stairways, elevators, escalators, and mezzanines) when improvements to surface transit could move vastly more people while costing less.[27]

Other critics of the subway have stated that the problem is not the concept of the subway but its poor design. It dead-ends deep beneath Chinatown rather than exiting at a north or northwest portal to connect to a wider transit system. The civil grand jury reported that the subway design makes it impossible to consider a Geary subway line in the future.[28] The 38-Geary is the city's busiest bus line, carrying over fifty-four thousand passengers a day, and Geary rail has been part of San Francisco's rapid transit plans for almost a century. Moreover, as designed (and approved by the SFMTA) the Central Subway lacks direct connectivity to the proposed Transbay Terminal located four blocks from the alignment, which will have future high-speed rail and future electrified Caltrain service. The configuration also lacked direct, seamless connectivity to BART and the Muni Metro lines at Market Street, which is the city's transit spine. Transferring between the subway and these lines will require a five-minute, one-thousand-foot walk and navigating of eight stories of escalators, elevators, or stairs. The current Third Street light-rail alignment merges directly into the existing Muni Metro tunnels under Market, albeit after taking a circuitous route along the Embarcadero. That the subway dead-ends with poor connectivity means that its benefits are geographically limited.

Despite all of these objections, in 2011 the SFMTA board unanimously voted to award a $233-million tunnel contract to commence work on the subway, even as the federal government commitment was uncertain owing to a three-year delay of reauthorization of federal transportation policy and a Republican-controlled House that was openly hostile to transit funding. In that light and with no secure federal funding agreement assured for the project, the Board of Supervisors voted unanimously to divert $57 million in Prop K funds to buy tunnel-boring machines and start the tunneling process.[29] With no discussion of the merits of the project or of the recent civil grand jury report critiquing it, the board allotted these funds even as Muni struggled with deferred maintenance and rationing of routes. In 2011 the California Public Utilities Commission, which regulates rail transit safety, reported that Muni had a poor safety rating because of deferred maintenance of its tracks.[30] What's more, at least $163 million in funding had not been identified even though federal regulations required that it come from local sources. In response, the SFMTA was contemplating a so-called Prop K loan as well as skimming from other parts of the transit budget. This was exactly what opponents had warned against, namely, that the subway would swallow up already inadequate sales tax funds, meaning other transit-first projects would be deferred or canceled. What compels such powerful momentum for allocating scarce sales tax revenues, already spreading the burden, to such a flawed project when there are obvious financial problems at Muni?

Vested interests such as the Chinatown Chamber of Commerce and the building trades union expect the project to generate jobs and thus support the project. But the subway also happens to connect significant real estate developments such as the massive Mission Bay redevelopment and surrounding upscale urban infill in the Eastern Neighborhoods, the Moscone

Convention Center and Yerba Buena Gardens in South of Market, and the Union Square area, the Bay Area's premier upscale retail district, and so has considerable support from representatives of these concentrations of capital (see figure 5). The Central Subway might improve mobility somewhat between parts of Chinatown and the southeastern part of the city, but it also will enhance wealth in specific largely neoliberal locales.

As currently manifested, the Central Subway is revanchist. It reflects not a more integrated, egalitarian, citywide approach to transit funding but a steering of public investment, such as limited sales tax revenue, to specific privileged spaces. In other words, San Francisco is investing in an expensive new rail line that enhances land values in a specific corridor identified as being profitable rather than in a more mundane improvement of overcrowded bus routes. Under contemporary neoliberalism, municipal government prioritizes an urban transportation policy, in this case the Central Subway, that enhances business competitiveness and provides a foundation for gentrification, which increases real estate values.[31]

When crafting the Prop K expenditure plan, SPUR and the Chamber of Commerce ensured that the language in the plan identified the Central Subway as a signature project, and the SFMTA called the Central Subway the highest priority transit project in San Francisco. SPUR titled the Central Subway a legacy project, and key political representatives, including Mayor Newsom, Congresswoman Pelosi, and Senator Feinstein used their influence to lobby for the $950 million in federal funding for the project.[32] This amount provides only 60 percent of the needed funding, and the remainder must be found locally. The State of California does supply some support (at the expense of other needs in San Francisco such as the transit-first policies in the *TEP Implementation Plan*), but state support, too, is unstable. Prop K became the default local option.

The Prop K sales tax renewal was enthusiastically promoted by SPUR, the Chamber of Commerce, BOMA, and the San Francisco Democratic Party establishment, including Pelosi. SPUR characterized the tax as the "single most important source of transportation funding" in San Francisco and promoted it as efficient, balanced, and responsible.[33] BOMA, representing large downtown building owners, reiterated that Prop K would enhance the city as an international destination and commercial center, acknowledging the real estate value incurred by such projects as the Central Subway.[34] The neoliberal, entrepreneurial, and revanchist discourse argued that Prop K resources should be captured and spent where they might make the city and business more competitive. What the sales tax renewal did not provide was resources for Muni's mainline day-to-day operations. And while funds could go to Muni's vision of capacity expansion, little has come of that.

Meanwhile, the impetus for the Central Subway is oddly a consequence of San Francisco's conservative politics of mobility as well. While some conservatives balk at the cost of the subway, and nationally there is widespread conservative opposition to federal funding of public transit, in the case of the Central Subway local conservative discourses about automobility have fatefully provided the rationale for the subway. Ingenuously, the SFMTA celebrates the notion that the subway will speed up car traffic because it will remove slow, crowded buses from one of the densest transit streets in the city, Stockton Street, which has three bus lines carrying seventy-three thousand people a day.[35] By moving transit underground, the logic is that more space will be open to cars. When progressives suggest making Stockton a transit-first street, merchants and business interests insist on preserving parking and automobile access and oppose improvements. At a fundamental level the essentialization of automobility necessitates that no politician promote the idea of removing cars from Stockton Street, around Union Square, the Moscone Center, or Mission Bay. Instead, the subway makes more room for cars.

Many transit advocates believe that connecting the Central Subway westward on Geary Street or northward on Columbus Avenue in North Beach would legitimize the expense of the subway. The North Beach option has had little public vetting, but conservatives have a long history of opposing rail transit and even modest bus rapid transit on Geary Boulevard (Geary Street turns into Geary Boulevard west of Van Ness Avenue). Part of the original BART plan, rail on Geary was dropped in the 1960s to cut costs in the face of a lack of federal and state assistance. Conservative opposition to rapid transit on Geary contributed to the failure of the Muni bond in 1966, and in the 1970s neighborhoods in the Geary corridor associated rapid transit with the redevelopment of high rises. When BART revisited rail rapid transit on Geary in 1972, neighborhood groups continued this line of opposition. In the late seventies conservatives opposed even a study for electrifying the Geary bus line, again associating that with a stealth policy for accommodating higher density. The defeat of electrification led to studies of rail in the 1980s, and in 1988 Muni proposed surface rail in the median of Geary Boulevard from the ocean to the vicinity of Van Ness Avenue, where trains would enter a subway and connect to Market Street.

In 1989 the Geary rail proposal was included in San Francisco's first transportation sales tax referendum, although it was prioritized for further study and design, not construction. Once again merchants opposed rail because it threatened parking and roadway capacity, and residents on the corridor charged it was yet another disguised attempt to increase density. By the time of the Prop K referendum in 2003, language regarding Geary shifted to bus rapid transit rather than rail. Yet the objections of conservatives continue today in regard to bus rapid transit proposals, and as of 2012 Geary remains largely as it looked in the early 1960s when it was widened to six lanes. Any proposal to rethink a west portal for the Central Subway would likely be challenged by conservatives. Moreover, a Columbus Avenue option, which is a much narrower street than Geary, would undoubtedly provoke opposition from motorists and merchants seeking to preserve parking and car access in that corridor.

The juxtaposition of conservative politics opposing rail on Geary Boulevard and the politics of concentrating wealth in neoliberal spaces along the subway route has all but assured the dead-end variation of the Central Subway. Heightening the momentum, however, progressives on the Board of Supervisors, despite having a majority between 2000 and 2010, were loath to alienate social justice advocates in Chinatown who also supported the subway. That reluctance has severely widened the fissures within the ranks of progressives. It has made it difficult to organize for a comprehensive progressive transit vision, much less to lobby for Prop K funds to be redirected from the subway to the bus system. Superimposed on this political dynamic, the bundling of the Central Subway with other projects desired by progressives, such as bicycle lanes and traffic calming, meant that progressives by and large unintentionally, perhaps silently, endorsed the subway. Yet in the end this important project, largely revanchist in its intention, privileges very specific neoliberal geographies while preserving conservative visions of automobile access and undermines progressives' vision for Muni.

To further amplify this revanchism, future Prop K funds could be bonded to underwrite the subway. As of 2011 the city could bond $842 million for shovel-ready projects like the subway, but, significantly, this would be paid back with an additional $858 million in interest over a thirty-year period.[36] A boon to bankers, such an arrangement would exhaust already scarce resources for transit, as debt finance would exceed the actual amount expended on infrastructure. Yet with the SFMTA letting a $233-billion contract to construct the Central Subway tunnels, effectively locking in the subway, the city could find itself on a slippery slope of bonding for the project if federal, state, and other local funds come up short.

Beyond Prop K and the Central Subway, it is apparent that the spread-the-burden approach has not provided the level of funding needed to keep downtown San Francisco functioning for capital interests that acknowledge more funding is needed from somewhere. As Muni continues its "downward spiral," to quote a SPUR report, neoliberals and conservatives have promoted other revanchist tactics to further address Muni's financial problems, including system efficiency, reforming the work rules of transit operators, tightening enforcement of fare evasion, and the use of entrepreneurial approaches such as creating premium fares on buses, and, ultimately perhaps, private transit.[37]

Revanchist Efficiency

Together with debate about municipal fiscal discipline comes a discussion about Muni's efficiency as a transit system. Originally part of the transit-first approach, system efficiency involves squeezing more service out of Muni with less funding, offering speed and the opportunity for expanding the capacity of transit without having to procure more vehicles. The logic of system efficiency is that if the average travel time for a typical bus run is halved, hypothetically the number of round trips a bus operator can make is doubled, saving on labor while extracting more capacity out of the system. Further optimization of the system can be achieved by expanding proof of payment (POP) to minimize dwell times at transit stops, using global positioning systems and other technologies to track and route vehicles (reflecting a cornucopian emphasis on technology), and eliminating some bus stops along some transit routes to reduce stop and go. In this vein, the TEP identifies fifteen transit corridors where 75 percent of daily boardings occur, most of which serve the downtown, and the SFMTA proposes to convert them into so-called rapid corridors by using transit-first treatments and the consolidation of bus stops.

In part, SFMTA's TEP and the modest *TEP Implementation Plan* include progressive visions of transit first, including those of making it possible for people to live in the city without owning a car and creating transit spaces that support basic livability principles and benefit the collective social good. Yet the objectives of progressives—the collective public good—are not the same as the neoliberal and conservative objectives of the TEP. The neoliberal transit policy of improving system efficiency involves getting more out of each service hour of operation, and, while within the general ambit of transit first together with progressives, the underlying rationale for neoliberals is a businesslike emphasis on productivity, that is, making it cheaper to operate for each mile of service. For conservatives, who use

transit in very select situations such as high-quality commuter rail or express buses, system efficiency is a way to analyze transit lines case by case
and provide government support for ones that are "efficient" and to eliminate those that are not.[38] Commuter services that bypass congestion, such
as grade-separated railways, are efficient and preferred over slow, crowded
urban buses. Having generally higher fares, commuter rail and commuter
bus service also produce higher farebox recovery, and so conservative
discourse about efficiency leans toward privileging rail and premium bus
service. For example, commuter-oriented rapid transit like BART exacts
a farebox recovery of 65 percent and Caltrain 48 percent, compared to
Muni's 24 percent recovery rate for diesel buses and 30 percent for electric
trolley buses.[39]

What is not considered efficient are low-ridership routes that serve
neighborhoods (what Muni calls community connectors) or routes with
a high number of bus stops that accommodate seniors, children, and
the disabled. Progressives want to do both: bolster a rapid network with
transit-first infrastructure, while simultaneously providing a basic level of
service to special communities that need it. Neoliberals and conservatives
seek to dispense with or at least minimize the latter.

Bus stop consolidation is an instance in which progressive visions of the
TEP can collide with the revanchist neoliberal and conservative visions of
transit. For example, in 2004, as the TEP process was getting under way,
the SFMTA proposed to eliminate a handful of closely spaced bus stops
to increase the operating speeds of the 38-Geary bus, as noted, the city's
most heavily patronized bus route and identified as a rapid corridor in the
TEP. The proposal focused on the inner Geary segment, in the Tenderloin
between Van Ness Avenue and Union Square, and included removing one
lane of car traffic to create a transit-only lane, widening the transit-only
lane, installing more efficient passenger loading zones called bus bulbs
and removing five bus stops. The proposal was expected to reduce the
overall travel time for the 38-Geary by two minutes.

For progressives bus stop consolidation erupted into a confusing social
justice issue as low-income seniors and disabled residents of the Tenderloin, organized through community groups like the Tenderloin Neighborhood Development Corporation and backed by some progressives on the
Board of Supervisors, protested the removal of bus stops. Other progressives supported removal because it benefited the population of low- and
middle-income transit passengers using the 38-Geary line but residing
to the west, beyond Van Ness Avenue. After an emotional set of public
hearings, the stop consolidation debate was settled when it was agreed

upon to remove some stops and retain others. The outcome set a precedent for difficult debates about Muni bus stops in following years. Low-income, elderly, and disabled passengers would persistently object to stop consolidation proposals such as that eventually proposed in the TEP and that are now part of the *TEP Implementation Plan*. Most significant, bus stop removal divides progressives. *StreetsblogSF,* reflecting views of the sustainable mobility movement, contends that stop consolidation would not harm low-income and disabled riders but would benefit hundreds of thousands of daily riders while helping to implement transit first.[40] Yet social service providers and community organizers insist on preserving bus stops, at least in specific places, reflecting their conceptualization of Muni as a public service and social service, not an optimized, efficient, rational commuting system. The tension within progressivism is aggravated by the limited resources available to deploy the TEP plan. In an ideal world, both kinds of services would be provided.

The consolidation of bus stops is made more complicated in that it complements broader route consolidation and rationalization proposals that have revanchist undertones. The *TEP Implementation Plan* still awaits lengthy environmental review and will continue to be vetted, but a hint of how it could be used to advance revanchist ends occurred in late 2009, when SFMTA used the data provided by the TEP to rationalize the system in the wake of the two-year, $129-million budget shortfall.[41] Using the background studies that informed the *TEP Implementation Plan,* the SFMTA identified six allegedly inefficient bus lines for elimination and thirty-seven lines on which service was decreased or consolidated with other routes; in other words, lines that had low ridership were inefficient and should be cut immediately. As a 10 percent service cut was implemented, SFMTA simultaneously rerouted service to the 38-Geary, adding a 15 percent capacity increase and more frequent bus service during peak hours. To be sure, improved service on the city's busiest bus line was sorely needed, and it benefited over fifty-four thousand daily riders with diverse income and racial demographics.

The SFMTA, in defending the restructuring and rationalization of Muni, argued that the cuts to service on specific low-ridership routes would have happened eventually, since the forthcoming *TEP Implementation Plan* included cutting less productive routes and shifting the capacity to routes that needed increases in frequency and capacity. Yet the TEP, originally intended to implement transit first, was being used to optimize the system in a revanchist manner. This rationalizing of routes through a restructuring of service to prioritize the rapid network is consistent with neoliberal and conservative discourses that mobility should be allowed to develop with the efficacy of the market rather than for goals separate from the market—such as serving populations that are isolated but dependent on transit.

If the city is hoping to wean motorists from their cars by achieving the 30–30–40 mode split, cutting service, even in relatively low ridership routes, is counterproductive. It begs the question: Were the ridership levels on these routes low because the service was poor to begin with, including such irritating factors as less frequency, less reliability, or fewer hours of service? What would ridership levels look like if these routes had high frequency, all-day and late-night service with high reliability? Moreover, what would demand for these services look like if parking were substantially reduced throughout the city while car-travel lanes were removed, creating space for bicycle lanes and transit lanes? Or what if there were a regional gasoline tax, a congestion charge, or other measures that priced automobility closer to its real social cost, thus producing higher demand for transit? Surely reducing the footprint of transit service, however inefficient that service might seem now, is not creating a template necessary for carrying 1.4 million daily passengers in the future, which is the city's estimate of what it would take to reach emissions reduction goals (see chapter 6). It will only make it harder to rebuild and accomplish that goal.

Disciplining Bus Drivers

Transit is capital intensive but also expensive to operate, and for systems like Muni up to $200 million in operating costs are for labor, including salaries, health insurance, and pensions (this figure covers only the two thousand Muni operators, not the twenty-seven hundred other employees of the SFMTA).[42] When the Great Recession of 2008–12 resulted in considerable cuts in state support for transit, coupled with declining local tax revenue, increased fuel costs, and decreases in federal aid, agencies like Muni sought concessions from their operators' unions, a volatile undertaking that has a major bearing on the politics of mobility. The economic crisis not only debilitated public transit at a time when it needed to expand but also drew attention to long-standing structural problems with the agency's labor arrangement and provided a political opportunity to discipline labor.

Paralleling the tactics of spreading the burden and implementing system efficiency, in 2010 Muni's financial crisis bled into a long-standing class struggle over salaries and work rules. That struggle was set against the backdrop of the national discourse about public employee unions, such as the elimination of collective bargaining in Wisconsin in 2011. Instead of seeking ways to expand public transportation and attract more riders, either through restricting driving by reallocating street space or through obtaining new revenues by taxing real estate or automobiles, neoliberals, joined by conservatives and even some unwitting progressives, engaged in a campaign that scapegoated the drivers and operators of Muni and invoked antiunion and revanchist discourses about transit workers.

In 2010 a neoliberal–conservative alliance put Muni's labor contract on the ballot, which not only aligned labor unions and progressive allies against their traditional neoliberal and conservative opponents but also pitted the union against a decidedly nonsympathetic class of younger, hip tech workers and creative workers, many of whom shared some broader progressive social values but not a sense of labor history. The creative class invoked neoliberal and conservative discourses about transit workers, who were characterized as having bloated salaries, political patronage, and work rules that don't reflect commensurate salaries. As part of the broader program of system efficiency, the language of disciplining labor further divided and confused progressives. Sustainable transportation activists had less sympathy for the workers than community organizers and ethnic social justice organizations, who felt more solidarity with the largely black, Latino, Asian, and female union. This important ethnic and gender dimension of the politics of transit must be laid bare.

As described earlier, despite the largest fare increase in a century and service cuts in 2009, in early 2010 the SFMTA projected an additional midyear, $17-million shortfall and a $45-million shortfall later that year owing to further cuts in state spending, continued declining sales tax revenue collected by the city, and increased operating costs because of healthcare and salary formulas. SFMTA quickly proposed reducing service frequency on almost every bus route in the city by adding one to two minutes between each run on busy lines and by adding five or ten minutes between the arrival of buses on other lines, further rationalizing service. Not surprisingly, the SFMTA excluded more increases in parking meter rates or expanding of parking meter hours, which progressives had lobbied for, and, needless to say, a TAD was not mentioned. By February 2010 the rhetoric surrounding Muni's financial problems pointed to the operators and their contract with the city.

Mayor Newsom, loath to raise parking rates while seeking higher statewide office (he was courting suburban voters and wanted to avoid being

seen as anti-car), framed the Muni crisis as a trade-off between fare increases and labor concessions.[43] Labor's acquiescence to some of the work
rules and to salary concessions would offset the counterproposal to increase fares on Muni's discount passes and, furthermore, would enable
Muni to restore some of the service eliminated in 2009. Echoing the may-
or, the executive director of SPUR chimed in that "the first and foremost
concern for Muni should be labor reform."[44] Neoliberals' strategy was to
pit labor against progressive social service providers and their low-income
clients, leaving motorists and wealthy landowners out of the discussion.
Fearing backlash against the union, the leadership of the Transport Workers Union (TWU)-250A negotiated labor concessions to avert an increase
in the cost of low-income transit passes, but the rank and file in the union
voted against the agreement. Some suggested that operators were unclear
or misinformed and hinted that the union's leadership failed to explain the
negotiation. Still other union members said the proposal was too vague,
did not ensure against future layoffs, and offset labor costs rather than
providing other revenues to fix the structural problem at Muni. The union
then asked for a binding agreement promising no future layoffs if they
ratified the proposal. But no labor agreement was reached, and in April
2010 the SFMTA board voted 4–3 to cut Muni service.

In the SFMTA's view, the primary issue involved the complicated work
rules governing bus drivers during weekday, off-peak, midday, and late-
evening transit service, when ridership demand was less and Muni reduced the deployed fleet from 630 buses to 430 buses.[45] Historic labor
agreements forbade the hiring of part-time drivers only for peak period
runs and instead required that all drivers work a minimum eight-hour day
and forty-hour week. When midday or late evening demand fell, many
drivers were idled on standby and were thus unproductive yet paid their
full salary. In 2010 an audit of Muni operations found that some bus routes
had up to three hours of standby time built in to their operations and overall roughly 20 percent of Muni's expenditure on salary went to standby.[46]
To be sure, some drivers shuffled among routes during off-peak hours,
worked special events, and performed various duties, but others were simply idled, and still others often ended up working unscheduled overtime,
even after being idled, because they replaced drivers who were on sick
leave or were absent. Unscheduled overtime amounted to 25 percent of
all overtime pay, and 15 percent of drivers' absences was unscheduled.[47]
The audit placed less emphasis on how congestion and police activity,
for example, street closures and stalled buses while drivers enforced fare
evasion, often resulted in unscheduled overtime, and it did not analyze

the causes of unscheduled absenteeism, such as health issues and family emergencies.

All transit systems have the conundrum of idled workers during off-peak operations, and the audit of daytime bus operations found that standby is necessary and inevitable in order to have professional, well-trained, and healthy operators. However, the audit suggested that Muni could save $3 million annually, or 2.5 percent of the annual SFMTA budget, if the work rules for standby operators and overtime were tightened via a rethinking of scheduling and avoidance of overtime that overlaps with standby. Beyond these minor budget fixes the audit compared Muni's standby policies with those of peer agencies and suggested that Muni compared unfavorably. Yet the peer agencies were allowed to hire part-time drivers and thus had labor arrangements different from those of Muni, although no peer system eliminated the standby issue entirely.

The technicality of scheduling aside, the audit hinted that longer-term, deeper savings could be found if Muni were able to hire flexible, part-time drivers instead of full-time drivers. While the audit suggested SFMTA analyze the causes of absenteeism, it nevertheless left considerable ambiguity and contributed to the public's perception that drivers were lazy and, as public sector employees, abused the system. This, then, was the crux of neoliberal and conservative political antagonism toward labor. Using the rhetoric of efficiency, coupled with the objectionable alternative of raising the price of automobility on innocent motorists, a neoliberal–conservative coalition emerged to reform Muni labor practices on the basis of flexibility and ending bus drivers' absenteeism. What neither the audit nor the broader neoliberal–conservative discourse around it offered was a vision of what Muni might look like if all of the 630 peak-time buses operated throughout the day.

Incensed that Muni drivers allegedly abused overtime rules and sick leave and lazed around union parlors at midday, coupled with the obvious solution of hiring part-time drivers during peak periods, paid signature gatherers had little trouble gathering seventy-five thousand signatures to put Muni labor reform on the November ballot.[48] Ironically, signature gathering was conducted at Sunday Streets events, and many unwitting progressives joined in the scapegoating of Muni drivers. However, the real outrage against the labor union came from the conservative west side, where car-driving grocery shoppers were easily intercepted to sign the petition. Thus was born Proposition G, titled "Transit Operator Wages."[49]

Steering away from the complicated and muddy scheduling and work rules, Prop G focused on a simpler labor formula, established by San Francisco voters as a charter amendment in 1967, which guaranteed automatic pay increases for drivers rather than raises negotiated through collective bargaining.[50] Coincidentally, the 1967 measure was also known as Prop G and, was approved by 55 percent of voters and supported by the mayor, most elected officials, labor unions, and Muni management. It was widely celebrated as a labor peace because there was considerable labor unrest at Muni, the result of operators not being paid as well as other city employees; local leaders had sought to avoid a strike like the one that shut down New York City transit for twelve days in 1966.[51] The formula devised in 1967 was deemed necessary by management because it reduced not only the high turnover rate of drivers but also the overall cost of retraining workers, making Muni more competitive with other employers for good, long-tenured, experienced professional drivers. Paradoxically, given that the discourse about labor in 2010 was centered on efficiency, the charter amendment of 1967 was characterized as a fair means of optimizing the system.

The charter amendment called for Muni drivers to be paid a salary no higher than the average of the top two highest-paid transit agencies in the nation. The automatic wage formula made working for Muni a solid middle-class opportunity in a city that, relative to other cities, had higher housing costs. Over the following forty-three years Muni operators never went on strike over their contract (New York City, by comparison, has had at least three major multiday strikes since 1966). However, in 2007, with parking reform and Muni's seemingly perpetual crisis in the air, the charter was again amended as part of the aforementioned Prop A, which mandated the GHG reductions for San Francisco's transportation system, redirected parking revenue directly to Muni (instead of to the general fund), and protected new parking policies (see chapter 4).

Labor underwrote a substantial part of the successful Prop A campaign and provided manpower for canvassing and phone banking during that campaign. Labor resources also countered the well-endowed Prop H campaign financed by the Gap founder Don Fisher, which was aimed at tossing out San Francisco's new parking reforms. In return for labor's activism on Props A and H, a compromise was made with labor to eliminate the wage ceiling made in 1967 and instead make it a floor. Muni drivers would now be paid "not less" than the average of the two highest wage schedules in the nation. Additionally, in exchange for the revision in the formula, there was an understanding that TWU would reconsider the work rules and weigh how to incorporate flexible, that is, part-time, drivers. In November 2007, Prop A passed with 55.6 percent voter approval, and Prop H failed.

Despite success at the ballot box and apparent political alignment around labor-sustainable transportation, subsequent years saw more deep cuts to service, fare increases, and increased parking charges. After the rank and file of the drivers' union rejected proposals to scale back wages and reform work rules voluntarily, public dissatisfaction with the union was manifested yet again, in Prop G in 2010. Above all, Prop G eliminated the automatic wage formula created in 1967 and amended in 2007. The provision guaranteeing that Muni drivers had the second-highest operator wages in the country was removed, and new labor agreements were to be reached through collective bargaining rather than set automatically. As in the case of most labor processes in the United States, if SFMTA management and the union reached an impasse over the labor contract, binding arbitration was required.

Prop G directed the labor contract mediator to prioritize system efficiency over bus drivers, such that if it was found that working conditions conflicted with management's notion of how the system should be run, system optimization trumped the operators. For example, drivers could be made to bear more responsibility for the time it took buses to move through the car traffic that slows Muni down. The arbitration language emphasized how to extract more from labor in order to run the system more efficiently but did not address congestion or the fare collection system that imposed long dwell times on many routes.

Throughout the summer of 2010 and leading up to the election in November, public discourse about Prop G focused on animosity toward the operators' union rather than on the deeper structural problems of how public transportation was funded.[52] Proponents of Prop G tapped into the widespread public identification with individual stories of rude drivers and being passed up at bus stops for no apparent reason and manipulated this into a pseudo-populist good governance reform movement. In a large percentage of affluent riders, the wider discourse served to alienate transit workers from the city's erstwhile progressive creative class. Proudly "leading the charge," SPUR stressed that Muni's "workplace culture" was the central issue,[53] that is, a culture of people not showing up for work and union rules that make it impossible to have enough drivers at peak times but too many at off-peak. The reforms in Prop G, according to SPUR, were modest and common-sensical.[54]

SPUR cocreated a "Fix Muni Now" campaign with a populist emphasis and produced a slick television advertisement showing regular people being passed up by crowded trains while drivers demanded more money.[55] The conservative Coalition for San Francisco Neighborhoods demanded that drivers be disciplined for absenteeism, while "Plan C," representing homeowners who opposed more pricing of automobiles, campaigned in favor of the charter amendment. "Rescue Muni," the transit reform organization that championed Prop E in 1999, argued that Muni's problems originated in overpaid workers and that Prop G was the "first step to ending Muni's downward spiral."[56] Despite its populist veneer, Prop G was largely financed by well-endowed benefactors such as the Chamber of Commerce, BOMA, the Golden Gate Restaurant Association, the San Francisco Association of Realtors, the Committee on Jobs, a downtown corporate political organization, and an assortment of other corporate interests that together contributed at least $466,000 to promote the proposition.[57] In other words, while it was framed as a populist campaign, few of the benefactors were the grass-roots, small donors that the Prop G proponents implied undergirded the initiative.

Meanwhile, the ad hoc, fragmented nature of progressive politics resulted in an opposition to Prop G that was barely organized. The Muni drivers' union, the TWU-250A, in opposing the measure, tried to make the case to the public that the union was open to eliminating the automatic pay increase if other measures, such as management's salaries, were added to the ballot initiative.[58] Organized labor, including the San Francisco Labor Council and AFL-CIO, rallied behind the TWU-250A, as did the *San Francisco Bay Guardian,* which opined that the city needed a fair, omnibus measure that contained some labor reforms but also funding for Muni from business elites.[59] The *Guardian* pointed out that Prop G gave too much discretion over work rules and safety to binding arbitration and that an arbitrator could force optimization of the system over safety. City-wide progressive organizations like the Harvey Milk Democratic Club, Chinese Progressive Association, and an array of social service and low-income advocates also opposed Prop G. Some progressives on the Board of Supervisors charged that it was racist because it was led by wealthy white elites and targeted mainly minority drivers.[60] Race was undoubtedly a factor. The TWU-250A, a largely minority organization, has a history reaching back to the 1970s as a place for good-paying jobs for African Americans and, later, for Asian Americans and for women as well. Some in the TWU-250A asked, Would a workforce of mostly white workers have been treated the same way?

In a sign that progressive labor politics were waning in the city, an assortment of traditionally reliable progressive organizations remained silent on Prop G. The San Francisco Democratic Central Committee, which was controlled by progressives at the time and crafted the party's local positions, excluded Prop G from its ballot mailer, which went to hundreds of thousands of voters in the city. Yet the party took progressive positions on many other controversial issues, for example, endorsing the legalization of marijuana and opposing a statewide ballot that threatened to repeal the state's global warming laws. Revealing just how sensitive Prop G was, the Democratic Central Committee was openly opposed to another neoliberal labor reform measure on the ballot that year but chose to remain mute on Prop G.

Fundamentally, in a city with a high population of nonunionized, creative class tech workers, the TWU-250A was not able to convince voters that its stance was also about preserving social benefits for everyone. Further, Muni's drivers were the only public employees' union in San Francisco that spurned the city's requests for givebacks, wage freezes, and other measures to help close the city's gaping budget deficits.[61] Particularly workers in the volatile tech sector often face greater insecurity and more severe cutbacks than unionized civil servants, and so the creative class technocrats had little sympathy for public sector unions. Instead, the TWU-250A's class advocacy looked selfish, a bloated union demanding the highest salary in the nation while tech workers were shifting around for work, laid off, fired, and then rehired with no security. More broadly, however, the focus on transit operators in 2010 came at a time of growing national backlash against public sector unions. Unions were being charged with collecting excessive salaries and enjoying generous benefits packages, and thus local and state governments could not afford basic physical infrastructure.[62] The *New York Times* reported that in 2010 national sentiment toward public sector unions was diminishing, and unions were under assault even in union-friendly states like California and New Jersey. Rather than being angry at banks and millionaires, public anger was seemingly directed at unions, even as public salaries were shown to be equal to or lagging behind private sector salaries. The *Times* characterized the situation as a "race to the bottom": as more and more people resented benefits since they themselves would never have them, the private sector increasingly paid fewer benefits.[63]

On November 2, 2010, Prop G passed with 64 percent voter approval. The SFMTA immediately identified $14 million as coming from the reforming of labor rules and cost savings. When the current labor contract expired, SFMTA would be permitted to negotiate for part-time drivers and other reforms. In March 2011 the TWU-250A filed an appeal against Prop G in state court, and that May asked the Federal Transit Administration (FTA) to intervene by holding back the federal share of money for the

Central Subway. The union assumed that the FTA, under federal mandates to recognize the collective bargaining rights of unions, would withhold federal funds from the SFMTA if collective bargaining was determined by an arbitrator. Meanwhile, the union voted to authorize a strike, while the union leadership negotiated with the SFMTA for a new contract.

In June 2011 the defeated TWU-250A leadership reached a tentative agreement that saved Muni $38 million in labor costs over the next three years.[64] The agreement included a three-year wage freeze, decreased overtime, and new opportunities for hiring part-time operators to help cover the busy morning and evening commute runs and special events. Significantly, the agreement introduced, for the first time at SFMTA, a two-tiered compensation system whereby all future hires will pay 2.5 percent of their salary into their pension. This practice, in which new workers receive less pay than incumbent workers and inferior benefits, is not just a way to reduce costs while avoiding a full-scale fight with existing employees; in addition, it creates a lack of solidarity within the union between senior workers and new workers, and it plays one generation of transit workers off against another.[65] The rank-and-file transit workers rejected the agreement with a vote of 994 to 488, but immediately the designated arbitrator concluded that the workers had to accept the proposed agreement, and the city attorney threatened action against the union if it went on strike or disrupted service. Union leaders signed the arbitration award.

Nevertheless, in the aftermath of this agreement the original Prop G proponents were disappointed in the outcome because they had sought a deeper, 10 percent wage cut, reduction in nighttime pay, and an end to paid lunch breaks as well as reductions in benefits.[66] The *San Francisco Chronicle* continued to characterize the TWU-250A as "union power run amok."[67] All indicators were that the revanchist strategy toward labor would remain a centerpiece of neoliberal and conservative transit politics in San Francisco.

Disciplining Riders: The Politics of Fare Evasion

Dwell time at bus stops, by Muni's calculation, accounts for 15 to 30 percent of the time it takes for a bus to complete a full round-trip run.[68] At every bus stop passengers are required to board at the front, where the driver can screen potential fare evaders. At seventy passengers per hour, Muni has the nation's highest density of boardings for any given bus run, and passengers' front-door boarding renders the system slow and inefficient.[69] To remedy this inefficiency transit industry experts recommend deploying a universal POP fare-collection scheme with automated vending machines at every transit stop; passengers are encouraged to use prepaid discounted passes so that passengers can board at every door and reduce dwell times. POP is already used on the Muni Metro light-rail lines, where passengers pay in advance before entering the railway and can board vehicles at any door. While expensive to implement, POP has proven extremely beneficial in cities around the world where transit ridership is high and the quality of service is excellent.[70] In the long run the savings in operator costs balance the frontloaded coast of deploying POP, and it is also beneficial for bus operators because it relieves them of the obligation to police fare evaders, which can be a very stressful and distracting aspect of driving a bus.

Progressive transit advocates, SPUR, and Muni planners have advocated systemwide POP, but the city has been reluctant, seeing costs, logistics, and uncertainty about how to deal with fare evasion as obstacles. Bus drivers have developed an unspoken tradition, one rooted in a progressive view of transit as a public service and in solidarity with passengers, of opening the rear doors of buses on busy routes and at crowded stops. This practice, which SFMTA called a "culture of backdoor boarding," informally and unofficially speeds up bus service while providing more dignity to passengers, especially those holding discounted passes.[71] But it enrages many critics of Muni operators, who, deploying neoliberal and conservative discourses, express their belief that rampant fare evasion is responsible for much of Muni's financial woes and that bus drivers are derelict in their duty to responsibly police the system. SFMTA responds that it may seem self-evident to just force all boardings at the front of vehicles, but that an immediate shift to exclusive front-door boarding would result in longer times at stops and slower travel times, especially at peak commute periods. Enforcing fare validation would slow the system down, deepening the system's inefficiency.

The juxtaposition of dwell time at bus stops and fare evasion creates a dilemma for Muni, and a vitriolic politics of fare evasion swirled around Muni's larger budget debates between 2000 and 2010. The rhetoric surrounding fare evasion invoked the broken-windows theory, which holds that disorder invites more disorder, for example, that youth evading fares leads inevitably to minor vandalism then to property theft and violence.[72] Among the 42 percent of Muni passengers from the middle and upper classes there was widespread resentment toward the presence of unkempt, apparently homeless passengers, unpleasant odors, and annoyance with loud conversations. That attitude permutated into politically charged suspicion of rampant fare evasion by the lower classes. The perception that drivers tolerate fare evasion by opening all doors, allowing rear-door boarding of buses, folded into a lack of conservative and neoliberal political support for finding new revenue for Muni, as newspapers reported that fare evaders were bilking the system of millions of dollars annually.[73] Muni, the discourse contended, needed to get its fare collection in order before parking prices were raised or new transit fees were assessed. To dampen the perception of brazen criminals not paying their fair share, the SFMTA, in anticipation of a new in-house policing effort, conducted a thorough study of fare evasion in 2008 and 2009. Stoking the flames of discontent, the study of fare evasion in 2009 concluded that roughly 9.5 percent of passengers on Muni had an expired transfer, were misusing a discount pass by lying about their age or disability, or, in the vast majority of cases, simply had no evidence they had paid the fare.[74] In other words, fare evasion amounted to upward of $19 million in uncaptured revenue, and on some of the city's busiest bus routes, such as those along the streets of the Mission and Bayview, fare-evasion rates were 15 percent and higher.[75] In its analysis of the culture of backdoor boarding on the Geary, Mission, and Bayview bus routes, the study concluded that fare-evasion rates of riders entering at the rear were 55 percent. Operators made little effort to enforce payment, sometimes for security reasons but also because it could be overwhelming, and, to expedite travel times, they ignored fare evasion at the rear. Revealingly, the study reified POP because fare evasion was low on Muni Metro lines that were regularly patrolled by roving fare inspectors (before 2009 fare inspectors did not patrol the bus system).

Yet rather than emphasize that full POP was good public policy, or that many passengers simply forgot to properly scan their fare card in the new fare-reader machines, or that reader machines malfunctioned, or that passengers' transfers expired while they waited for buses, the study was used as a baseline to measure the before and after of intensive policing against fare evaders on key bus routes. Unwittingly, the report served to inform a politics of fare evasion that echoed broader revanchist discourses about quality-of-life crimes that, if left unchecked, would lead to further criminal activity. In response, the SFMTA invoked a discourse of fostering a "culture of fare compliance" and public respect for the system.

In July 2009, just as the study of fare evasion was released, the SFMTA initiated "concentrated enforcement efforts" with teams of unarmed fare-evasion inspectors accompanied by armed police officers targeting bus routes identified as having endemic fare evasion.[76] This meant saturation enforcement was directed toward the 38-Geary and routes in the Mission,

Bayview, and southern neighborhoods with high percentages of low-income, transit-dependent African American, Latino, and Asian populations and, in many cases, with considerable language barriers and immigration issues. Progressives from advocacy organizations that stressed social services and immigrants' rights were outraged, as the stings resulted in what they perceived as the unfair stigmatization of people who could not afford the seventy-five-dollar fine, which were levied even if the passenger had not intended to evade the fare.

People Organized to Win Employment Rights made a high-profile case out of a Latina mother who was humiliated by police and hauled off a bus in the Mission because her transfer had expired.[77] Calling the targeted enforcement reactionary, progressive Latino and Asian community organizers asserted that the stings were too strict for those with expired transfers or who juggled complicated child care and family obligations and that police racially profiled immigrant riders who did not speak English. The stings criminalized low-income people and youth for taking public transportation and focused the burden of Muni's financial troubles on the poor. Community organizations protested the enforcement at City Hall, raising concerns with progressive members of the Board of Supervisors, and leveraged a response from the city's Immigration Rights Commission that asked police and fare inspectors to undertake sensitivity training.[78]

In May 2010 the saturation enforcements were suspended largely because of protests. SFMTA compared data from the results of the enforcements with the study of fare evasion from 2009 and pronounced that the effort was a success.[79] Systemwide fare evasion declined from 9.5 percent to 8.6 percent between July 2009 and March 2010 after 326,293 inspections during 130 enforcement operations and 1,276,593 regular inspections. In total, 28,169 citations were issued to people who did not have valid fares, and the agency collected $1.7 million in citations. Yet 60 percent of citations remained unpaid, and activists charged that, relative to the financial needs of Muni, these results showed that massive police force brought little in return except harassment of the poor. Using police on Muni, for example, cost above $11 million per year, since the SFMTA was required to reimburse the police department for shifting officers to Muni. People Organized to Win Employment Rights and other advocates pointed out that during the almost year-long enforcement operation the SFMTA raised fares and slashed service, disproportionately impacting the poor (the fare increased by fifty cents to two dollars), while policing youth and immigrants—effectively disciplining low-income riders for the system's larger troubles.

Acknowledging that enforcement could be improved with sensitivity training of fare inspectors and police, the discourse around fare evasion also revealed that SFMTA's motive for the enforcement operation was twofold. Recouping lost fares as a means of instilling fiduciary confidence was only part of the equation. The enforcements were also a potent response to—arguably accommodation of—revanchist discourses about public transit. In this case urban elites use revanchist policies to sanitize transit, as Muni is often identified as a space in the city in need of reclamation from minor quality-of-life offenders because fare evasion, as a quality-of-life crime, eventually leads to deeper criminal activity. Police who are checking POP can also enforce against disorderly passengers, eating on buses, taggers, and the homeless. Based on the theory that minor violations were creating a sense of disorder that invites more serious crime and creates a sense of fear, the police presence was welcomed because it inevitably led to capturing people with arrest warrants, illegal immigrants, and people carrying weapons. Such thinking may have a grain of truth in it, but it ignores that, when compared to citywide crime statistics, crime on Muni was low—the system was not an exceptional space for criminal activity in the city.[80] Despite that fact, surveys show that between 50 and 60 percent of riders feel unsafe on Muni in some way, and this is in part owing more to inflammatory revanchist discourses about low-class riders than to reality.[81]

Progressives, too, including community organizers working for low-income transit riders, seek a safe, clean, pleasant transit experience. Yet they have a different strategy for achieving it. Some argue that collecting fines and paying police is a diversion of resources that could be better used by implementing a full POP system that brings about significant time savings and system efficiencies. An all-door POP system staffed by sensitive, multilingual, well-trained ticket inspection officers who lack powers of arrest might be implemented fairly. In the short term, until universal POP is implemented, progressives have suggested that Muni allow all-door boarding on key high-volume routes by having ticket agents preemptively collect fares or verify transit passes, much like airport security checkpoints. Some progressives have even lobbied the Board of Supervisors and SFMTA to grant free transit to youth between the ages of five and seventeen, which would avert the criminalization of youth fare evaders.[82]

Further complicating the discussion of a universal POP, however, is San Francisco's struggle over homelessness. On any given night there are between eleven thousand and fourteen thousand homeless people in San

Francisco, many of whom use Muni. Moreover, 80 percent of the city's single resident occupant hotel units (often used by transient homeless people) are concentrated near the Civic Center BART and Muni Metro Station. This area is ground zero for the next wave of redevelopment in the city, as Twitter and the Black Rock Arts Foundation, the sponsor of Burning Man, relocate nearby.[83] There is deep suspicion that universal POP will not work, at least in certain parts of the city like the Civic Center, unless there is policing.

Although progressives forced the city to implement sensitivity training and to relax the saturation approach, revanchist transit policies remain pronounced in the discourse over Muni fare evasion. In July 2011 the fine for fare evasion was increased from seventy-five to one hundred dollars, and the SFMTA expects the increased collection of fines to help balance the budget in the near future, suggesting the likelihood of more saturation campaigns. Neoliberals and conservatives see the problem with Muni not just as unreasonable labor militancy by the transit operators' union, but also as unruly passengers who are mostly poor and should be disciplined or relegated off the system through fare increases so that the middle and upper classes can enjoy a pleasant ride. The transit system needs to be "cleaned up" in order for it to be more livable and for transit-oriented development to be able to maximize profit in places like Mid-Market. Just as upscale bars and boutiques displace services for the poor to make way for the neoliberal vision of the livable city, so some of Muni's passengers must be disciplined and removed.

Premium Transit

Neoliberalism envisions a mobility system shaped by pricing and markets rather than by regulation and collective action, consistent with the broader agenda of the privatization of space and market-based pricing of public access to space. Conservatism envisions the reluctance of people to ride crowded, slow buses, but support for commuter rail and express buses if they are of high quality and exclude undesirables and the poor. These neoliberal and conservative perspectives on transit converge in the recent proposal of a two-tiered transit system in the Bay Area. For example, SPUR has recommended that new revenue for Muni could come from establishing premium fares on Muni Metro lines and on the proposed rapid bus lines in the TEP as well as on future bus rapid transit on Geary or Van Ness Avenue.[84] The rest of the system would remain economy class, as in the case of congestion charging and high-occupant toll lanes.

While this scheme for creating premium transit service has yet to be implemented in the city, there are some examples of what form such a system might take. Premium-service, privately operated bus operations have proliferated among large high-tech software and biotech companies in the Bay Area, enabling well-to-do commuters to avoid interaction with Muni or other public transit systems, while enjoying more direct service than that of conventional public transit. These private, employer-provided regional buses offer a glimpse of what a two-tiered premium or privatized transit system might look like.

In 1980, 9 percent of commuters in San Francisco left the city every day to go to work. In 2010 outbound commuters approached 25 percent, suggesting that parts of San Francisco were functioning as a bedroom community for suburban employment centers like Silicon Valley.[85] Owing to regional political fragmentation, Muni cannot provide intercounty service and thus is not the travel mode of choice for many of these commuters. And although Caltrain and BART offer some regional service, the sprawling locations of these firms often make regional rail impractical or at the very least time-consuming owing to unavoidable multiple transfers to local buses. So in noteworthy ways the provision of private transit is an immediate reaction to poor regional transit connections. But many of these poor connections are also the result of land use decisions by these corporations, which are characterized by dispersed, automobile-oriented campuses that are disconnected from adjacent communities and lack robust transit.

Furthermore, as noted in previous chapters, many employees in the technology sector shun living in suburbia and prefer the city of San Francisco. Although most reverse commuters drive, increasingly thousands are using luxury buses provided by third-party contractors for Google, Yahoo, Facebook, Apple, Genentech, E-Bay, and an expanding array of Silicon Valley firms. Every weekday employees are shuttled between San Francisco and suburban corporate campuses, and urban-based workers are provided an easy commute that also allows them to work on the bus. Many of these $2-million, forty-five- to fifty-passenger buses have wireless Internet access, iPod and laptop plug-ins and docking stations, televisions, restrooms, leather seats, and tabletops for working; some include even attendants handing out coffee and pastries to morning commuters. The shuttles have rules of etiquette, such as limiting cellphone conversations to work-related calls and speaking in a low voice. Each passenger is guaranteed a seat, and most buses fill with commuters who spend their time working, surfing the Web, or watching television.

These luxury buses are reducing the amount of VMT that would occur if these employees drove to the sprawling office parks. In one survey, 63 percent of passengers said they would drive alone were it not for the private bus service.[86] This equated to 375,000 round-trip solo-driving commutes avoided that year. Moreover, 28 percent of the respondents in the survey did not own a car, a figure on a par with San Francisco's rate of 30 percent car-free household ownership in 2010. In 2012 the *Wall Street Journal* published a profile of wealthy tech workers residing in San Francisco: living car-free in walkable neighborhoods with corporate shuttle service was a highly desired lifestyle of this class stratum.[87] At first glance there might seem to be an environmental benefit from these buses. However, many respondents said that the availability of the shuttle impacted their choice to live in the city rather than in the suburbs closer to work. This increases residents' overall demand for longer distance travel, albeit while living in a city that affords the choice of not owning a car.

Beyond an altruistic environmental benefit, some commuter bus service results from mandates for regional air quality and congestion mitigation. Large employers that generate thousands of commuting trips are required by the regional air quality and transportation agencies to implement schemes that manage transportation demand so as to reduce driving. They cannot allow all of their employees to arrive at work via a single-occupant automobile and are obligated to enforce such restrictions through the zoning code, environmental law, and building permits. For example, South San Francisco, home to a large cluster of biotech firms, required Genentech to provide 30 percent of commuters with alternatives to driving. Under that mandate Genentech has reached a 35 percent mode split of non–solo driving, much of which was achieved through carpooling and luxury buses.[88]

The provision of private transit is not limited to suburban firms. Downtown employers like Levis, Adobe, LinkedIn, and the Gap supply shuttles for employees, suggesting that more than just poor regional transit connections undergird their logic. This "shadow industry solution" to declining public transit is an expression of neoliberal and conservative inclinations to abandon the public realm, in this case public transit.[89] Restricted to employees who must show identification, the proliferation of these buses is creating a premium transit system for workers of elite firms, while enabling spatial secession from the poor, homeless, and all of the other annoyances expressed on blogs complaining about Muni patrons.[90]

Over the long term, the privatized commuting arrangement may accentuate revanchist transit policy. Fundamentally it creates an erstwhile pro-transit constituency among tech workers and wealthy professionals who favor environmental awareness and, more broadly, a framework of livability. Yet this class is seceding from the public and in due time may embrace policies that starve public transit as they resist taxes and fees that fund public transit. Privatized transit constitutes a resolution to the muddled labor union work rules like those found in Muni. In these systems drivers are flexible, can work part time, and are largely unorganized compared to the TWU-250A.[91] Furthermore, already scarce federal and state transit funds potentially may be opened to private corporate transit providers, meaning even less funding of Muni and other urban transportation systems. A recent study of Bay Area corporate shuttles recommended that the private shuttle entities pursue federal air quality funds and local development impact fees, among other public revenues.[92] Perhaps most egregious, in March 2012 evidence emerged that a major national private carrier, Veolia, lobbied the United States House of Representatives to encourage federal funding of private transit and of measures to accelerate privatization of transit.[93] Some private transit providers are envisioning a lucrative future for their industry.

All indications are that premium private transit is expanding. As Bay Area transit agencies strain under declining revenues, deferred maintenance, and deep federal and state cuts, one Bay Area transit contractor has rapidly expanded to over two hundred vehicles and more than one hundred drivers, increased daily ridership to more than six thousand people a day, and grew 30 percent a year between 2005 and 2010. The SF-CTA reports that Google had doubled its shuttle bus commuters, and the Mission Bay shuttles carry up to twelve thousand riders every weekday.[94] Moreover, in 2011 and 2012 real estate listings for some neighborhoods in the Victorian Belt began to mention their proximity to private shuttle bus routes, and anecdotally some observers have suggested that such proximity increases rents by up to $400, while the *Wall Street Journal* reports a 20 percent premium on new condominium sales in the area.[95] All of this foreshadows a potential transit future in which a premium system serves the wealthy in first-class coaches—and in premium livable neighborhoods—and a dilapidated, economy-class system serves the lower classes that are gentrified out of the core.

The Gentrification of Transit?

San Francisco's development class recognizes that transit is needed for the marketing of neoliberal visions of livability and especially for the intensive upscale redevelopment of the downtown. As part of the critical infrastructure for the production and circulation of capital, transit must be recaptured from progressive policies that envision the system as a social service and instead optimized for the functioning of the private market and to enhance the value of private property. For conservatives, secessionist discourses about automobility are intertwined with broader intolerance of progressive policies toward homelessness and mental illness. That rhetoric translates into efforts to contain quality-of-life crimes and to impose sanitizing of the transit system through saturation police tactics on Muni routes, fortification and surveillance of transit stations, and the incremental discontinuation of inefficient local transit programs that support the urban underclasses, such as by raising discounted fares and defunding social programs that subsidize transit usage.

Through emphasis on regressive sales taxes that invariably concentrate wealth, system efficiency that rations service, the disciplining of labor and unruly riders, and nascent privatization of transit, public transit, and especially Muni, is where revanchist discourses bluntly meet the politics of mobility in San Francisco. This revanchism is disorienting to a progressive politics of mobility. Progressives endorsed the regressive sales tax and have had a confusing approach to the Central Subway, which concentrates scarce funds in a limited geography to generate wealth for elite landowners. Rifts between social justice advocates and sustainable transportation advocates characterize progressives' juggling of system efficiency through the removal of bus stops and route consolidation. Faced with revanchist policies toward public sector unions, sustainable transportation advocates have grown alienated from Muni's bus drivers, and progressives have given mixed signals on debates about fare evasion. Progressives support the environmental benefits of private commuter buses but have stood by while tech workers embrace privatized transit to the peril of public transit and a potential declining constituency for public funding. As transit is captured from low-income people who depend on it, through the proliferation of increased fares, policing, and perhaps eventually market-rate pricing and segmentation of the system, the gentrification of the city may spread to the gentrification of transit.

CONCLUSION

San Francisco as
National Bellwether

Pessimistic political realities notwithstanding, if sustainable urban transportation is to work for people, many disparate pieces must come together in a synchronized way. Reducing automobility requires not only good transit, but higher-density, walkable residential patterns, more public spaces rather than private space, and more mixed uses within the urban fabric instead of single-use districts. Bicycling has enormous potential for short-range urban trips but needs good transit as a regional complement. Safe, practical walking and bicycling require that cars not only be slowed and tamed but also that they be less obtrusive, bulky, and menacing. Concomitantly, if urban transit is to flow smoothly, less urban space should be allocated for the moving and parking of cars. San Francisco is an important national bellwether because many of the attributes of the city have the potential to be synchronized in these ways. The city's population density and evolving policies vis-à-vis the car are arguably more in line with what truly needs to be done to address urgent problems of GHG emissions, energy policy, and social concerns about mobility.

San Francisco is an exceptionally livable city by many indicators and has a very high, one might say, insatiable demand for new housing because of this. It is a city where one can choose to live without a car and remain functional and comfortable, something atypical of most American cities. However, despite having 30 percent car-free households and the highest transit ridership west of the Mississippi River, today San Francisco has one of the highest densities of automobile registrations in the United States, at over nine thousand motor vehicles per square mile. As stressed in the introduction, this apposition of many car-free households and high transit ridership juxtaposed against high vehicle density is a critical issue for the livability movement to consider. People might be able to choose to live without a car, but they continue to be affronted and burdened by their neighbors' choices to continue to own and use cars. Transit is slowed in traffic, bicycling remains hazardous for the less nimble, and walking in the city can be a dangerous obstacle course. San Francisco embodies both what the livability movement is trying to achieve and what can go wrong.

In the political process, loud opposition to removing car space and parking permeates the discourse on mobility in San Francisco. The preservation of automobility is often justified on claims that transit systems are slow and impractical and that bicycling is unsafe and things are too far apart to walk. All of this is true to a certain extent in parts of San Francisco, especially in the Bay Area region, but it is a self-reinforcing feedback cycle. To break the cycle requires a rethinking of urban space and perhaps a moment of inconvenience for the motorist. This is exactly the situation San Francisco finds itself in in the opening decades of the twenty-first century: it is poised to break the cycle.

In San Francisco breaking the cycle includes a bold discussion around a future 30–30–40 mode split between cars, transit, and bicycle/walking, respectively, and a mandate to reduce GHGs to 80 percent of levels in 1990. The city has practical ideas about implementing transit first, expanding Muni to double its current capacity, and, through persistent progressive activism, could Connect the City (as proposed by the SFBC) by building a network of cycle tracks, removing more segments of freeways, and reducing the amount of available parking as well as reforming traffic engineering in ways that limit automobility. These are all vital to the broad livability agenda, and in an era of paltry national leadership on global warming and energy security progressive San Franciscans continue to see it as their global civic duty to be out front and to inspire others to break the cycle.

Ideology Matters

Yet breaking the cycle cannot be accomplished by transcending ideology or hoping it goes away. There is no apolitical, dispassionate, objective, and unbiased professionalism in transportation, despite the insistence by many scholars, planners, engineers, policymakers, and advocates that transportation can be separated from ideology. There are deeply embedded assumptions involved in mobility debates, and these are ideological. Obviously, there are people who hold strong, internally consistent beliefs, beliefs backed by coherent ideologies like progressive, neoliberal, or conservative, and who do not go back and forth on different models or values from issue to issue. These include sustainable transportation advocates, who delineate progressive values of actively discouraging automobility; developer and business elites, who champion neoliberal policies of pricing automobility and space; and small merchants and property owners with conservative positions on the necessity of the automobile and the need for government to intervene in order to protect automobility. But perhaps the majority of persons do not recognize coherent ideologies in themselves. Many people are inconsistent and as voters may apply different parts of ideologies for different issues at different times. Ideologies can overlap, exhibit some degree of fluidity, and be hard to pin down sometimes. Yet this does not mean that ideology is absent.

Ideology can be an unconscious expression of underlying ideas and beliefs exerted not through visible force but through the willing acquiescence of citizens to accept their status by approving of and agreeing to abide by cultural, social, and political practices and institutions. In the United States the ubiquity of automobility can make the act of driving seem apolitical and cloak the reality that ideology and political choice are inherently connected to driving. Claims of nonideological, nonpartisan, objective mobility shroud the true sociopolitical nature of mobility. The broad ambit of this book, by way of examining the case study of San Francisco, is to provide some transparency as to how transportation is structured by ideology. For example, the loose, ad hoc neoliberal–progressive détente in San Francisco included rapprochement over freeway removal, parking pricing, and transit-oriented urban infill as well as recognition that traffic engineering techniques such as LOS must be reformed. These are specific examples, but they can be compared to situations in other cities, and I hope readers will undertake such a comparison. The high profile reallocation of streets in New York City, such as took place in Times Square and in the investment in the High Line greenway, occurred under a neoliberal mayor but had progressive mobility undertones, by which new bike lanes are juxtaposed against luxury housing that includes parking in otherwise transit-rich Manhattan. One can see the progressive mobility vision deployed in Chicago, Portland, and Seattle, where strong progressive mobility discourses intersect with the promotion of livability as a strategy of entrepreneurial economic development, thereby luring the creative class while putting the underlying moral purposes aside but not entirely dismissing them.

San Francisco's politics of mobility also demonstrates some of the pitfalls of the national détente over mobility between progressives and neoliberals. The livability policies promoted by national environmental and transportation advocacy organizations are rooted in progressive challenges to automobility and the belief that government can affect positive change in cities while also addressing climate change and resource conservation. Yet livability sounds a neoliberal chord with decidedly revanchist purposes—reclaiming the city for business, for the creative class, that is, the middle and upper classes, and for the functioning of the private market and private property—rather than notions of collective, public, egalitarian livability. To neoliberals, livability is a premium physical arrangement and the commodification of quality of life, including the walkability and transit accessibility of neighborhoods.

If livability is to be fair, it must avoid the revanchist tendencies emerging. Walkable, bicycle- and transit-oriented gentrification with premium off-street parking and private commuter transit is livability for the elite and is not progressive. This is a reality that progressives in San Francisco and elsewhere must judiciously navigate. Sustainable transportation advocates who boast that livability is legitimized because walkable places have high real estate values somewhat undermine the progressive city.

San Francisco has as well instances of conservative rhetoric about automobiles and the city. While the city is not a bastion of broader conservative ideology, when one deconstructs the politics of mobility, one finds potent discourses invoking a conservative essentialization of automobility and resistance to the regulation and pricing of automobility. Conservative language is by no means as pronounced as it may be in metropolitan areas like Atlanta, Houston, Los Angeles, or even in Bay Area suburbs, but it is present and it does contribute to the production of space in the city. The conservative discourse seeks public policies that preserve automobile access, protests efforts to reallocate street space for other modes, opposes efforts to densify around public transit, and advocates that all new development have abundant and inexpensive parking.

Like neoliberalism, conservative discourse invokes a revanchism toward lower classes, toward labor unions, and toward the provision of public transit besides high-quality express commuting. Tellingly, conservative discourse balks at neoliberal proposals to price automobility through congestion charging, increased tolls, and increased parking pricing. While neoliberals do not want to see a TAD underwriting Muni, conservatives do not want to see expansion of parking pricing or congestion pricing to underwrite Muni. In San Francisco—and arguably in other cities with a progressive sheen—this conservative tenor must be acknowledged and confronted.

On the other hand, there are sustainable transportation movements beyond San Francisco that exhibit many of the progressive characteristics found there. In the South, for example, progressives are promoting livability, albeit one with a southern character, such as the New Urbanism, which at its core invokes southern urbanism as found in New Orleans, Charleston, and Savannah. Atlanta has had a long struggle with sprawl and a lively discourse about transit justice and gentrification, just as San Francisco has but perhaps not as loud. Even Detroit has recently had its share of a livability discourse, with proposals for light rail and a growing bicycling movement. I hope this case study of San Francisco, admittedly a unique place and home to a sharper radical edge, offers inspiration but also context and a useful template for how the rest of America can begin rethinking the car, transit, bicycling, and urban space.

Obviously neither conservatives nor neoliberals are inclined to provide the leadership necessary to meet the challenges stemming from the contemporary mobility system, including climate change, resource scarcity, and broader concerns about local, national, and global equity. Conservative mobility posits that unfettered movement is a prerequisite of individual liberty and freedom and that government should proactively accommodate it, mainly by car. This even when such an act requires generous, inefficient subsidy or when it undermines broader, collective environmental and social goals. Neoliberal mobility, which is fundamentally based on using not regulation but pricing, privatization, and the efficacy of the market to determine mobility, is by design not going to point toward an urban space shaped by a public good, environmental stewardship, and social equity. While ambiguous about automobility, in the contemporary context of San Francisco neoliberals believe that providing spaces for automobiles is necessary for increasing the profit in lucrative urban infill real estate—they promote walkable livability but with parking that brings a premium.

Unlike neoliberals and conservatives, progressives believe that personal responsibility toward oneself includes social responsibility in mobility choices. Progressive mobility, if prepared to use government to limit the overall amount of automobility in cities, is capable of questioning the premises of the need for excessive, unfettered movement and of the destructive resource consumption patterns that go to support that kind of movement. Yet it remains to be seen if San Francisco's progressives will be able to overcome the profound barriers that complicate sustainable transportation. The situation regarding Muni and access to affordable housing in the city is without a doubt frustrating and discouraging. This is a reality that progressives in San Francisco must change. What can be done to secure a more progressive, livable city without making it exclusive?

Obviously a reform of California's limitations on local taxation, such as Prop 13, would be helpful. Reducing voter thresholds for new taxes from a two-thirds to a simple majority gives progressives a better opportunity to provide stable, long-lasting funding to expand Muni and create a more robust affordable housing fund. Assuming progressives muster simple majorities to support new taxes and fees, which is conceivable in San Francisco, this could enable the city to employ transportation assessments on commercial land, on parking, and on automobiles, all in ways that can help underwrite the expansion transit capacity, discourage driving, and shift travel to transit and other modes. The affordable housing conundrum could also be addressed through statewide tax reform, as initiatives for affordable housing can also possibly garner simple majority support locally but are stymied by the two-thirds requirement.

Yet conservative and neoliberal forces, locally and statewide, make the task of dispensing with Prop 13 and other statewide measures seem insurmountable. No one—no academic, politician, or pundit—has yet shown how to rid the state of the albatross of Prop 13, although there is widespread agreement that it should be dispensed with or at a minimum reformed in a way that taxes commercial land rather than residences. But the intransigence of the political system should not stop one from asking, What might a progressive mobility system look like if San Francisco got beyond these impediments?

A Map of Progressive Mobility

A thorough and meticulously prescriptive map of every mode in every section of the city would be an interesting presentation, but that would require a separate book and might not be of much use to anyone besides policy wonks in San Francisco. A more feasible approach here is to ask what people, as individuals and collectively, could be doing to lay a foundation for a more detailed map of progressive mobility in cities.

Perhaps the most important short-term endeavor for progressives is to take a moment to reassess why they are driving, for most progressives do own cars and do drive them. All but two of the progressive members of

San Francisco's current Board of Supervisors own and drive cars, as do many social justice advocates, professional planners, and community organizers. Even two leading proponents of removing the Central Freeway owned cars. Car ownership is a puzzling question considering that fundamentally progressive values include a variant of personal responsibility that includes social responsibility. Rather than pure self-interest and a laissez-faire, free market, which assumes that seeking individual self-interest will maximize everyone's interests, progressive values center on collective, cooperative approaches. At their core, automobiles are atomistic, privatized, individualistic forms of mobility that undermine arrangements based on cooperation. Driving a car under unfettered conditions is a form of mobility that usurps public space and crowds out mobilities that are more egalitarian, such as public transit, or that enable more community building social interaction, such as bicycling and walking.

From a global justice perspective, which many American progressives take, consider that the number of motorized vehicles is increasing rapidly and that nations like China and India will not sit idly by while the United States produces a disproportionate amount of pollution while consuming a disproportionate amount of global resources in order to have unfettered automobility. Progressives who acknowledge this reality and yet do not question their own driving might want to think about this.

The current fetish with a green car is not a solution. There has been very little truthful accounting of what the energy system or ecological footprint of a green car system would look like. It is doubtful that there is a realistically viable substitute for oil that can provide the levels of automobility that Americans and increasingly the middle class worldwide expect while also meeting existing industrial and residential energy consumption patterns. Shifting the world's fleet of automobiles to electric cars, hydrogen fuel cells, or biofuels will draw energy away from our industrial, residential, and food systems or it will require an entirely new layer of energy production. Tremendous amounts of energy are required to produce substitutes for petroleum, and the nuclear, solar, wind, and geothermal capabilities to produce that energy are unreliable or unrealistic at the levels at which global automobility is forecasted. Progressive should ask themselves, What kind of future does this make?

Progressive mobility, given the urgency and pressing need for change, is ultimately car-free mobility. Progressives must strive toward eliminating their personal car ownership and shift to a car system that resembles a cooperative utility, modeled on city car share or other communal car programs and use cars only as a last resort.

Yet it is naive to expect that progressives will immediately give up their cars. Many of them live in sprawl and have little choice, while others claim to be juggling too many obligations or have concerns about safety, for example, many adult women do not feel safe navigating the city at night and many fit adults feel unsafe cycling in mixed traffic. Let us set aside the legions of excuses and just assume many people might intend to give up car ownership at some point in the future but for whatever reason will not now give up driving. There are still constructive things people can do. For example, they can develop a progressive code of motoring conduct.

Progressive motoring conduct would entail a fundamental rethinking of the emphasis on speed in everyday life. Reallocating street space will no doubt slow down automobiles and is the crux of the debate about reforming LOS, which, as noted earlier, is a measurement of delay at intersections that reflects the notion that motorists have the right to speed through the city with minimal delay (see chapter 5). In progressive mobility, avoidance of the delaying of automobiles should not trump safe, wide bicycle lanes and smoothly flowing transit lanes. Ultimately, speed is an issue of justice, and progressives should be careful about characterizing it, as neoliberal pricing strategies do, as a commodity. Rather than enable the wealthy to pay for faster speeds through, for example, premium high-occupant toll lanes, congestion charging, and high-priced curbside parking using smart phones, all cars should be made to travel slowly in the city; further, the city should be made navigable at no greater than fifteen miles per hour, a speed deemed not only to be comfortable on calmed pedestrian streets but also to minimize injury and fatalities when there are collisions. Setting a citywide speed limit of fifteen miles per hour decreases the utility of a car, for it makes crossing town by car an exceptionally longer process. But the collective good of the city in a progressive mobility scenario takes precedence over individual desires for instant gratification and immediate access through speed.

When progressives defend what they perceive as their entitlement to high-speed car space, they inadvertently propagate a conservative essentialization of automobility and give politicians cover to do nothing. In San Francisco the defensive posture is especially characteristic of well-off people who reside in steep, hillside districts of the city and in places like green Marin County. These motorists often claim they have no choice but to drive, yet they fail to acknowledge that they chose to live in these hillside enclaves, thereby necessitating driving. Perhaps living on a hillside requires driving, but it can be done by following a progressive code of motoring conduct that means they cannot expect to speed across the city with few impediments or delays and then find ample free parking. Progressives have an obligation to drive slow, to expect to pay to drive and park, and to support reallocation of street space.

Progressive motoring conduct includes as well political action, and an important responsibility of progressives is to discontinue localized political resistance to reallocating of city streets. Attempts at traffic calming or pedestrian enhancements, for example, are diluted by anger over lost parking space or because many motorists simply do not want to slow down or take an alternative, perhaps round-about route. Individual motorists should tolerate the idea that the space of cars in cities must be reconfigured away from ample car space and toward the accommodating of public transit, cycling, and walking—here is where one has to start to break the self-reinforcing cycle. In San Francisco the broad progressive discourse might support transit first and bicycle space conceptually, but when it comes to the specific transformation of a particular street or to eliminating what is perceived to be an entitlement to parking, many progressives invoke a staunchly conservative essentialization of automobility. Every time a stretch of street is considered for change, angry motorists line up at city hall to protest the change.

The outcome, as outlined in this book, is a mobility stalemate whereby traffic is miserable, the buses move slowly largely because of traffic, and bicyclists find haphazard, fragmented bike lanes. Often cars double park in bike lanes, making cycling very unsafe. Even some progressive neighborhood organizations, fearing their access to on-street parking space will be curtailed, demand that new transit-oriented housing contain parking. Beyond the city this is a critical issue in the new *One Bay Area Plan,* which seeks to place hundreds of thousands of new housing units around transit nodes but has thus far failed to seriously rethink parking provision. If they contain even half of the parking per dwelling unit, these nodes will simply reflect the mobility stalemate experienced by San Francisco.

Resistance to change is expected from conservatives, who essentialize automobility, and from neoliberals, who seek profit, but progressives who engage in a local politics defending motoring are acting in a contradictory manner and ultimately defeating the broader progressive agenda. Progressives who continue to drive should step aside and cede space to other modes. Better yet, they must vocally endorse the removal of travel lanes and reductions in parking as a necessary step toward creating a truly progressive city. It is a matter of national security, resource conservation, and global justice, and these are all progressive values. The progressive motorist would still be able to drive, just more slowly, perhaps with less convenience than now, but over time the options of cycling, of walkable shopping, and improved public transit would synchronize more seamlessly.

Progressives must also think cautiously about the revanchist discourses surrounding low-class transit ridership and particularly transit operators. This major fissure does significant harm to the true aims of progressive mobility. Progressives need to avoid open, direct conflict with unions and instead focus on why wealthy downtown interests and the system of auto-mobility are not being held responsible for the transit finance conundrum. It would also befit the transit union to engage more directly and regularly in sustainable transportation advocacy and to join in the coalition seeking to reform how street space is allocated.

Regulating automobility through pricing is not a progressive solu-tion in the long run, for it simply leads to a two-tiered mobility system in which the wealthy drive and everyone else cedes part of the commons in order to allow that to happen. Pricing might be a necessary short-term approach to financing transit, if it is indeed used for that, but in the long term linking the financial future of transit to pricing automobiles means that at some level driving must continue to be encouraged. Rather than configure congestion pricing zones, the long-term progressive mobility system would simply reduce the spaces of automobility across the board and turn much of the city street space over to public green space, housing, and spaces for bicycling and transit. Pricing is perhaps a key short-term bridge loan but should be considered temporary in an enduring progres-sive mobility system.

Last, for those who do embrace a lifestyle that is car-free or at least not wholly dependent on a car or who do slow down and do advocate a sustainable transportation future, a deep social commitment and so-cial responsibility means patience, persistence, and political engagement. San Francisco's progressive politics of mobility reflects the core value of progressive sustainable transportation advocates that government should actively regulate and limit automobility and the recognition that this re-quires political action. Such rethinking of automobility required the de-termination of a core group that believed it was possible for San Fran-cisco—and the world—to change for the better. But the present urgency means that a progressive politics of mobility needs to be accelerated. The city must expand transit to carry 1.4 million passengers a day, double cur-rent levels, and must find the way to underwrite this soon, as it will take at least a decade to acquire equipment and ramp up to a holistic transit-first system. If the progressive view wins out, there is a chance for this kind of transformation, and judging from the trends in San Francisco that seems possible, but this is only one place. I hope others can apply the lessons of San Francisco that this book provides and consider how to implement progressive mobility in other cities. The time is urgent, the time is now, and rediscovering the poetry of the city demands it.

NOTES

Introduction

1. For a discussion of the political influence of beat poets in San Francisco and the city's broader role as a bellwether of dissent, see the editors' preface in James Brooks, Chris Carlsson, and Nancy Peters, eds., *Reclaiming San Francisco: History, Politics, Culture* (San Francisco: City Lights Books, 1998), vi–xi, and two essays in that collection: Nancy Peters, "The Beat Generation and San Francisco's Culture of Dissent," 199–215; and Richard Walker, "An Appetite for the City," 10–20. David Talbot's *Season of the Witch: Enchantment, Terror, and Deliverance in the City of Love* (New York: Free Press, 2012), narrates San Francisco's foreshadowing of a national culture war over same sex marriage, immigrant rights, free speech, critiques of the military, and urban environmentalism.

2. Lawrence Ferlinghetti, "San Francisco Poet Laureate Inaugural Address," in *San Francisco Poems* (San Francisco: City Lights Foundation, 2001), 12.

3. John Urry, "The 'System' of Automobility," *Theory, Culture, and Society* 21.4/5 (2004): 25–39.

4. Ferlinghetti, *San Francisco Poems,* 13.

5. Carla Marinucci, "Republicans Seek Inroads in Liberal San Francisco," *San Francisco Chronicle,* March 19, 2012, A-1. By comparison, Democrats make up 56 percent of the city's electorate.

6. Nancy Grimm, Stanley H. Faeth, Nancy E. Golubiewski, Charles L. Redman, Jianguo Wu, Xuemei Bai, and John M. Briggs, "Global Change and the Ecology of Cities," *Science* 319 (2008): 756–60; Peter Newman, Timothy Beatley, and Heather Boyer, *Resilient Cities: Responding to Peak Oil and Climate Change* (Washington, D.C.: Island Press, 2009).

7. Daniel Sperling and Deborah Gordon, *Two Billion Cars: Driving Towards Sustainability* (Oxford: Oxford University Press, 2009).

8. David W. Jones, "The Road to Sustainable Motorization," in *Mass Motorization and Mass Transit: An American History and Policy Analysis* (Bloomington: Indiana University Press, 2008), chapter 10. Similarly, Sperling and Gordon, *Two Billion Cars,* 217, argue that there can be an enlightened car policy.

9. Kenneth Deffeyes outlines peak oil in *Beyond Oil: The View from Hubbert's Peak* (New York: Hill and Wang, 2005), xi–xv. Dennis Kingsley and John Urry discuss the implications of peak oil on automobility in *After the Car* (Cambridge: Polity Press, 2009), 14–19.

10. Newman, Beatley, and Boyer, *Resilient Cities,* 27.

11. Mikhail Chester and Arpad Horvath, "Environmental Assessment of Passenger Transportation Should Include Infrastructure and Supply Chains," *Environmental Research Letters* 4 (2009): 1–8.

12. USDOE, *Transportation Energy Data Book: Edition 30* (Oak Ridge, Tenn.: Center for Transportation Analysis, Engineering Science and Technology Division, Oak Ridge National Laboratory, USDOE, 2011).

13. In 2009 the United States had 828 vehicles per 1,000 people. Given its population in 2012 of 1.343 billion and that rate of car ownership, China would have over 1.112 billion vehicles. Data on vehicles are from USDOE, *Transportation Energy Data Book 30*, table 3-5; China population figure is from "US Census International Population Database," www .census.gov/population/international/data/idb/country.php.

14. For good overviews of livability, see the websites of the Congress for the New Urbanism, Smart Growth America, and Transportation for America. These are some of the principal advocates of the livability agenda.

15. Newman, Beatley, and Boyer, *Resilient Cities.*

16. Joe Cortright, *Driven to the Brink: How the Gas Price Spike Popped the Housing Bubble and Devalued the Suburbs* (Portland: CEO's for Cities, 2008); Christopher Leinberger, "The Next Slum?" *Atlantic Monthly,* March 2008, 70–75.

17. The Partnership for Sustainable Communities program was established to coordinate the USDOT, the USEPA, and the Department of Housing and Urban Development. These federal agencies have the most direct impact on land use and transportation policies in the United States. See USEPA Office of Sustainable Communities, *Partnership for Sustainable Communities: One Year Progress Report* (Washington: USEPA, Office of Sustainable Communities, 2010).

18. Good overviews of SB 375 include Natural Resources Defense Council (NRDC) and California League of Conservation Voters, *Communities Tackle Global Warming: A Guide to SB 375* (San Francisco: NRDC, 2009), and John Darakijian, "SB 375: Promise, Compromise, and the New Urban Landscape," *UCLA Journal of Environmental Law and Policy* 371 (2009): 371–404.

19. ABAG and MTC, *Bay Area Plan: Initial Vision for Public Discussion* (Oakland: ABAG/MTC, 2011), 1–3.

20. For example, in 2011 the global financial services company Mercer ranked San Francisco as the city with the highest quality of living in the United States. See "2011 Quality of Living worldwide city rankings—Mercer survey," www.mercer.com/qualityoflivingpr #city-rankings.

21. USDOT and FHWA, *Summary of Travel Trends: 2009 National Household Travel Survey* (Washington: USDOT and FHWA, 2011).

22. SFMTA, *Transportation Fact Sheet November 2010* (San Francisco: SFMTA, 2010), and USDOE, *Transportation Energy Data Book: Edition 30.*

23. SFMTA, *Transportation Fact Sheet November 2010,* and USDOT and FHWA, *Summary of Travel Trends: 2009,* table 17.

24. SFMTA, *2011 Climate Action Strategy for San Francisco's Transportation System* (San Francisco: SFMTA, 2011). The National Household Transportation Survey of 2009 did not report results for mode split for all trips. Instead, see USDOT and FHWA, *Summary of Travel Trends: 2001 National Household Travel Survey* (Washington: USDOT and FHWA, 2004), table 9.

25. SFMTA, *Transportation Fact Sheet November 2010;* USDOT and FHWA, *Summary of Travel Trends: 2009,* table 25.

26. SFMTA, *2011 Climate Action Strategy.*

27. USDOT and FHWA, *Summary of Travel Trends: 2001,* table 9; SFMTA, *2011 Climate Action Strategy.*

28. SFMTA, *2011 Climate Action Strategy.*

29. SFMTA, *2008 San Francisco State of Cycling Report* (San Francisco: SFMTA, 2008).

30. David Binder, *Binder Research Poll on Bicycling in San Francisco* (San Francisco: David Binder Research, 2009).

31. SFMTA, *State of the SFMTA: Presentation to SFTA Board of Directors Workshop, September 21, 2010* (San Francisco: SFMTA, 2010).

32. Some dense suburbs adjacent to Los Angeles, such as Maywood and West Holly-wood, have densities higher than the overall density of San Francisco but are very small jurisdictions geographically and comparable to San Francisco neighborhoods. To be sure, parts of Los Angeles are also very dense.

33. SFPD, *2009 Housing Element Update for San Francisco* (San Francisco: SFPD, 2011).

34. SFMTA, *Transportation Fact Sheet November 2010.*

1. How We Get There Matters

1. Mark Rose, *Interstate: Express Highway Politics 1939–1989* (Knoxville: University of Tennessee Press, 1990), 42–43, discusses how federal highway engineers came to see them-selves as apolitical.

2. Jason Patton describes how many standard transportation planning metrics can be value laden, "A Pedestrian World: Competing Rationalities and the Calculation of Trans-portation Change," *Environment and Planning A* 39.4 (2007): 928–44. Peter Adey, *Mobility* (New York: Routledge, 2010), 104, argues that "to move is political" and that one must look at the wider ideological assumptions about mobility.

3. George Lakoff, *Moral Politics: How Liberals and Conservatives Think* (Chicago: University of Chicago Press, 2002), 14–15.

4. This veil of consensus invokes the concept of hegemony, drawing from Antonio Gramsci, *Selections from the Prison Notebooks* (London: Lawrence and Wishart, 1971). A succinct overview of hegemony can be found in Derek Gregory et al., *The Dictionary of Human Geography* (Malden, Mass.: Wiley-Blackwell, 2009), 327.

5. David Harvey, *Social Justice and the City* (Cambridge, Mass.: Blackwell, 1973), 18.

6. Mike Davis, preface to *City of Quartz: Excavating the Future in Los Angeles,* 2d ed. (London: Verso, 2006), xx.

7. David Harvey, "The Right to the City," *New Left Review* 53 (2008): 23–41.

8. Mimi Sheller and John Urry, "The New Mobilities Paradigm," *Environment and Planning A* 38 (2006): 207–26; Adey, *Mobility,* 31.

9. Henri Lefebvre, *The Production of Space* (Malden, Mass,: Blackwell, 1991).

10. Lakoff, *Moral Politics,* 114–16. In *Moral Politics,* Lakoff uses the mainstream political term *liberal* rather than *progressive* to describe people who support public education, social programs, environmentalism, etc. (21).

11. Richard De Leon, *Left Coast City: Progressive Politics in San Francisco, 1975–1991* (Lawrence: University Press of Kansas, 1992). See esp. chapter 1, "The Capital of Progressivism."

12. Timothy Redmund, "The Ultra-liberal City?" *San Francisco Bay Guardian,* August 15, 2008, www.sfbg.com/blogs/politics/2008/08/the_ultraliberal_city.html. Despite their criticism of capitalism, most progressives in San Francisco do not self-identify as socialists.

13. There is a robust literature on the historic role of progressives in San Francisco's highly politicized land use debates during the post–Second World War era and into the 1990s, including Bruce Brugmann and Greggar Sletteland, eds., *The Ultimate Highrise: San Francisco's Mad Rush toward the Sky* (San Francisco: San Francisco Bay Guardian Books, 1971); Frederick Wirt, *Power in the City: Decision Making in San Francisco* (Berkeley: Insti-tute of Government Studies, University of California Press, 1974); Allan B. Jacobs, *Making City Planning Work* (Chicago: American Society of Planning Officials, 1978); Manuel Cas-tells, "City and Culture, the San Francisco Experience," in part 3 of *The City and the Grass-roots: A Cross-Cultural Theory of Urban Social Movements* (Berkeley: University of Califor-nia Press, 1983); John H. Mollenkopf, *The Contested City* (Princeton: Princeton University Press, 1983); De Leon, *Left Coast City;* Chester Hartman, *City for Sale: The Transformation*

of San Francisco (Berkeley: University of California Press, 2002); Chris Carlsson and Lisa Ruth Elliot, eds., *Ten Years that Shook the City: San Francisco 1968–1978* (San Francisco: City Lights Foundation, 2011).

14. Richard Walker, *The Country in the City: The Greening of the San Francisco Bay Area* (Seattle: University of Washington Press, 2007), 15. See also William Issel, "'Land Values, Human Values, and the Preservation of the City's Treasured Appearance': Environmentalism, Politics, and the San Francisco Freeway Revolt," *Pacific Historical Review* 68.4 (1998): 611–46.

15. Michael T. Klare provides an excellent overview of oil as a source of conflict and violence in *Blood and Oil: The Dangers and Consequences of America's Growing Petroleum Dependency* (New York: Henry Holt, 2004). See a more recent overview by Klare in "The Energy Wars Heat Up," *The Nation*, May 10, 2012, www.thenation.com.

16. De Leon, *Left Coast City*, 18.

17. For an overview of the transit justice discourse, see POWER's website, www.peopleorganized.org.

18. Richard Walker, "Another Round of Globalization in San Francisco," *Urban Geography* 17.1 (1996): 60–94; Walker also discusses neoliberalism in the Bay Area, specifically how it set back environmental policies in the 1980s, in *The Country in the City*, 252.

19. For a general discussion of exchange value and the production of urban space, see John Logan and Harvey Molotch, "Place as Commodities," in *Urban Fortunes: The Political Economy of Place* (Berkeley: University of California Press, 1987); for a discussion of how business elites navigate the politics of mobility in another city, Atlanta, see Jason Henderson, "The Politics of Mobility and Business Elites in Atlanta, Georgia," *Urban Geography* 25.3 (2004): 193–216.

20. David Harvey, "The Urban Process under Capitalism: A Framework for Analysis," in *Readings in Urban Analysis*, ed. Robert Lake (New Brunswick: Center for Urban Policy Research, Rutgers University, 1983), 197–227.

21. Stephen Graham and Simon Marvin, *Splintering Urbanism: Networked Infrastructures, Technological Mobilities, and the Urban Condition* (New York: Routledge, 2001), 192.

22. David Harvey, "The Urbanization of Capital," in *The Urban Experience* (Baltimore: Johns Hopkins University Press, 1989), 21, 39–40.

23. Reid Ewing, Keith Bartholomew, Steve Winkelman, and Jerry Waters, *Growing Cooler: The Evidence on Urban Development and Climate Change* (Washington: Urban Land Institute, 2008).

24. Good overviews of SB 375 include Natural Resources Defense Council (NRDC) and California League of Conservation Voters (CLCV), *Communities Tackle Global Warming: A Guide to SB 375* (San Francisco: NRDC, 2009) and John Darakijian, "SB 375: Promise, Compromise, and the New Urban Landscape," *UCLA Journal of Environmental Law and Policy* 371 (2009): 371–404.

25. NRDC and CLCV, *Communities Tackle Global Warming*, 11.

26. Marvin, *Splintering Urbanism*, 143.

27. Harvey, *The Urban Experience*, 122. Harvey is invoking Crawford McPherson's *The Political Theory of Possessive Individualism* (Oxford: Clarendon Press, 1962).

28. Don Mitchell, "The SUV Model of Citizenship: Floating Bubbles, Buffer Zones, and the Rise of the "Purely Atomic" Individual," *Political Geography* 24.1 (2004): 77–100.

29. Adey, *Mobility*, 85.

30. The writings of Peter Gordon and Harry Richardson, based at the University of Southern California, inform the cornucopian strand of neoliberal mobility. See Peter Gordon and Harry Richardson, *Why Sprawl Is Good* (Portland: Cascade Policy Institute, 1997), and Peter Gordon and Harry Richardson, "Are Compact Cities a Desirable Planning Goal?" *Journal of the American Planning Association* 63.1 (1997): 95–106. Gordon and Richardson also have linkages to neoliberal think tanks such as the Reason Foundation.

31. Harvey, "Right to the City," 31–32.

32. Harvey, "Right to the City," 33.

33. Harvey, "Right to the City," 33–35.

34. Redmund, "The Ultra-liberal City?"

35. SPUR, "Critical Cooling: San Francisco Can Fight Global Warming through Smart Changes to Local Policy. What Can We Do to Lead the Way?" *SPUR Urbanist,* May 2009, 6–19.

36. Gabriel Metcalf, "50 Years of SPUR, 100 Years of Building a Better City: The Ironies of History," *SPUR Urbanist,* August 2009, 32–34.

37. Lakoff, *Moral Politics,* 13.

38. The columnist E. J. Dionne, in many writings on conservative politics in the United States, shows how conservatives look to government for key ambitions and goals. See, for example, "Conservatism Recast," *Washington Post,* January 27, 2002. David Frum, a former Republican Party operative, also argues that conservatives look to government to achieve many goals. See "Post–Tea Party Nation" *New York Times Magazine,* November 14, 2010.

39. The historian Shelton Reed, in a presentation at the University of Georgia in 2001 entitled *What's Southern about the South? . . . These Days,* discusses the power of churches and community organizations in the South. While San Francisco exhibits less of this conservative strain, the role in conservative evangelical thought in shaping U.S. transport policy does have consequences in San Francisco in that it frames the parameters of transit funding and road funding.

40. For discussion of how spatial secession impacts mobility in the peer city of Atlanta, see Jason Henderson, "Secessionist Automobility: Racism, Anti-urbanism, and the Spatial Politics of Automobility in Atlanta, Georgia," *International Journal of Urban and Regional Research* 30.2 (2006): 293–307.

41. Vukan R. Vuchic, *Transportation for Livable Cities* (New Brunswick: Center for Urban Policy Research, Rutgers University, 1999), 3.

42. Robert Bruegmann, *Sprawl: A Compact History* (Chicago: University of Chicago Press, 2005), 116; Brian Ladd, *Autophobia: Love and Hate in the Automotive Age* (Chicago: University of Chicago Press, 2008), 148.

43. See esp. James Dunn, "The Automobile and Its Enemies: The Making of a Policy Vanguard," in *Driving Forces: The Automobile, Its Enemies, and the Politics of Mobility* (Washington: Brookings Institution, 1998).

44. For example, see Jane Shaw and Ronald Utt, *A Guide to Smart Growth: Shattering Myths, Providing Solutions* (Washington: Heritage Foundation and the Political Economy Research Center, 2000). More recently the Heritage Foundation fanned Tea Party sentiments against livability in Wendall Cox, Ronald Utt, and Brett Schaefer, "Agenda 21 Should Not Divert Attention from Homegrown Anti-Growth Policies," December 2011, www.heritage.org/research/reports. For a collection of essays against livability, the Heritage Foundation maintains a page on smart growth at www.heritage.org/issues/housing /smart-growth.

45. Shaw and Utt, "Introduction," *A Guide to Smart Growth,* ix.

46. Essentialism is a concept used in cultural geography, sociology, anthropology, and ethnic studies that sees its broadest usage in the study of racism, gender inequality, and identity politics. This section on essentialism draws from Andrew Sayer, "Essentialism, Social Constructionism, and Beyond," *Sociological Review* 45.3 (1997): 453–87.

47. David Banister, John Pucher, and M. Lee Gosselin, "Making Sustainable Transport Politically and Publicly Acceptable: Lessons from the EU, USA, and Canada," in *Institutions and Sustainable Transport: Regulatory Reform in Advanced Economies,* ed. Peit Rietveld and Roger Stough (Cheltenham: Edward Elgar, 2007), 7.

48. Daniel Sperling and Deborah Gordon, *Two Billion Cars: Driving Towards Sustainability* (Oxford: Oxford University Press, 2009), 38.

49. Sperling and Gordon, *Two Billion Cars,* 240.

50. David W. Jones, "The Road to Sustainable Motorization," in *Mass Motorization and Mass Transit: An American History and Policy Analysis* (Bloomington: Indiana University Press, 2008), 126.

51. In *The City and the Grassroots,* 101, Manuel Castells hinted that the progressive–conservative alignment in San Francisco was also a space of coexisting cultures based in neighborhoods that were distinctive to one another.

52. Coalition for San Francisco Neighborhoods, "Where Am I Going to Park Downtown?" December 2005.

53. Lakoff, *Moral Politics,* 15.

54. David Goldfield, *Region, Race, and Cities: Interpreting the Urban South* (Baton Rouge: Louisiana State University Press, 1997).

55. San Francisco Board of Supervisors, Government Audit and Oversight Committee, "Hearing on the Relationship between Parking, Neighborhood Businesses, and Families, Part 1," June 11, 2007.

56. SFPD, *The Upper Market Community Workshop Series and Design Plan,* San Francisco: SFPD, July 23, 2007.

57. David Lee, "Storming the Gates: San Francisco's Emerging Chinese American Electorate" (M.A. thesis, San Francisco State University, 2003). Thirty-five percent of all voters in San Francisco are property owners; around 50 percent of Chinese American voters are property owners.

2. San Francisco's Mobility Stalemate

1. "Traffic volumes on the State Highway System, Route 1," Caltrans, 2009, www.dot. ca.gov/hq; Additional background data on 19th Avenue come from SFCTA, *19th Avenue/ Park Presidio Draft Final Report* (San Francisco: SFCTA, 2008), 1–3.

2. An analysis by the SFPD notes that many of the intersections on 19th Avenue are failing by conventional traffic engineering standards. See SFPD, "Roadway Network and Intersection Existing Conditions," *19th Avenue Corridor Study* (San Francisco: SFPD, 2010), III.13–III.15.

3. Katherine M. Johnson, "Captain Blake versus the Highwaymen: Or, How San Francisco Won the Freeway Revolt," *Journal of Planning History* 8.1 (2009): 56–83.

4. For good overviews of the postwar consensus on automobility in the United States, see Owen O. Gutfreund, *20th-Century Sprawl: Highways and the Reshaping of the American Landscape* (New York: Oxford University Press, 2004); Kenneth J. Jackson, *Crabgrass Frontier: The Suburbanization of the United States* (New York: Oxford University Press, 1985); and Mark H. Rose, *Interstate: Express Highway Politics 1939–1989* (Knoxville: University of Tennessee Press, 1990).

5. In addition to Johnson's, "Captain Blake," there are many good overviews of San Francisco's postwar freeway planning and revolts, including William Issel, "'Land Values, Human Values, and the Preservation of the City's Treasured Appearance': Environmentalism, Politics, and the San Francisco Freeway Revolt," *Pacific Historical Review* 68.4 (1998): 611–46; David W. Jones, *California's Freeway Era in Historical Perspective* (Berkeley: Institute of Transportation Studies, University of California, Berkeley, 1990); Kevin Starr, *Golden Dreams: California in an Age of Abundance, 1950–1963* (Oxford: Oxford University Press, 2009); Louis Nelson Dyble, *Paying the Toll: Local Power, Regional Politics, and the Golden Gate Bridge* (Philadelphia: University of Pennsylvania Press, 2009); Clifford Ellis, "Visions of Urban Freeways, 1930–1970" (Ph.D. diss., University of California, Berkeley, 1990); Herbert Goodwin, "California's Growing Freeway System" (Ph.D. diss., University of California, Los Angeles, 1969); Lawrence Jacobson, "The Effect of Political Pressure upon Freeway Route Decisions in San Francisco" (M.A. thesis, San Francisco State Col-

lege, 1972); William Lathrop, "San Francisco Freeway Revolt," *Transportation Engineering Journal* (February 1971): 133–44; and Seymour Adler, "The Political Economy of Transit in the San Francisco Bay Area, 1945–1963" (Ph.D. diss., University of California, Berkeley).

6. See Adler, "The Political Economy of Transit," 8, for the links to early twentieth-century Progressivism. Neil Smith, *The Endgame of Globalization* (New York: Routledge, 2005), 38, provides a more critical view of American Progressives' historical evolution, describing them as a historical "left-leaning immune system to socialism." As they evolved, Progressives absorbed socialist ideas yet dampened them as well; many Progressives were, in fact, antisocialist, as epitomized by President Woodrow Wilson, who was vehemently antisocialist but also believed government should regulate corporate monopolies.

7. Jones, *California's Freeway Era,* 290.

8. John H. Mollenkopf, *The Contested City* (Princeton: Princeton University Press, 1983), 120, quoting John Burby, *The Great American Motion Sickness; or, Why You Can't Get There from Here* (Boston: Little, Brown, 1971).

9. Jacobson, "Freeway Route Decisions in San Francisco," 58.

10. For Boston's freeway revolt, see Alan Lupo, Frank Colcord, and Edmund Fowler, *Rites of Way: The Politics of Transportation in Boston and the American City* (Boston: Little, Brown, 1971); on New York City, see Robert Caro, *The Power Broker: Robert Moses and the Fall of New York* (New York: Vintage Books, 1975); and Anthony Flint, *Wrestling with Moses: How Jane Jacobs took on New York's Master Builder and Transformed the American City* (New York: Random House, 2009); for Washington, D.C., see Zachary M. Schrag, *The Great Society Subway: A History of the Washington Metro* (Baltimore: Johns Hopkins University Press, 2006), 40–45.

11. Issel, "Land Values."

12. Jacobson, "Freeway Route Decisions in San Francisco," 160.

13. There is confusion about which of the proposed freeways was actually the Western Freeway. For example, in 1955 the Western Freeway was mapped as a short link connecting the Juniper Serra to the Panhandle and Presidio Freeways. In other iterations, the Western Freeway was mapped more extensively, as displayed in Jacobson, "Freeway Route Decisions in San Francisco," 48, 80, and discussed by Adler, "The Political Economy of Transit," 308. For the sake of simplicity, I consider the Western Freeway as the north–south freeway that parallels 19th and 7th Avenues, as discussed by Adler and Jacobson as well as by Issel, "Land Values."

14. Johnson, "Captain Blake." Detailed discussions of the west-side freeway revolt include Issel, "Land Values," Jacobson, "Freeway Route Decisions in San Francisco," and Lathrop, "San Francisco Freeway Revolt."

15. Jacobson, "Freeway Route Decisions in San Francisco," 78.

16. Richard DeLeon, *Left Coast City: Progressive Politics in San Francisco, 1975-1991* (Lawrence: University Press of Kansas, 1992), 18; Chester Hartman, *City for Sale: The Transformation of San Francisco* (Berkeley: University of California Press, 2002), 235.

17. Ellis, "Visions of Urban Freeways"; Goodwin, "California's Growing Freeway System"; Jacobson, "Freeway Route Decisions in San Francisco"; and Lathrop, "San Francisco Freeway Revolt."

18. Issel, "Land Values," 617.

19. Adler, "The Political Economy of Transit," 311–13.

20. Issel, "Land Values," 627; Goodwin, "California's Growing Freeway System," 446. The *Chronicle* led parallel objections to the infamous double-deck Embarcadero Freeway, built along San Francisco's deindustrializing waterfront, adjacent to the downtown financial district. Kevin Starr, *Golden Dreams,* called it the initial "flashpoint" that sparked rebellion against the consensus for freeways because it was built astride the architecturally significant Ferry Building and perturbed developers of the Golden Gateway Center, a lucrative redevelopment with views of the bay. Residents of San Francisco lamented the

structure when it was built, and the *San Francisco Chronicle* continued a sustained media attack on freeways and on highway engineers, keeping the issue prominent. The Embarcadero debate emboldened opposition to freeways in the city's neighborhoods.

21. See Lathrop, "San Francisco Freeway Revolt," and Adler, "The Political Economy of Transit," 311–13.

22. Richard De Luca, *"We the People!" Bay Area Activism in the 1960s: Three Case Studies* (San Bernardino: Borgo Press, 1994), 47–92; see also Goodwin, "California's Growing Freeway System," 461–64.

23. Adler, "The Political Economy of Transit," 316.

24. This sentiment was described by Sue Bierman, an active leader in the freeway revolts during the 1960s, who was interviewed by Wayne Schotten, July 11, 2006.

25. Issel, "Land Values."

26. Goodwin, "California's Growing Freeway System," 526–27.

27. Ibid., 481.

28. Louis N. Dyble, "Revolt against Sprawl: Transportation and the Origins of the Marin County Growth-Control Regime," *Journal of Urban History* 34.1 (2007), 38–66; Richard Walker, *The Country in the City: The Greening of the San Francisco Bay Area* (Seattle: University of Washington Press, 2007), 104.

29. Richard Baumbach and William Borah, *The Second Battle of New Orleans: A History of the Vieux Carré Riverfront Expressway Controversy* (Tuscaloosa: University of Alabama Press, 1981), 80.

30. Raymond A. Mohl, "Stop the Road: Freeway Revolts in American Cities," *Journal of Urban History* 30.5 (2004): 674–706.

31. Schrag, *The Great Society Subway*, 119.

32. Anthony Perles, *The People's Railway: The History of the Municipal Railway of San Francisco* (Glendale: Interurban Press, 1981), 199; Stephen Zwerling, *Mass Transit and the Politics of Technology: A Study of BART and the San Francisco Bay Area* (New York: Praeger, 1974), 89.

33. BART is a separate transit agency from Muni and provides regional commuter rail service, with stations in suburban areas miles apart from one another. In the city BART has a cluster of stations on Market Street situated to provide maximum accessibility to some of the highest value land in the Bay Area—land owned by the business elite of 1950s and 1960s.

34. Peter Hall, *Great Planning Disasters* (Berkeley: University of California Press, 1982), 110–17.

35. Adler, "The Political Economy of Transit," 5.

36. United States Congress, Office of Technology Assessment, *The Assessment of Community Planning for Mass Transit: Volume 8 – San Francisco Case Study* (Washington, D.C.: Office of Technology Assessment, 1976), 52.

37. Adler, "The Political Economy of Transit," 313–14, discusses how BART was conceptualized as a viable substitute to freeways by west siders, but he did not examine the debate beyond 1963.

38. To be sure, a simple majority of voters did endorse the concept of subways, suggesting public support for rapid transit, but funding for the rapid transit proposal had to garner two-thirds support under state law.

39. Perles, *The People's Railway*, 216–17.

40. Bruce Brugmann and Greggar Sletteland, *The Ultimate Highrise: San Francisco's Mad Rush toward the Sky* (San Francisco: San Francisco Bay Guardian Books, 1971).

41. DeLeon, *Left Coast City*, 41.

42. Jacobson, "Freeway Route Decisions in San Francisco," 6–7.

43. San Francisco's population declined from a peak of 776,000 in 1950 to 715,000 in

1970, and to a low of 678,000 in 1980. See SFPD, *2009 Housing Element Update for San Francisco* (San Francisco: SFPD, 2011), I-4.

44. Automobile density is calculated by dividing automobile registrations by 47.355 square miles (area of San Francisco). For automobile registrations, see MTC, *Auto Ownership in the San Francisco Bay Area 1930–2020* (Oakland: MTC, 1999), table 11.

45. SFPD, *Transportation: Conditions, Problems, and Issues* (San Francisco: San Francisco Planning Department, 1971), 213.

46. MTC, *Auto Ownership in the San Francisco Bay Area*, table 13.

47. Dan Solomon provides a lengthy discussion of the confluence of these grids in "The Twelfth Map," in *Global City Blues* (Washington, D.C.: Island Press, 2003), 131–44.

48. Mary Brown, "Shifting Landscapes of Mobility: The Spatial Reconfiguration of the Mission District to Accommodate Automobility" (M.A. thesis, San Francisco State University). Brown is referring to an oral history by Max Kirkberg and newspaper accounts. The protests were about the potential loss of housing rather than a critique of automobility.

49. SPUR, *Building a New Muni* (San Francisco: SPUR, 1973), 2–3.

50. SFMTA, *Transit Effectiveness Project, Briefing Book* (San Francisco: SFMTA, 2006), 6–8.

51. Donald Appleyard, *Livable Streets* (Berkeley: University of California Press); Donald Appleyard and Mark Lintell, "The Environmental Quality of City Streets: The Residents' Viewpoint," *Journal of the American Planning Association* 38.2 (1972): 84–101; and Donald Appleyard, "The Environmental Quality of City Streets: The Residents' Viewpoint," in *Transport Sociology: Social Aspects of Transport Planning*, ed. Enne de Boer (Oxford: Pergamon, 1976), 51–70.

52. Appleyard, *Livable Streets*, 15–19.

53. Ibid., 27.

54. Ibid., 97.

55. Ibid., 15–19, 150.

3. The Second Freeway Revolt

1. Removal of the Embarcadero Freeway was considered in 1963, and in the 1980s the city studied demolition. In 1986 a ballot initiative over removal failed to get citywide voter approval. See Carl Nolte and Reginald Smith, "S.F. Votes to Save the Freeway," *San Francisco Chronicle,* June 4, 1986.

2. American Society of Engineers, "2009 Report Card for America's Infrastructure," www.infrastructurereportcard.org/report-cards (see esp. the sections on bridges, 74–81, and roads, 98–105).

3. Congress for the New Urbanism, *2012 Freeways without Futures* (Chicago: Congress for the New Urbanism, 2012).

4. John H. Mollenkopf, *The Contested City* (Princeton: Princeton University Press, 1983), 17, referring to all of the Western Addition, of which Hayes Valley is a part.

5. Volumes calculated from "Map of Twenty-Four-Hour Traffic Flows on Principal Streets and Highways, 1966–1968," in SFPD, *Transportation: Conditions, Problems, and Issues* (San Francisco: SFPD, 1971), 74.

6. Kandace Bender, "Loyalty Up for Grabs in Mayoral Free-for-All," *San Francisco Examiner,* April 28, 1995; Warren Hinckle, "The Last Freeway Battle," *The Independent,* April 1, 2003; Zusha Elinson, "In the Bay Area, Trains Are Powered by Myths," *New York Times Bay Area Edition,* July 2, 2011, www.baycitizen.org/transportation. There is also much political intrigue about the promise of a subway to Chinatown in exchange for the Embarcadero removal(see chapter 7).

7. FHWA and Caltrans, *San Francisco Central Freeway Replacement Project: Environmental Assessment* (Washington: FHWA, 1997), 17. This did not include traffic on Franklin, Gough, or Van Ness, which remained substantially high.

8. Ibid.

9. For the narrative of the Agnos defeat, see Richard DeLeon, "Postscript, the 1991 Mayoral Election and Beyond," *Left Coast City: Progressive Politics in San Francisco, 1975–1991* (Lawrence: University Press of Kansas, 1992).

10. Martin Danyluk and David Ley discuss the ideological differences found in separate waves of gentrification, "Modalities of the New Middle Class: Ideology and Behavior in the Journey to Work from Gentrified Neighborhoods in Canada," *Urban Studies* 44.11 (2007): 2195–2210.

11. Patricia Walkup, personal interview, December 2005. Walkup led the public safety organizing in Hayes Valley, led campaigns to remove the Central Freeway, and helped found the Hayes Valley Neighborhood Association (HVNA).

12. Elizabeth Crane, "Neighbors Organize—Everyone Benefits," *Castro Star,* August 1996.

13. Jonathan Marshall, "Traffic Supplants Crime atop Bay Poll, Packed Freeways Are No. 1 Concern," *San Francisco Chronicle,* January 23, 1997.

14. A good overview of the sprawl debate of the 1990s can be found in Reid Ewing, "Is Los Angeles–Style Sprawl Desirable?" *Journal of the American Planning Association* 63.1 (1997): 107–26, and, in the same issue, a counterpoint argument by Peter Gordon and Harry Richardson, "Are Compact Cities a Desirable Planning Goal?" *Journal of the American Planning Association* 63.1 (1997). For examinations of the sprawl debate in Atlanta, see Jason Henderson, "The Politics of Mobility and Business Elites in Atlanta, Georgia," *Urban Geography* 25.3 (2004): 193–216, and for Portland, see Carl Abbott, "The Portland Region: Where City and Suburbs Talk to Each Other—and Often Agree," *Housing Policy Debate* 8.1 (1997): 11–51.

15. Martin Wachs, "The Political Context of Transportation Policy," in *The Geography of Urban Transportation,* 2d ed., ed. Susan Hanson (New York: Guilford Press, 1995), 269–86.

16. Jim Klein and Martha Olsen, *Taken for a Ride,* New Day Films, 1996, www.newday.com/films/Taken_for_a_Ride.html.

17. Walkup, personal interview.

18. Mitch Reid, "Devil's Slide Dilemma: Save Our Coast or Pave Our Coast," *San Francisco Chronicle,* February 9, 1996. Patricia Walkup had an extensive file on the Devil's Slide controversy, including ballot language and legal papers from environmentalists who sued Caltrans.

19. The early evolution of Critical Mass is described in a volume edited by Chris Carlsson, *Critical Mass: Bicycling's Defiant Celebration* (Oakland: AK Press, 2002); see also Aaron Golub and Jason Henderson, "The Greening of Mobility in San Francisco," in *Sustainability in American Cities: Creating the Green Metropolis,* ed. Matthew Slavin (Washington, D.C.: Island Press, 2011), 113–32.

20. Carolyn Diamond, Ann Lee Harris, and Roger Boas, "The Best Central Freeway Plan," *San Francisco Chronicle,* July 18, 1996.

21. David Lee, "Storming the Gates: San Francisco's Emerging Chinese American Electorate" (M.A. thesis, San Francisco State University, 2003), 72. Lee discussed how, in 2000, Asians, of which Chinese Americans are the largest group, made up 55 percent of voters in the Sunset and 49 percent of voters in the Richmond.

22. Ibid.

23. The Six Companies were an anticommunist affiliate of the Kuomintang and despised leftist politics.

24. John King, "Protests Growing over Central Freeway Closure," *San Francisco Chronicle,* January 24, 1997.

25. Subcommittee of the Peer Review and Technical Advisory Panel for the Seismic Evaluation and Strengthening of the San Francisco Double Deck Freeway Viaducts, "Letter to Mr. James W. Van Loben Sels, Director, Caltrans: Seismic Retrofit of the Central Freeway Viaduct in San Francisco," December 6, 1995. In early 1996 there was extensive front-page media coverage of the Caltrans warnings; for example, see Greg Lucas and Catherine Bowman, "Central Freeway Plan Gets Green Light: Brown OKs Removal of Quake-vulnerable Deck," *San Francisco Chronicle,* February 7, 1996, and Gerald D. Adams and George Raine, "S.F. Sets Course for New Midtown Gridlock," *San Francisco Examiner,* February 8, 1996.

26. Greg Lucas and William Carlsen, "S.F. Freeway to Close for Six Months, Traffic Nightmare Expected during Retrofit," *San Francisco Chronicle,* February 24, 1996.

27. James W. van Loben Sels, Director, Caltrans, "Letter to Mayor Willie Brown Regarding Seismic Retrofit of Central Freeway," February 13, 1996.

28. Edward Epstein, "Freeway Traffic Dips in S.F., Oakland: Caltrans Credits Central Freeway Gridlock Warnings," *San Francisco Chronicle,* September 4, 1996.

29. Caltrans, *Central Freeway Closure: Initial Traffic Impacts—Final Report* (Oakland: Office of Highway Operations, Caltrans District 4, 1996), 1–7.

30. John King, "Brown Pledges to Unclog Central Freeway Detour Traffic," *San Francisco Chronicle,* March 12, 1997.

31. *San Francisco Chronicle,* Editorial, "Re-open the Central Freeway," March 13, 1997. On Haight Street merchants, see Rachel Gordon, "City Says "No Thanks' to Fell Street Off-Ramp," *San Francisco Examiner,* March 14, 1997.

32. Rescue Muni, "Letter to the Editor, Rescue Muni Review," *San Francisco Chronicle,* March 27, 1997.

33. FHWA and Caltrans, *San Francisco Central Freeway Replacement Project;* see esp. "Traffic and Circulation, 44–55.

34. Ibid., 62.

35. Alex Barnum, "All Options for Central Freeway Draw Wrath in S.F. as 300 Attend Raucous Session Sponsored by Caltrans," *San Francisco Chronicle,* April 24, 1997.

36. The State of California requires every county with a population of over two hundred thousand to have a "congestion management agency." In San Francisco that agency is the SFCTA. Created in 1989 by referendum, the SFCTA also oversees the management of the city's transportation sales tax and coordinates funding to the various local transportation programs, such as Muni. It is the fiduciary agent for transportation in the city, separate from SFMTA for political reasons beyond the scope of this discussion. The Board of Supervisors is the committee that governs the SFCTA, and any member of the board can ask the SFCTA to conduct transportation studies.

37. SFCTA, *Strategic Analysis Report 97-1: Central Freeway Alternatives* (San Francisco: SFCTA, 1997), 1–9.

38. SFPD, *Civic Center Study* (San Francisco, SFPD, 1994): 98 and 101.

39. Ibid., 67.

40. Ibid., 101.

41. Van Loben Sels, "Letter to Mayor Willie Brown."

42. Larry D. Hatfield, Gerald Adams, Gregory Lewis, "Deal Near on Fixing Central Freeway," *San Francisco Examiner,* February 7, 1996.

43. Ephraim Hirsch, "Neighbors Want the Central Freeway to Become a Bad Memory," *San Francisco Examiner,* March 13, 1996. Hirsch chaired the CFCTF.

44. John King and Greg Lucas, "Brown Wants Freeway Ramps Demolished, Proposal Could Snarl S.F. Traffic for Years," *San Francisco Chronicle,* March 26, 1996.

45. Gerald Adams, "Central Freeway Fix, Replacement Plan Draws Critics," *San Francisco Examiner,* June 5, 1996.

46. *San Francisco Chronicle,* "Groups Seeks to Halt Demolition of Freeway," May 16, 1996; Carolyn Diamond, Ann Lee Harris, Roger Boas, "The Best Central Freeway Plan," *San Francisco Chronicle,* July 18.

47. The city hired Jacobs and MacDonald after the CFCTF explicitly asked that the duo get involved.

48. San Francisco Department of Elections, "Prop H: Central Freeway," *City and County of San Francisco Voter Information Pamphlet and Sample Ballot, Consolidated Municipal Election,* November 4, 1997 (San Francisco: Department of Elections), 82–96.

49. Ibid., "Proponents' Arguments and Paid Arguments in Favor of Proposition H," 86.

50. *San Francisco Chronicle,* Editorial, Prop. H: A Freeway Folly," October 29, 1997.

51. Willie Brown Jr. and Sue Bierman, "Why Central Freeway Ballot Proposal Is a Dead End," *San Francisco Chronicle,* November 3, 1997.

52. The San Francisco Department of Elections presents historic voter turnout data at www.sfgov2.org/index.aspx?page=1677.

53. Edward Epstein and Ramon G. McLeod, "New S.F. Voter Bloc Shows Clout: Chinese Americans Were Key to Freeway Retrofit Ballot Victory," *San Francisco Chronicle,* November 6, 1997; Chuck Finnie, "Central Freeway Win a West Side Story," *San Francisco Examiner* November 6, 1997.

54. Edward Epstein, "Central Freeway Work Should Start, Finish Early: Funding for Project Nearly All in Place," February 20, 1998. The same state senator also submitted paid arguments in favor of Prop H.

55. San Francisco Department of Elections, *Proposition E: Central Freeway, City and County of San Francisco Voter Information Pamphlet and Sample Ballot, Consolidated Municipal Election, November 3, 1998* (San Francisco: Department of Elections), 87.

56. Caltrans, *Central Freeway Fact Sheet* (Oakland: Caltrans District 4, Office of Highway Operations), 1.

57. Chuck Finnie, "High Road or Low Road: Prop E Will Determine if Central Freeway Is to be Rebuilt or Replaced," *San Francisco Examiner,* October 27, 1998.

58. David Binder, "SF Propositions Results, Presentation to SPUR, Nov 4, 1998."

59. SFCTA, *Strategic Analysis Report: Implications of Relocating the Central Freeway Touchdown Ramps* (San Francisco: SFCTA), 1.

60. Rachel Gordon, "One More Vote for Central Freeway?" *San Francisco Examiner,* June 18, 1999.

61. San Francisco Department of Elections, *Proposition J: Central Freeway Replacement, City and County of San Francisco Voter Information Pamphlet and Sample Ballot, Consolidated Municipal Election, November 2, 1999* (San Francisco: Department of Elections), 175.

62. Chester Hartman, *City for Sale: The Transformation of San Francisco* (Berkeley: University of California Press, 2002), 268.

63. The geography of the MOBNP area expands well beyond this intersection and was delineated by planners because it reflected the potential for transit-oriented infill around Muni Metro stations as well as infill opportunities on former land parcels that were once part of the freeway.

64. Some transportation scholars posit that gentrification and increased land values are indicators of the benefits of freeway removal. For example, see Robert Cervero, "Transport Infrastructure and Global Competitiveness: Balancing Mobility and Livability," *Annals of the American Academy of Political and Social Science* 626.1 (2009): 210–25. Cervero discusses the place-making aspects of the removal of the Embarcadero and the Central Freeway, invoking Richard Florida's thesis of the creative class and suggesting that the gentrification of Hayes Valley was a good outcome of freeway replacement.

65. In 2012 San Francisco had the most expensive housing in the nation, owing largely to a new tech boom. See Nancy Keates and Geoffrey Fowler, "The Hot Spot for the Rising Tech Generation," *Wall Street Journal,* March 16, 2012.

4. Between Walkability and Freeways

1. SFPD, *2010 San Francisco Housing Inventory* (San Francisco: SFPD, 2011), 5.

2. HVNA formally registered as a tax-exempt nonprofit organization in 2000; before that the organization existed informally, mostly centered on the freeway and public safety issues.

3. The Hayes development was based on financing from the dot-com boom; the project stalled after the dot-com crash in 2000 but was resuscitated in 2005 and completed in 2009.

4. Olle Hagman, "Morning Queues and Parking Problems: On the Broken Promises of the Automobile," *Mobilities* 1.1 (2006): 63–74.

5. Good overviews of the space consumed by parking include Jonathan Barnett, *Redesigning Cities: Principles, Practice, Implementation* (Chicago: American Planning Association, 2003), 50–52; Todd Littman, *Parking Requirement Impacts on Housing Affordability* (Victoria, B.C.: Victoria Transportation Policy Institute, 2004), 10; John Jakle and Keith Sculle, *Lots of Parking: Land Use in a Car Culture* (Charlottesville: University of Virginia Press, 2004), 1–9; Donald Shoup, *The High Cost of Free Parking* (Chicago: American Planning Association, 2005), 12.

6. Shoup, *The High Cost of Free Parking*, 12, makes a similar estimate based on automobile ownership rates in 2000. This estimate includes U.S. Census estimate of world population (www.census.gov/main/www/popclock.html) and USDOE, *Transportation Energy Data Book 30*, table 3-5, for the estimate of vehicle ownership in the United States in 2009 and assumes 335 square feet per off-street parking space.

7. USEPA, *Parking Spaces/Community Places: Finding the Balance through Smart Growth Solutions* (Washington: USEPA, 2006), 11.

8. Shoup, *High Cost of Free Parking*, 93–94, 152.

9. SFPD, "Feasibility of Citywide 1:1 Parking: Presentation to the San Francisco Board of Supervisors, Government, Audit and Oversight Committee," July 23, 2007.

10. SFPD, *Getting It Right: Rethinking San Francisco's Parking Requirements* (San Francisco: SFPD, 2002), 5.

11. Ibid., 4–5. See also Shoup, *High Cost of Free Parking*, 152.

12. The *San Francisco Chronicle* reported in 2007 that garage inserts cost an average of $100,000 but increased a home's value by $180,000. See Lili Weigert, "Garages Add Value, Stress for S.F. Homeowners," *San Francisco Chronicle*, September 9. See also SFPD, *Getting It Right*, 4; SFPD, *Feasibility of Citywide 1:1 Parking*; Shoup, *High Cost of Free Parking*, 152–53, discusses the impact parking has on affordable housing.

13. Wenyu Jia and Martin Wachs, "Parking and Affordable Housing," *Access* 13 (1998): 22–25.

14. San Francisco does exempt senior housing, special needs housing, and single-occupant residential hotels from the 1:1 requirement.

15. SFMTA, *Transportation Fact Sheet November 2010*, 8. This figure includes both on-street and off-street parking. There is no full accounting of the space of parking in San Francisco.

16. SFPD, *2009 Housing Element*, 41.

17. ABAG and MTC, *Bay Area Plan: Initial Vision for Public Discussion* (Oakland: ABAG/MTC, 2011), 61–63.

18. Duany-Plater-Zyberk and Company, *Smartcode V8* (Miami: DPZ, 2006), 41.

19. Shoup, *High Cost of Free Parking*, 135.

20. Table 11 in DPZ, *Smartcode V8*, 25.

21. SFPD, *Market and Octavia: An Area of the General Plan of San Francisco* (San Francisco: SFPD, 2008), 2.

22. Ibid., 63–68.

23. When the draft plan was officially adopted in 2008, the area had 10,500 existing housing units and 23,000 people.

24. In many typical suburban jurisdictions throughout the Bay Area and across the United States, too, the minimum parking requirements are even higher than this 1:1 ratio. For example, in most U.S. cities and suburbs residential off-street requirements mandate more than one parking space per housing unit (often two or three), and many zoning codes delineate the parking requirements based on the number of bedrooms.

25. See "Zoning District Table" in ibid., 8.

26. The most important progressive organization promoting parking reform was and still is Livable City. Established in 2002 by the executive director of the SFBC, Livable City emphatically lobbies for reduced parking as one of its central platforms. See www.livablecity .org/campaigns/parking.html.

27. World Environment Day refers to the culminating event, which occurs annually on June 5, but in most instances the hosts incorporate a week of activities celebrating WED. See www.unep.org/wed/about.

28. One exception was a panel called "Cities on the Move: Environmental Urban/Public Transportation Strategies from around the Globe," which was hosted by the SFBC but was located at the San Francisco Public Library.

far from the main event.

29. The development is known locally as 1844 Market Street and is in a prominent location adjacent to the Lesbian, Gay, Bi-Sexual and Transgender Center.

30. As in the case of the aforementioned The Hayes, construction of the Market Street project was delayed in part because of the global financial decline. In 2012 a new developer took interest, and construction began.

31. This subject was discussed on January 12, 2006, at a meeting between HVNA and the supervisor who had taken on the task of mediating between the developer and HVNA.

32. The project was appealed and litigated, unsuccessfully, by historic preservationists, who argued that the entire complex of buildings was historically significant and that the city should be saving the buildings and promoting adaptive reuse of them. Like the other large infill projects discussed here, 55 Laguna went into limbo when the developer went bankrupt, and not until 2011 did a new developer seek to resuscitate the project.

33. Jia and Wachs, "Parking and Affordable Housing," 22–25.

34. Paul Knox, "The Restless Urban Landscape: Economic and Sociocultural Change and the Transformation of Metropolitan Washington, DC," *Annals of the Association of American Geographers* 81.2 (1991): 181–209; Richard Florida, *Cities and the Creative Class* (New York: Routledge, 2005).

35. Alex Marshall, *How Cities Work: Suburbs, Sprawl, and the Roads Not Taken* (Austin: University of Texas Press, 2000), 31.

36. San Francisco Board of Supervisors, Government Audit and Oversight Committee, *Hearing on the Relationship between Parking, Neighborhood Businesses, and Families, Part 1 & 2*, June 11 and July 23, 2007.

37. *San Francisco Business Times*, "Our View: Disappearing Kids Illustrate SF Family Flight," June 24, 2011.

38. That the downtown parking reform leapfrogged the MOBNP should not be surprising given that land use planning beyond the downtown has traditionally been more difficult. Previous to the MOBNP, the city conducted little visionary planning beyond the downtown because of neighborhood opposition to densification. See Richard DeLeon, *Left Coast City: Progressive Politics in San Francisco, 1975–1991* (Lawrence: University Press of Kansas, 1992), esp. chapter 4, "The Birth of the Slow Growth Movement and the Battle for Proposition M."

39. *San Francisco Bay Guardian*, Editorial, "Downtown Calls the Shots," February 23,

2006; Charlie Goodyear, "Supes Delay Limiting Parking for New Buildings Downtown," *San Francisco Chronicle,* February 15, 2006; Steven Jones, "Records Show How Newsom Opposed Downtown Parking Limitations and Supported a Developer-Written Alternative at the Urging of Business Community Elites," *San Francisco Guardian,* February 9, 2006; Jim Lazarus (Senior Vice President/Public Policy, San Francisco Chamber of Commerce), "Letter to the Editor: Unfriendly Parking Rules," *San Francisco Chronicle,* February 22, 2006.

40. In the spirit of full disclosure, I add that I was involved in this appeal and the broader parking debates presented here.

41. The Planning Commission, albeit with close votes, decided to deny conditional uses for excess parking at 555 Fulton Street, 2001 Market Street, and 25–35 Dolores Street.

42. Tom Radulovich, Executive Director, Livable Cities, personal interview, May 2007.

43. San Francisco Board of Supervisors, *Hearing on the Relationship between Parking, Neighborhood Businesses, and Families, Part 1* (San Francisco: SFBOS, June 11, 2007).

44. Coalition for San Francisco Neighborhoods, "Where Am I Going to Park Downtown?" *CSFN Newsletter,* December 2005.

45. Mimi Sheller, "Automotive Emotions: Feeling the Car," *Theory, Culture, and Society* 21.4/5 (2004): 221–42.

46. San Francisco Board of Supervisors, *Hearing, Part 1.*

47. SFPD, *Feasibility of Citywide 1:1 Parking: Presentation to the San Francisco Board of Supervisors, Government, Audit and Oversight Committee,* July 23, 2007; SFPD, *The Upper Market Community Workshop Series and Design Plan San Francisco,* September 11, 2007.

48. In 2003 and 2004 the debate about parking policies in the *Housing Element* was frequently in the local news. For example, see Adriel Hampton, "Supe Enters Housing War: Hall Calls for Nov. Ballot Initiative in Development Fight," *San Francisco Examiner,* July 19, 2004; Judith Berkowitz, "Housing and Urban Land Use: Coming Soon to Your Block—Manhattan," *San Francisco Chronicle,* October 7, 2003; James Temple, "Housing Hopes Hammered: Opponents Try to Nail Door Shut on Citywide Plan," *San Francisco Business Times,* January 16, 2004; Ken Garcia, "A Plan for Living: San Francisco's Housing Plan Is Almost as Dense as It Is Dumb," *San Francisco Chronicle,* October 20, 2003.

49. San Francisco Department of Elections, *Proposition H: Parking Regulations, City and County of San Francisco Voter Information Pamphlet and Sample Ballot, Consolidated Municipal Election, November 6, 2007* (San Francisco: Department of Elections, 2007), 84–93.

50. SFPD, *Planning Department Assessment of Proposition H, Parking Regulations,* Memo to Department of Elections, July 27, 2007, 19.

51. Like that over the *Housing Element,* the debate over Proposition H had plenty of media coverage, including Joshua Sabatini, "S.F. Parking Debate in Overdrive," *San Francisco Examiner,* August 8, 2007; John Diaz, "Worst of Politics, Worst of Policy," *San Francisco Chronicle,* October 21, 2007.

52. San Francisco Department of Elections, *Proposition A: Transit Reform, Parking Regulations, and Emissions Reductions, City and County of San Francisco Voter Information Pamphlet and Sample Ballot, Consolidated Municipal Election, November 6, 2007* (San Francisco: Department of Elections, 2007), 38–47.

53. Steven Jones and Tim Redmund, "Fisher Fails: New Progressive Coalition Stops Downtown's Attack on Transit and Sets the Stage for Next Year's Board Fight," *San Francisco Bay Guardian,* November 14, 2007.

54. Remarks of Rodney Fong, Planning Commissioner, at the City Planning Commission hearing on 25–35 Dolores Street, April 7, 2011.

55. The project, 1050 Valencia, was delayed in September 2010 owing to opposition by the Liberty Hill Neighborhood Association, which opposed zero parking.

5. "We Are Not Blocking Traffic, We Are Traffic!"

1. Pucher and Buehler, "Making Cycling Irresistible," 1–57, provide a detailed overview of the components required for creating bicycle space.

2. Latest membership reported in June 2012.

3. USDOT, *The National Bicycling and Walking Study: 15-year Status Report* (Washington: USDOT, 2010), 6.

4. Alliance for Biking and Walking, *2012 Benchmarking Report* (Washington: Alliance for Biking and Walking, 2012), 205; Mark Byrnes, "Is Bicycle Commuting Really Catching On? And If So, Where?" www.theatlanticcities.com/commute. For broader overviews of the rise of cycling in the United States, see John Pucher and Ralph Buehler, "Making Cycling Irresistible: Lessons from the Netherlands, Denmark, and Germany," *Transport Reviews* 28.4 (2008): 1–57; Harry J. Wray, *Pedal Power: The Quiet Rise of the Bicycle in American Public Life* (Boulder: Paradigm, 2008); and Jeff Mapes, *Pedaling Revolution: How Cyclists Are Changing American Cities* (Corvallis: Oregon State University Press, 2009).

5. SFMTA, *2011 Bicycle Count Report* (San Francisco Bicycle Program, San Francisco: SFMTA, 2011), 9; David Binder, *Binder Research Poll on Bicycling in San Francisco 2009* (San Francisco: SFBC, 2009). The low range is reported by SFMTA and derived from U.S. Census, American Community Survey data. The high range was reported by SFMTA in *2008 San Francisco State of Cycling Report* (San Francisco: SFMTA, 2009), 9.

6. SFMTA, *2008 San Francisco State of Cycling Report,* 9; SFMTA, *2011 Bicycle Count Report.*

7. SFMTA, *San Francisco Bicycle Plan* (San Francisco: Bicycle Program, SFMTA, 2005), I-7.

8. USDOT, *The National Bicycling and Walking Study,* 2.

9. City of Oakland, *Oakland Bicycle Master Plan* (Oakland: Community and Economic Development Agency, Bicycle Program), 30.

10. Wray, *Pedal Power,* 207.

11. Ibid., 6–11.

12. Jennifer Dill and Kim Voros, "Factors Affecting Bicycling Demand: Initial Survey Findings from the Portland, Oregon, Region," *Transportation Research Record, Journal of the Transportation Research Board,* 2031, 2007, 12.

13. SFPD, *Improvement Plan for Transportation: The Comprehensive Plan of San Francisco, a Proposal for Citizen Review* (San Francisco: SFPD, 1971), 17.

14. David Snyder, personal interview, June 2008. Snyder reestablished the SFBC, was executive director until the early 2000s, and is now director of the California Bicycle Coalition.

15. There are two ways of measuring LOS for automobiles. Intersection LOS evaluates vehicle delay at intersections on city streets. Vehicle/capacity LOS measures the throughput of vehicles per hour and per lane on a particular roadway segment or on a freeway. I consider only intersection LOS because it is the metric that is challenged in San Francisco.

16. Transportation Research Board, *Highway Capacity Manual 2000* (Washington: National Research Council, Transportation Research Board, 2000), chapter 2, 2–4.

17. Brian Smith, former Board Member, SFBC, personal interview, June 2010.

18. Ted White, "Reels on Wheels," in *Critical Mass: Bicycling's Defiant Celebration,* ed. Chris Carlsson (Oakland: AK Press, 2002), 147.

19. Rigo, "First Critical Mass Rides Take Over Downtown San Francisco," exhibit titled "Backtracking 1994–1985," May 11–June 16, 2007, Luggage Store, San Francisco.

20. Carlsson, *Critical Mass.*

21. Ibid., 75–76. Not all participants had progressive values. A libertarian and even an anarchist bent characterized some participants.

22. Josh Switzky, "Riding to See," in Carlsson, *Critical Mass,* 186–92.

23. Cheryl Brinkman, personal interview, San Francisco, June 2010. Brinkman was the president of Livable City and an organizer of Sunday Streets. She also served as a commissioner on the SFMTA between 2010 and 2013.

24. Carlsson, *Critical Mass,* 8.

25. The documentary filmmaker Ted White chronicled the confrontation of 1997 in his film "(We Aren't Blocking Traffic,) We Are Traffic! A Movie about Critical Mass," 1999, www.tedwhitegreenlight.com/cm.htm.

26. Paul Dorn, "Pedaling to Save the City," *Journal of the Urban Institute, San Francisco State University* (1998), 7.

27. Martin Wachs, "Creating Political Pressure for Cycling," *Transportation Quarterly* 52.1 (1998): 6–8.

28. Snyder, personal interview. At this point the SFBC was distancing itself as the official sponsor of the rides and was supporting them only surreptitiously. The SFBC insisted that Critical Mass was leaderless and an entity in its own right. However, key leaders in the SFBC were regular participants.

29. Michael Salleberry, *Valencia Street Bicycle Lanes: One Year Evaluation.* (San Francisco: Department of Parking and Traffic, 2000), 2.

30. The SFBC makes sought-after endorsements in local elections.

31. Rachel Gordon, "Car 'Critical Mass' Protest Is a Bust: More Pro-Bicycle Demonstrators than Frustrated Auto Drivers Show Up," *San Francisco Examiner,* July 23, 1999.

32. SFBC, "Our History," www.sfbike.org/?about. See also David Darlington, "A Truly Critical Mass," in *San Francisco Magazine,* www.modernluxury.com.

33. Bert Hill, Chair, Bicycle Advisory Committee, personal interview, July 2008.

34. SFCTA, *Strategic Analysis Report on Transportation System Level of Service Methodologies* (San Francisco: SFCTA, 2003), 15.

35. Review of Policy Framework for SF Bike Plan presented to West of Twin Peaks Council & Greater West Portal Neighborhood Association, January 31, 2005.

36. Phred Dvorak, "San Francisco Ponders: Could Bike Lanes Cause Pollution?" *Wall Street Journal,* August 20, 2008.

37. *Coalition for Adequate Review and Rob Anderson v. City and County of San Francisco,* Superior Court of California, 505509, 2006, 4.

38. Tom Radulovich, personal interview, July 2008.

39. Good historical overviews of the politics in traffic engineering include Paul Barrett and Mark Rose, "Street Smarts: The Politics of Transportation Statistics in the American City 1900–1990," *Journal of Urban History* 25.3 (1999): 405–33, and Peter Norton, *Fighting Traffic: The Dawn of the Motor Age in the American City* (Cambridge: MIT Press, 2008), 201–4.

40. Mark Rose, *Interstate: Express Highway Politics 1939–1989* (Knoxville: University of Tennessee Press, 1990), 42–43. Rose never mentions the concept of LOS in his book but discusses traffic engineering politics and ideologies at length.

41. Wayne Kittelson, "Historical Overview of the Committee on Highway Capacity and Quality of Service," *Transportation Research Circular E-C018, 4th International Symposium on Highway Capacity,* 2001, 12. Kittelson is quoting remarks by Howard Hanna in meetings about highway planning in 1964. Today, six levels are used in LOS analysis, but in the early development there were five).

42. In the summer of 2011, as the *One Bay Area Vision* process got under way, Tea Party activists based in Bay Area suburbs began to protest the plans. They invoked the conspiratorial rhetoric stoked by national conservatives like those at the Heritage Foundation. For example, see www.theeastbayteaparty.com. The protests continued through 2012. See Tom Barnidge, "Sustainable Growth—Boon or Bane for Contra Costa Residents?" *Contra Costa Times,* January 29, 2012, www.contracostatimes.com/ci_19847976.

43. Aaron Bailick, "SFMTA Delays Fell and Oak Bikeways to Spring 2013 to Create More Parking," *StreetsblogSF,* January 20, 2012, http://sf.streetsblog.org.

44. Part of the Fell Street cycletrack was installed in late 2012.

45. Aaron Bailick, "Two-Way Haight Street Project Would Speed Up 6, 71 Muni Bus Lines," *StreetsblogSF,* June 21, 2011, http://sf.streetsblog.org; and "SFMTA Board Approves Two-Way Haight Street Project," October 19, 2011, http://sf.streetsblog.org.

46. Niko Letunic and Chris Ferrel, *Establishing Thresholds of Significance under CEQA: Final Memorandum to the SFCTA* (San Francisco: Eisen | Letunic, 2007), 27, and Niko Letunic and Chris Ferrel, *Strategy for Implementing a New CEQA Threshold of Significance: Technical Memorandum to the SFCTA* (San Francisco: Eisen | Letunic, 2008), 10.

47. Ironically, in the early 1980s progressives actually used LOS to contest new office towers in downtown San Francisco. In this case LOS was used as evidence to help establish impact fees on new office towers, as described by Sue Hestor, personal interview, August 2008. Hester was the land use attorney for San Franciscans for Reasonable Growth.

48. Local analysis applies only to city-owned streets. State-owned streets are subject to state analysis.

49. California Governor's Office of Planning and Research, *Thresholds of Significance: Criteria for Defining Environmental Significance* (Sacramento, OPR, 1994), 2.

50. SFCTA, *Automobile Trips Generated: CEQA Impact Measure and Mitigation Program* (San Francisco: SFCTA, 2008).

51. Rachel Hiatt, "An Alternative to Auto LOS for Transportation Impact Analysis," paper presented at the Transportation Research Board Annual Meeting, January 2006. Paper #06-2306, 19.

52. The National Complete Streets Coalition is made up of an array of professional societies and national advocacy organizations ranging from the American Association of Retired Persons (AARP) to the Institute of Transportation Engineers, and Smart Growth America (see www.completestreets.org/who-we-are).

53. Barbara McCann and Suzanne Rynne, *Complete Streets: Best Policy and Implementation Practices* (Chicago: American Planning Association, 2010).

54. SPUR, *Multimodal Planning at MTA* (San Francisco: SPUR, 2004), 12.

55. In March 2012 the city released a draft nexus study of the relationship between future development and future transit crowding and transit travel times. This study will inform the scheduling of fees on future development, but ironically must itself undergo extensive environmental review. That environmental review will take over one year, and legislation is not expected until late 2013, at the earliest. The intention is to replace LOS analysis in CEQA with this 20-year transportation mitigation program. See Cambridge Systematics, *San Francisco Transportation Sustainability Fee Nexus Study, Draft Report Prepared for SFMTA* (Oakland: Cambridge Systematics, 2012). The SFPD has also created a website for the proposal at www.sf-planning.org.

56. SFBC, "Year in Review," *Tube Times,* Summer, no. 136, 2011, 9–10.

57. When a sitting mayor is elected to another office before completing his or her term, San Francisco law requires that the president of the Board of Supervisors, together with a majority on the board, appoint an interim mayor until the next mayoral election, which in this case was in November 2011.

58. Rebecca Bowe and Steve Jones, "Chiu's Choice: The Man Who Presided over the End of the Progressive Era at City Hall Needs to Decide Whose Side He's Really On," *San Francisco Bay Guardian,* June 14, 2011.

59. Technically speaking, Livable City was the non-profit fiscal agent of Sunday Streets, and not SFBC.

60. Brinkman, personal interview.

61. Rachel Gordon, "New S.F. Study: Phase-in Market St. Car Ban," *San Francisco Chronicle,* 10 May 2009.

62. SFMTA, *Pilot Study of Required Right Turns on Eastbound Market Street* (San Francisco: SFMTA, 2010), 2.

63. Rachel Gordon and Jill Tucker, "Ruling Paves Way for San Francisco Bike Lanes," *San Francisco Chronicle,* August 7, 2010.

6. Transit First?

1. The 5 percent figure comes from USDOT and FHWA, *Summary of Travel Trends: 2009 National Household Travel Survey* (Washington: USDOT and FHWA, 2011), 42, and data on metropolitan area transit mode split come from U.S. Census Bureau, *Commuting in the United States: 2009* (Washington: Department of Commerce, U.S. Census Bureau, AC-15, 2011), 8.

2. U.S. Census, *Commuting in the United States,* 8. Los Angeles's transit commute is 6.6 percent.

3. SFMTA, *Transportation Fact Sheet November 2010;* U.S. Census, *Commuting in the United States,* 8.

4. The following figures on downtown San Francisco are drawn from the SFPD, *The Downtown Plan: 2010 Annual Monitoring Report* (San Francisco: SFPD, 2011), esp. 3–5, 12–13.

5. MTC, *Census Transportation Planning Package 2000* (Oakland: MTC, 2003). Public transportation includes BART, Caltrain, ferries, AC Transit (serving East Bay cities), and Golden Gate Transit (serving Marin County).

6. ABAG and MTC, *Bay Area Plan: Initial Vision for Public Discussion* (Oakland: ABAG/MTC, 2011), 1–3.

7. Ibid.

8. ABAG and MTC, *Scenario Analysis and Targets Scorecard* (Oakland: ABAG/MTC, 2011), 2.

9. SFMTA, *2011 Climate Action Strategy for San Francisco's Transportation System* (San Francisco: SFMTA, 2011), 11. The built environment accounts for 64 percent of the city's emissions.

10. SFMTA, *SFMTA 2009 Climate Action Plan: Draft for Public Review* (San Francisco, SFMTA, 2008), 19, 62–63.

11. ABAG and MTC, *Scenario Analysis and Targets Scorecard,* 2.

12. Prop A was a counterinitiative to Prop H, the parking initiative (see chapter 4).

13. SFMTA, *2011 Climate Action Strategy,* 13. The benchmark year of 1990 is used because that was the year global CO_2 emissions reached 350 ppm, considered a sustainable volume. Most climate change planning focuses on 1990 levels as a goal.

14. Ibid., 30. The benchmark year of 2035 is used because this is the planning horizon for the regional transportation planning agency that allocates funds to localities. SFMTA has not offered a similar mode split for 2050.

15. Good discussions of transit-first policies include Transportation Research Board, *Making Transit Work: Insights from Western Europe, Canada, and the United States* (Washington: Transportation Research Board, National Research Council, 2001), and Andrew Nash and Ronald Sylvia, *Implementation of Zurich's Transit Priority Program* (San Jose: Mineta Transportation Institute, San Jose State University, 2001).

16. SFMTA, *Transit Effectiveness Project Briefing Book* (San Francisco: SFMTA, 2006), 2-2.

17. SFMTA, *2009 Climate Action Plan,* 19.

18. This includes an increase in the number of vehicles and changing the configuration of streets.

19. Sharon Green Associates and AECOM, *Fare Free Muni System Feasibility Analysis for the SFMTA* (San Francisco: Sharon Green and Associates, 2008), ES-3.

20. SFMTA, *2011 Climate Action Strategy*, 36.

21. Complete streets schemes would also include bicycle lanes, pedestrian space, and other public spaces, but transit would be a large component.

22. SFMTA, *Draft Transit Effectiveness Project Implementation Strategy* (San Francisco: SFMTA, 2011) 1–4.

23. Rachel Gordon, "SF Muni Plans 50-cent Fare Increase in July," *San Francisco Chronicle*, May 1, 2009.

24. Michael Cabanatuan and Rachel Gordon, "Muni Is Actually Worth $11 Billion," *San Francisco Chronicle*, August 6, 2010.

25. Federal Transit Administration, *2010 National State of Good Repair Assessment* (Washington: FTA, 2010), 1.

26. American Public Transit Association, *Impact of the Recession on Public Transportation Agencies* (Washington: APTA, 2010), 8.

27. MTC, *2009 Annual Report: Transit in Transition* (Oakland: MTC, 2010), 4–7.

28. Ibid., 6–7.

29. Matthew Roth, "Streetsblog Recap on Budget," San Francisco Transit Riders Union Board Meeting, December 2010.

30. "House Bill Makes Deep Cuts to Transit, Biking and Walking," Transportation for America, July 14, 2011, http://t4america.org.

31. Peter Schrag, *Paradise Lost: California's Experience, America's Future* (New York: New Press, 1998), 14 and esp. 129–88.

32. Richard Walker, "The Golden State Adrift," *New Left Review* 66.6 (2010): 15.

33. Chester Hartman, *City for Sale: The Transformation of San Francisco* (Berkeley: University of California Press, 2002), 311–18, provides a good overview of the 1980s transit finance debates.

34. Ibid., 316.

35. Peter Straus, personal interview, November 2010. Straus was a Muni planner from 1974 to 2010.

36. San Francisco Department of Elections, *Proposition O: Downtown Transit Assessment District Preparation, City and County of San Francisco Voter Information Pamphlet and Sample Ballot, Consolidated Municipal Election, November 8, 1994* (San Francisco: Department of Elections, 1994), 204–17.

37. Hartman, *City for Sale*, 317.

38. The arguments against Prop O can be read in the voter information pamphlet, San Francisco Department of Elections, *Proposition O*, 204–17.

39. Today SPUR also argues that a TAD would make downtown San Francisco less competitive with suburban office developments, and that this would lead to more sprawl.

40. Compared to other transit systems in the United States, Muni has a higher share of middle- and upper-class riders. Evidence of this was anecdotal but widely acknowledged until 2006, when the TEP study revealed that 42 percent of regular Muni riders had a higher-than-average annual income (above forty-five thousand dollars). See SFMTA, *Transit Effectiveness Project Briefing Book*, esp. 3-2 and 3-6.

41. Beginning in late August 1998 and for the rest of that fall, stories about Muni's computer system and its reliability appeared in newspapers almost every day. For example, Lynda Gledhill, "Fitful Service Antagonizes Muni Riders: Long Waits Overshadow New Method of Payment," *San Francisco Chronicle*, August 25, 1998; Edward Epstein, "Woes Worsen for Muni Riders: Metro System Foul-ups Outrage Drivers, Public," *San Francisco Chronicle*, August 27, 1998; Edward Epstein and Lynda Gledhill, "Brown Lashes Out at Muni Honchos," *San Francisco Chronicle*, September 3, 1998; Lynda Gledhill, "Muni Relapses, Just When It Seemed to Be on the Mend," *San Francisco Chronicle*, September 9, 1998; Edward Epstein, "S.F. Mayor Creating Task Force to Probe Muni Woes," *San Francisco Chronicle*, September 18, 1998.

42. Hartman, *City for Sale,* 317.

43. Ibid., 318.

44. Rachel Gordon and Michael Cabanatuan, "Muni Reaches Tentative Pact with Operators Union," *San Francisco Chronicle,* June 1, 2011.

45. Rachel Gordon, "Paying the Price for Riding the Bus: Muni, AC Transit Passengers Face Higher Fares Today," *San Francisco Chronicle,* September 1, 2003.

46. Rachel Gordon, "Muni Chief Could Get Big Raise: Fares Went Up 2 Months Ago," *San Francisco Chronicle,* October 22, 2003.

47. Liam O'Donoghue, "Bus Stop: Public Outcry Delays Muni Cuts, but Battles Still Loom over Slashed Service and New Taxes," *San Francisco Bay Guardian,* April 28, 2004; Katia Hetter, "Muni Refuses to Cut Services: Board Deadlocks on Declaring Emergency," *San Francisco Chronicle,* April 21, 2004; Sara Zaske, "Muni Battle Forges Ahead: Progressives Urge Stronger Resistance to Bus Service Cuts," *San Francisco Examiner,* April 22, 2004.

48. SPUR, "Downward Spiral," *SPUR Urbanist,* September 2005, 1.

49. SFMTA, *Potential Balancing Plans for the MTA FY06 Budget* (San Francisco: SFMTA, 2005) 1–8.

50. This section draws from my observations at the SFMTA Board public hearing on February 28, 2005, at San Francisco City Hall.

51. This figure was presented by Jeffrey Tumlin, principal of Nelson Nygaard Consulting, at a presentation at SPUR in 2002.

52. Matt Smith, "Unbalanced Budgeting: SF Public Parking Rates Insanely Subsidized," *San Francisco Weekly,* February 16, 2005, www.sfweekly.com.

53. Casey Mills, "*Examiner's* Muni Story Misses the Bus," *Beyond Chron,* February 17, 2005, www.beyondchron.org/news.

54. Advocates from the Coalition for Transit Justice held rallies in front of City Hall on February 1, 2005 and February 28, 2005.

55. Charlie Goodyear, "Rowdy Supes' Meeting on Muni's Big Deficit," *San Francisco Chronicle,* May 25, 2005.

56. See the SFMTA's "SF Park" website, at http://sfpark.org.

57. Michael Cooper and Jo Craven Mcginty, "A Meter So Expensive, It Creates Parking Spots," *New York Times,* March 16, 2012. In 2012 SF Park won a Sustainable Transportation Award from the Institute for Transportation and Development Policy, see, www.itdp.org /news.

58. Evan Halper, "Budget Deal Would Include Steeper Car Fees," *Los Angeles Times,* November 21, 2008.

59. The withdrawn funds included Muni operations but also funds for streets and other urban services. In 2010 voters approved a statewide ballot initiative that prohibits the shifting of gas tax funds to the state general fund, and it was anticipated that Muni would recover some state operating assistance. When Schwarzenegger reduced the VLF, the state became even more reliant on bonding and debt financing for transportation, and localities became more dependent on sales taxes, both more regressive than the VLF. The VLF was based on the value of automobiles, and so wealthier persons with more expensive cars paid more, making the VLF a progressive form of taxation.

60. José Gómez-Ibáñez, "Big City Transit Ridership, Deficits, and Politics," *Journal of the American Planning Association* 62.1 (1996): 30–41. See also Transport for London, *Central London Congestion Charging Impacts Monitoring, 6th Annual Report* (London: Transport for London 2008), 13–14.

61. Benjamin Ross, "Stuck in Traffic: Free-Market Theory Meets the Highway Lobby," *Dissent* (Summer 2006), www.dissentmagazine.org. David Levinson, "Equity Effect of Road Pricing: A Review," *Transport Reviews* 30.1 (2010): 33–57.

62. SFCTA, *Mobility, Access, and Pricing Study: Final Report* (San Francisco: SFCTA, 2010), www.sfcta.org/images/stories.

63. Ibid., 53.

64. Alexandria Rocha, "S.F. Panel Touts Toll to Tame Traffic," *San Francisco Examiner,* July 27, 2007; *San Francisco Chronicle,* Editorial, "S.F. on Wrong Road with Congestion Toll Idea," December 15, 2010; Michael Cabanatuan, "S.F. Supes Back Away from 'Southern Gateway' Toll," *San Francisco Chronicle,* December 15, 2010.

65. Associated Press, "Lawmakers Drop Plan to Charge Manhattan Motorists: Proposal Faced Objections from Legislators of Suburbs, Outer Boroughs," April 8, 2008; Owen Gutfreund, "Pick on the Big Guys," *New York Times,* April 9, 2008; Gene Russianoff, "Take an Alternate Route," *New York Times,* April 9, 2008.

66. SFCTA, *Mobility, Access, and Pricing Study,* 25–31.

67. Rachel Gordon, "Economy Wallops S.F.'s Big Muni Overhaul Plan," *San Francisco Chronicle,* December 8, 2008.

68. The riders' union has web postings at www.sftru.org.

69. SFMTA, *2011 Climate Action Strategy,* 37.

70. SFPD, *Transportation Sustainability Program,* www.sf-planning.org.

7. Disciplining Muni

1. Neil Smith, *The New Urban Frontier: Gentrification and the Revanchist City* (London: Routledge, 1996), 42–44.

2. Neil Smith, "New Globalism, New Urbanism: Gentrification as Global Urban Strategy," *Antipode* 34.3 (2002): 429, 437, 442–43; Stacey Murphy provides a good overview of revanchism with regard to homelessness in San Francisco, " 'Compassionate' Strategies of Managing Homelessness: Post-Revanchist Geographies in San Francisco," *Antipode* 41.2 (2009): 310–14.

3. Super-gentrification refers to the transformation of an already mostly gentrified neighborhood or city into an even more exclusive and expensive enclave. See Loretta Lees, "Super-gentrification: The Case of Brooklyn Heights, New York City," *Urban Studies* 40.12 (2004): 2487. Originally referring to global cities like New York and London, where a very wealthy financial class spread into areas previously gentrified by the middle class, super-gentrification can be observed in San Francisco with the onslaught of the new rich social network and tech worker class in the Victorian Belt, particularly in neighborhoods like the Castro, the Mission, Noe Valley, Hayes Valley, and also in the South of Market district.

4. SFPD, *The Downtown Plan: 2010 Annual Monitoring Report* (San Francisco: SFPD, 2011), esp. 3–5, 12–13.

5. For example, sustainable transportation advocates involved in planning for high-speed rail have proposed that I-280 south of downtown be removed because it interferes with the rail alignment plans. See Bryan Goebel, "Will SF Tear Down That Freeway? 280 Removal Study for HSR Moves Forward," *StreetsblogSF,* May 19, 2011, http://sf.streetsblog.org.

6. SFPD, *San Francisco Socio-Economic Profile, 2005–2009 American Community Survey* (San Francisco: SFPD, 2011), esp. section on Supervisor District 6, which includes most of the downtown, South of Market, and Mission Bay, 35–37.

7. In 2004, SFMTA expanded the five-dollar-per-square-foot TIDF to include retail and other downtown commercial space, not just offices. Yet it is still a flat rate, collected only once (compared to an annual tax assessment), and is not indexed to inflation.

8. SFMTA, *Draft Transit Effectiveness Project Implementation Strategy* (San Francisco: SFMTA, 2011), 1–4.

9. Rachel Gordon, "Fare Boost a Muni Talking Point," *San Francisco Chronicle,* February 15, 2008. In 2012 the new Transportation Sustainability Program, discussed in chapters 5 and 6, was presented as a potential new impact fee for transit, but is still several years from adoption.

10. San Francisco Department of Elections, *Prop K: Sales Tax for Transportation, Voter*

Information Pamphlet, November 4 2004 Election (San Francisco: Department of Elections, 2003), 143–60.

11. SFCTA, *Prop K Strategic Plan Update* (San Francisco: SFCTA, 2009), 1. In 2009 the SFCTA was cautioning that federal and state funds may not be that forthcoming.

12. Funds can be used for temporary start-up operations for new projects.

13. See Institute on Taxation and Economic Policy, *Who Pays: A Distributional Analysis of the Tax System in All 50 States* (Washington: Institute on Taxation and Economic Policy, 2009), 4. To be sure, San Francisco does not have a sales tax on food purchased at grocery stores, so the regressive impact of sales taxes on the poor is not as pronounced as elsewhere.

14. For example, high-income households make as much as 2½ times as many trips as low-income households. See USDOT, *Summary of Travel Trends,* 2011, 18.

15. Interviews with several progressive transportation advocates and planners stressed this point.

16. San Francisco Department of Elections, *Prop K: Sales Tax for Transportation,* 145.

17. Like the mayoral election of 1999 that determined the outcome of the Central Freeway, the election of 2003 was a high-profile mayor's race in which the progressive candidate, Matt Gonzalez, who was also president of the Board of Supervisors, was challenging the neoliberal Gavin Newsom. Progressive voters helped force Newsom into a runoff with Gonzalez. although there were also other candidates drawing votes and keeping Newsom from receiving a simple majority.

18. *San Francisco Bay Guardian,* "November 2003 Endorsements," October 15, 2003, www.sfbg.com.

19. This project, the Doyle Drive Replacement, or Presidio Parkway, is a $1-billion capacity expansion (from four to six lanes) and is basically a freeway approach between Lombard Street and the Golden Gate Bridge. As of 2011 it drew at least $68 million in Prop K funds. There was criticism of the project from some sustainable transportation advocates who argued it should have deployed congestion charging tolls to finance the project and should not have included capacity expansion.

20. San Francisco Department of Elections, *Prop K: Sales Tax for Transportation,* 147–48.

21. Cecilia Vega, "S.F. Chinatown Subway Plan Gets Agency's Nod," *San Francisco Chronicle,* February 20; Matthew Roth, "As Central Subway Funding Deadline Looms, Chinatown Rallies Support," *StreetsblogSF,* November 17, 2010, http://sf.streetsblog.org; Zusha Elinson, "In the Bay Area, Trains Are Powered by Myths," *New York Times,* July 2, 2011, www.baycitizen.org/transportation/story.

22. A sampling of supportive public comments and letters from Chinatown activists can be seen in FTA and SFPD, *Central Subway Final Supplemental Environmental Impact Statement and Final Supplemental Environmental Impact Report Response to Comments Volume II* (San Francisco: FTA and SFPD, 2008), esp. 3-22, 3-47, 3-196 to 3-201.

23. Gerald Cauthen, "Going Underground in Chinatown," *San Francisco Chronicle,* April 7, 2008.

24. *San Francisco Examiner,* "One Man's Plan: Stockton Bus-Only Lanes," July 18, 2007. For extensive critiques of the subway, see "Save Muni," at https://sites.google.com/a/save-muni.com/save-san-francisco-s-muni. Defenders of the subway point out that the federal money allocated can be spent only on the subway and that if canceled or modified the city would lose the money.

25. *Sierra Club Yodeler,* "Chinatown Transit Solution Is Long Overdue," July 10, 2011, http://theyodeler.org/?p=1350#respond.

26. Save Muni, https://sites.google.com/a/savemuni.com/save-san-francisco-s-muni/

27. Civil Grand Jury, City and County of San Francisco, *Central Subway: Too Much Money for Too Little Benefit* (San Francisco: Superior Court of California, City and County of San Francisco, 2011), 58.

28. The SFMTA maintains that future light rail to Geary is possible, and that the Central Subway will be designed to accommodate crossing tracks at Geary for this purpose. The Civil Grand Jury Report claims that the design of the Union Square Station makes that impossible.

29. SFCTA, *San Francisco County Transportation Authority Board Resolution No. 12-07: Allocate $57,213,174 of Prop K funds to Central Subway* (San Francisco: San Francisco County Transportation Authority, 2011).

30. See California Public Utilities Commission, www.cpuc.ca.gov/PUC. SFMTA and the CPUC reached a settlement in May 2012 whereby SFMTA agreed to accelerate maintenance on its tracks.

31. Stephanie Farmer describes a similar situation in "Uneven Transportation Development in Neoliberalizing Chicago," *Environment and Planning A* 43 (2011): 1154–72.

32. See SPUR comment in FTA and SFPD, *Central Subway EIR Response to Comments,* 2:4–9.

33. San Francisco Department of Elections, *Prop K: Sales Tax for Transportation,* 146.

34. Ibid., 148.

35. Save Muni argues that Muni will not be able to remove the Stockton buses because the subway does not serve needs further north of its alignment, and so will either have to operate duplicative service in the corridor or force passengers to switch from bus to train in Chinatown. See also Aaron Bialick, "Stockton Bus Riders Take a Back Seat to Central Subway Construction," *StreetsblogSF,* January 12, 2012, http://sf.streetsblog.org.

36. SFCTA, 2009 *Prop K Strategic Plan Update,* 2.

37. SPUR, *The Downward Spiral,* 1. To be sure, SPUR has yet to propose privatizing Muni.

38. Paul Weyrich and William S. Lind, *Conservatives and Mass Transit: Is It Time for a New Look?* (Washington: Free Congress Foundation, 1997), 23.

39. American Public Transit Association, "National Transit Database, Fare Passenger and Recovery Ratio," www.apta.com/resources/statistics/Pages/NTDDataTables.aspx.

40. Bryan Goebel, "SFMTA Releases Bus Stop Consolidation Plan," *StreetsblogSF,* November 3, 2010, http://sf.streetsblog.org.

41. In California, transit expansion such as the proposed *TEP Implementation Plan,* requires environmental review, as do bicycle lanes. However, cutting transit service does not require environmental review because when a transit agency declares a fiscal emergency, it is cleared of having to analyze the impacts of the cuts.

42. Muni and all American transit systems, because of the market-oriented structure of healthcare, have to dedicate significant resources to the healthcare of transit operators. In many European countries as well as Canada, urban transit agencies have far lower healthcare costs and do not have to include healthcare as part of labor negotiations. Muni's TEP acknowledges this in one small paragraph, meanwhile measuring worker productivity against a cost metric that includes very expensive healthcare costs (see SFMTA, *Transit Effectiveness Project Briefing Book* [San Francisco: SFMTA, 2006], 5–7).

43. Rachel Gordon, "Muni Operators Reject Concessions," *San Francisco Chronicle,* February 17, 2010.

44. Will Reisman, "Solving SFMTA's Solvency Crisis," *San Francisco Examiner,* February 8, 2010.

45. San Francisco Board of Supervisors Budget Analyst, "Executive Summary," *Limited-Scope Performance Audit of the SFMTA* (San Francisco: Budget Analyst, 2010), ii.

46. Ibid., iii.

47. Ibid., vi.

48. The *San Francisco Chronicle* pointed out that this represented the most signatures ever obtained for a ballot initiative. See Rachel Gordon, "SF Prop. G Backers Call It Mandate to Reform Muni," *San Francisco Chronicle,* November 8, 2010.

49. San Francisco Department of Elections, *Proposition G: Transit Operator Wages, City and County of San Francisco Voter Information Pamphlet and Sample Ballot, Consolidated Municipal Election, November 2, 2010* (San Francisco: Department of Elections, 2010), 108–15.

50. San Francisco Registrar of Voters, *Propositions, Arguments, and Statement of Controller November 7th 1967: Proposition G, Charter Amendment Relating to Compensation of Platform Employees, and Coach and Bus Operators* (San Francisco: Registrar of Voters, 1967), 98–101.

51. Joshua Freeman, "Anatomy of a Strike: New York City Transit Workers Confront the Power Elite," *New Labor Forum* 15.3 (2006): 9.

52. *StreetsblogSF* provided good coverage of the campaign. See, for example, Matt Baume, "Elsbernd Muni Reform Measure Has Money and Signatures to Spare," July 2, 2010, http://sf.streetsblog.org; Matthew Roth, "Proposition G and the Fix Muni Syndrome," October 14, 2010, http://sf.streetsblog.org.

53. SPUR, "2010 Voter Guide, Ballot Analysis and Recommendations," *Urbanist* 10.497 (2010): 2.

54. San Francisco Department of Elections, *Proposition G: Transit Operator Wages,* "Rebuttal to Opponents' Arguments against Prop G," 111.

55. Most of the Fix Muni campaign materials were removed shortly after the campaign, but one television ad remained online as of April 2012: www.youtube.com/watch. Additionally, about half a dozen brochures and campaign mailers were distributed during the campaign, with statements from key organizations and notable local personages. Statements for and against Prop G can be found at San Francisco Department of Elections, *Proposition G: Transit Operator Wages,* 108–15.

56. Rescue Muni, "Why We Support the Elsbernd Amendment," www.rescuemuni.org.

57. Rachel Gordon, "Muni Reform Petition Goes to City Hall," *San Francisco Chronicle,* July 2, 2010. See also October 4, 2010, campaign finance filing by San Franciscans for a Better Muni, with the San Francisco Ethics Commission, http://nf4.netfile.com.

58. The TWU-250A removed campaign materials from its website after the campaign. Arguments against Prop G can be reviewed at San Francisco Department of Elections, *Proposition G: Transit Operator Wages,* 108–15.

59. *San Francisco Bay Guardian,* "Endorsements 2010: San Francisco Ballot Measures, No on G," October 5, 2010, www.sfbg.com/2010/10/05/endorsements.

60. Will Reisman, "Supes Spar over Muni Wages," *San Francisco Examiner,* April 28, 2010; Dick Meister, "The Pummeling of SF Labor," *San Francisco Bay Guardian,* October 1, 2010, www.sfbg.com/bruce/2010/10/01.

61. Rachel Gordon, "SF Prop. G Backers Call It Mandate to Reform Muni," *San Francisco Chronicle,* November 8, 2010, and Rachel Gordon, "Muni Operators Overwhelmingly Reject Contract," *San Francisco Chronicle,* June 9, 2011.

62. David Brooks, "The Paralysis of the State," *New York Times,* October 12, 2010.

63. Michael Powell, "Public Workers Facing Outrage as Budget Crises Grow," *New York Times,* January 2, 2011.

64. Rachel Gordon and Michael Cabanatuan, "Muni Reaches Tentative Pact with Operators Union," *San Francisco Chronicle,* June 1, 2011.

65. Freeman, "Anatomy of a Strike," 3.

66. Will Reisman, "Muni's Savings on Labor Less than First Projected," *San Francisco Examiner,* June 1, 2011.

67. *San Francisco Chronicle,* "Muni Operators Lose Touch with Economic Reality," June 10, 2011.

68. Michael Rhodes, "Speeding Up Muni by Letting All Aboard, Through Any Door," *StreetsblogSF,* March 19, 2010, http://sf.streetsblog.org.

69. Michael Rhodes, "To Reduce Delay and Fare Evasion, Muni Considers All-Door

Boarding," *StreetsblogSF,* October 21, 2009, http://sf.streetsblog.org. SFMTA, *Proof-of-Payment Study on San Francisco's Buses, Light Rail, and Streetcars* (San Francisco: SFMTA, 2009), 22.

70. Andrew Nash and Ronald Sylvia, *Implementation of Zurich's Transit Priority Program* (San Jose: Mineta Transportation Institute, San Jose State University, 2001), 27–28; Transportation Research Board, *Making Transit Work: Insights from Western Europe, Canada, and the United States* (Washington: TRB, National Research Council, 2001), 69, 163.

71. SFMTA, *Proof-of-Payment Study,* 22.

72. San Francisco Office of the Controller, *Addressing Crime and Disorder on the Municipal Railway: A Case Study on Data-Driven Policing in the Ingleside District* (San Francisco: Office of the Controller, City Services Auditor, 2009), 10.

73. A smattering of newspaper articles includes Charlie Goodyear, "Muni Addresses Fare Evasion on Buses," *San Francisco Chronicle,* March 2, 2005; Rachel Gordon, "No Fare: Cheats on Muni," *San Francisco Chronicle,* February 27, 2007; Michael Rhodes, "Fare Evasion Is Down as Muni Steps Up Collection Effort," *StreetsblogSF,* May 5, 2010, http://sf.streetsblog.org; Will Reisman, "Fare Evasions Still High in San Francisco as Muni Loses $19M in 2010," *San Francisco Examiner,* April 5, 2011.

74. SFMTA, *Proof-of-Payment Study,* 50. SFMTA surveyed forty-one thousand passengers and rode what amounted to eleven hundred vehicle runs on different routes to observe patterns of fare evasion.

75. SFMTA, *Proof-of-Payment Study,* 6–7.

76. Michael Rhodes, "SFPD Conducting First Citywide 'Operation Safe Muni' Sting Today," *StreetsblogSF,* November 4, 2009 http://sf.streetsblog.org; Rhodes, "Fare Evasion Is Down."

77. PODER, "A Mother's Fight for Transportation Justice," *Powering Up* (Winter 2010): 1–2.

78. Rigoberto Hernandez, "Immigrants Say Officers Harass Them on Muni," *Mission Local,* March 9, 2010 http://missionlocal.org. Matthew Roth, "SFMTA Hones Enforcement, But Minority Rights Groups Still Leery of Stings," *StreetsblogSF,* August 16, 2010, http://sf.streetsblog.org.

79. The data presented here come from an SFMTA staff presentation on May 5, 2010, titled "Fare Evasion Proof of Payment Program." The activist statements are from the public comment that followed the presentation.

80. Office of the Controller, *Addressing Crime and Disorder on the Municipal Railway,* 4.

81. Ibid., 4–6.

82. Bryan Goebel, "Broad Coalition Calls on SFMTA to Provide Free Muni Youth Passes," *StreetsblogSF,* September 20, 2011, http://sf.streetsblog.org. In 2010 the Board of Supervisors adopted a resolution endorsing free youth fares. In April 2012 SFMTA proposed a pilot program for free youth fares.

83. Murphy, " 'Compassionate' Strategies of Managing Homelessness," 317–18.

84. SPUR, "Muni's Billion Dollar Problem," *SPUR Newsletter* 3.447 (2006): 17.

85. SFCTA, *The Role of Shuttle Services in San Francisco's Transportation System* (San Francisco: SFCTA, 2011).

86. Ibid., 7.

87. Nancy Keates and Geoffrey Fowler, "The Hot Spot for the Rising Tech Generation," *Wall Street Journal,* March 16, 2012.

88. Krute Singa and Jean David Margulici, *Privately-Provided Commuter Bus Services: Role in the San Francisco Bay Area Regional Transportation Network* (Berkeley: California Center for Innovative Transportation, University of California, 2010), 45.

89. Matt Baume, "New Study Recommends Augmenting the Benefits of Private Shuttle Service," *StreetsblogSF,* July 26, 2010, http://sf.streetsblog.org.

90. www.munidiaries.com provides a "love–hate" perspective on Muni.

91. Singa and Margulici, *Privately-Provided Commuter Bus Services,* 21.

92. Ibid., 37–41.

93. Angie Schmitt, "Advocates: Private Transit Giant Lobbied House to Weaken Public Transit," Streetsblog Capitol Hill, March 9, 2012, http://dc.streetsblog.org.

94. SFCTA, *The Role of Shuttle Services in San Francisco's Transportation System,* 6.

95. Carolyn Said, "S.F. Apartment Rent Rises as Vacancy Rates Fall," *San Francisco Chronicle,* August 11, 2011; Keates and Fowler, "The Hot Spot for the Rising Tech Generation."

INDEX

NOTE: Page numbers with an italic *f* indicate a figure.

AC Transit, 221n5
Adler, Seymour, 44, 45
Affordable Housing Alliance, 83
AFL-CIO, 46, 180
Agnos, Art, 58–59, 65, 83
Aids Housing Alliance, 103
Alice B. Toklas LGBT Democratic Club, 75, 79, 83
Alliance for Bicycling and Walking, 114
Alliance for Golden Gate Park, 82
American Institute of Architects and Urban Ecology, 63
American Society of Engineers, 55
Ammiano, Tom, 83–85, 149
anti-bicycle movement, 3, 82, 121–28, 138, 219n42
antidensity movement, 34, 48
Apple, 188
Appleyard, Donald, 52
Association of Bay Area Governments (ABAG), 106–7
Association to Simplify Traffic and Abate Congestion (ASTAC), 63–64, 67, 73–76, 78
Atlanta, x, 196
automobility, 1–6; automobile industry bailouts in, 144; car-ownership rates and, 9–10, 13, 197–98, 204n13, 216n6; definition of, 2; environmental considerations of, 6–9; essentialist views of, 17–18, 33–34, 37, 41, 52–53, 69, 99, 169, 194, 195, 199–200, 205n4, 207n46; family values and, 35, 99, 104–5, 126; freeway revolts against, 41–46; government's role in, 30, 31, 32, 151–53; green cars in, 20, 95, 96, 111; ideological dimension of, 17–18, 20,

24–28, 30, 31–33, 71–72; intersection level of service (LOS) in, 116–17, 123–32, 199, 218n15; in low-density sprawl, 8, 13, 62, 90; MOBNP's challenge of, 93–95; political contestation of, 3–6; possibility of change in, 16, 192–202; pricing of, 151–59, 174, 201, 223n59; replication in developing world of, 7, 92, 198; of San Francisco residents, 9–15, 45, 49, 65–66; small-business rhetoric on, 36; subsidized infrastructure for, 151–53. *See also* parking policies
auto trip generation (ATG + 1) proposal, 128–32

backdoor boarding, 183–84
Ball, Andy, 107
basic mobility networks, 26, 28. *See also* premium mobility networks
Bay Area, 13
Bay Area Rapid Transit System (BART), 47–49, 53, 142, 210n33, 221n5; farebox recovery in, 172; Geary Street plan of, 169–70; regional connectivity of, 167, 188; times required to travel by, 52
Bay Bridge, 54
Bayshore Freeway (U.S. Highway 101), 42
Bayview-Hunters Point, 81
beat poets, 1–3
Bechtel Corporation, 47
bicycling, 2, 20, 112–38, 192; advocacy movements for, 21, 22, 60, 63, 112, 114–20; conflict with parking policies of, 126–27; Connecting the City plan for, 135–38, 193; Critical Mass rides for, 115–20, 133, 137–38, 212n19, 219n25, 219n28; education on, 114;

bicycling *(continued)*
    family values in, 133, 136–37; integration
        with mass transit of, 113; legal support
        for, 114; LOS and environmental review
        of plans for, 121–32; in the 19th Avenue
        neighborhood, 39; opposition to, 3, 121–28,
        138, 219n42; politics of, 16, 25, 36, 114–15;
        progressive-neoliberal hybridized views
        on, 133–37, 138; rates of, 10–11, 113, 114,
        133; recreational use of, 115, 136–37; San
        Francisco's plan for, 119–23, 138; on side-
        walks, 39; space allocations for, ix–x, 3, 36,
        112–20, 133–37, 200; Sunday Streets events
        for, 136–37, 177, 219n23, 220n58; in transit-
        first policies, 115, 116, 148–49; utilitarian
        use of, 113, 114–15
Bierman, Sue, 69, 75, 78, 83, 96–97
bike boxes, 114
bike lanes, ix–x, 3, 36, 114, 115–17, 133
Black Rock Arts Foundation, 187
Bloomberg, Michael, 135
Brando, Marlon, 1
Brinkman, Cheryl, 219n23
Brown, Amos, 83
Brown, Willie, 1, 72–74, 78, 83; Critical Mass
    crackdown by, 119–20; on Proposition
    H, 75
Building Owners and Management Associa-
    tion (BOMA), 147, 149, 168, 180
Burning Man, 96–97
Burton, John, 83
bus bulb-outs, 39, 172
Bush, George H. W., 146
Bush, George W., 109
bus stop consolidation, 172–73
bus system. *See* Municipal Railway (Muni)
    system

California: priority development areas in,
    9; Sustainable Communities and Climate
    Protection Act (SB 375) in, 8–9, 25, 27–28,
    125, 132
California Academy of Sciences, 68, 78
California Citizen's Freeway Association, 46
California Department of Motor Vehicles, 154
California Highway Patrol, 154
California Office of Planning and Research,
    127
California Public Utilities Commission, 167
California State Department of Transporta-
    tion (Caltrans): on the Central Freeway,
    55, 60, 66–70, 72–73, 77–78, 80; mandate
    for local cooperation of, 60, 63; proposed
        freeways of, 40–42; regional highways of,
        38; on 19th Avenue stalemate, 39–40
Caltrain, 142, 167, 172, 188, 221n5
capitalism: Keynesian view of, 42, 47, 49;
    mobility economy of, 24, 125; unregulated
    forms of, 160. *See also* neoliberal ideology
    of mobility
car-free approaches, 94, 99–104, 193, 198–202
Carlsson, Chris, 118
cars: car-free mobility and, 99–104, 192–93,
    198–202; density rates of, 53, 193, 211n44;
    green technology for, 20, 34, 95, 96, 111,
    198; ownership rates of, 9–10, 13, 197–98,
    204n13, 216n6; sustainability goals for,
    10–11. *See also* automobility
Castells, Manuel, 208n51
Castro neighborhood, 58, 106, 224n3
Central Freeway, 36, 54–86, 142; boulevard
    alternatives to, 55, 67–68, 73–74, 78–81,
    214n47; Chinese-American faction on,
    65–66, 76–77, 79, 81–84, 212n21; design
    and building of, 56–58; earthquake dam-
    age to, 54–55, 64; environmental impact
    assessments of, 68–70; geography of revolt
    against, 77f; livability debates on, 55, 74;
    neighborhood activism against, 60–64,
    67, 69–71, 73–74, 77f, 79, 83, 212n11; new
    development options for, 70–74; politics
    of possibilities in, 84–86; Proposition E on
    alternatives to, 78–81; Proposition H on
    rebuilding of, 74–79, 221n12; Propositions
    I and J on rebuilding of, 81–84; rebuild
    movement for, 64–70, 72–73, 77–78,
    79–80; removal of, 59, 64, 67–74, 84–86
Central Freeway Citizens' Advisory Com-
    mittee, 81
Central Freeway Citizens' Advisory Task
    Force (CFCTF), 61–62, 73–74
Central Freeway Coalition, 64–65, 73–74
Central Subway, 34, 165–71, 181–82, 191,
    226n28
Cevero, Robert, 214n64
Chinatown: Central Freeway debates in, 81;
    Embarcadero Freeway access to, 58–59;
    progressive politics in, 65, 66; proposed
    subway service to, 165, 166–68, 170
Chinatown Chamber of Commerce, 167
Chinatown Community Development
    Center, 22, 165
Chinese-American politics of mobility,
    36, 208n57; in Central Freeway debates,

65–66, 76–77, 79, 81–84, 212n21; on the
   Embarcadero removal, 58–59
Chinese Progressive Association, 79, 180
City Lights bookstore, 1
Civic Center neighborhood, 187
Civic Center venues, 72
class contexts, 201; of freeway revolts, 43–45,
   57–58; of mass transit use, 16, 160–61,
   222n40; neoliberal perspectives on, 28–30;
   of parking policies, 110–11, 153; progressive perspectives on, 21, 22; of transit fare
   evasion, 183–90; of transit labor struggles,
   175, 180; of transportation sales taxes,
   225nn13–14
2011 Climate Action Plan, 165
climate change, 24–25, 29
Clinton, Bill, 29, 146
Coalition for Adequate Review (CAR), 3,
   123–24
Coalition for San Francisco Neighborhoods,
   35, 75, 78, 104–5, 107, 122, 179–80
Coalition for Transit Justice, 153, 223n54
Coalition of Ninety-Nine Percent, 123–24
Coalition of San Francisco Business and
   Neighborhood Communities Impacted by
   Prostitution, 61
Coalition to Save the Central Freeway, 66
Cole Valley neighborhood, 76
CO_2 levels, 6–8
Committee for Sensible Transportation Solu-
   tions (No on H), 75–76
Committee on Jobs, 29, 180
Committee to Save the Central Freeway, 75
compact development, 8, 9, 111, 139–40;
   bicycling in, 113; livability principles of, 85,
   92; reducing automobility for, 29; vehicle
   miles traveled (VMT) and, 125, 131–32
complete streets movement, 129, 132, 220n51,
   222n21
congestion pricing, 154, 155–57, 201
Congress for the New Urbanism, 92
Connecting the City, 135–38, 193
conservative ideology of mobility, 4, 5, 30–36,
   195–96; antiurban rhetoric in, 32–33;
   on bicycling space, 121–28, 138, 219n42;
   of Chinese-American residents, 65–66;
   commercial and small business needs in,
   36, 105–9; essentialist views of automobility in, 104–10, 125–26, 195–96, 200; family
   values in, 35, 99, 109–10, 126; in freeway
   and transit revolts, 49, 55, 64–70; identity
   politics in, 34–35; individual responsibility

in, 30–31, 36, 196; on livability, 33; in Los
   Angeles, 18; of mid-twentieth century San
   Francisco, 44; on parking policies, 104–10,
   153; possessive individualism in, 31–32,
   105; on premium transit, 187–90; on Prop
   K and the Central Subway plan, 169–70;
   on public transportation, 145, 171–72,
   191; revanchist views on, 160; on role of
   government, 30, 31, 32, 207n38
Contra Costa County, 126, 219n42
Convention and Visitors' Bureau, 61
corporate liberals, 29
corporate shuttle service, 187–90
Council of Community Housing Organizations (CCHO), 22, 83
Council of District Merchants Associations,
   36, 105–9
Critical Car Mass, 82, 121
Critical Mass rides, 2, 63, 115–20, 133, 137–38,
   212n19, 219n25, 219n28
Crossover Drive, 38
curb cuts, 94, 103
curbside parking, 111
Cyclovia, 136
Cypress Freeway, Oakland, 54, 64, 75

Davies Symphony Hall, 58
Davis, Grey, 155
Davis, Mike, 18
Deepwater Horizon accident, ix–x
DeLeon, Richard, 49
Democratic Party, 79, 83
Democratic Women's Forum, 83
densification strategies, 11–13, 25, 36, 72, 86,
   196
Detroit, 196
Devil's Slide highway, 62–63, 212n18
de Young Museum, 78
Dionne, E. J., 207n38
downtown neighborhood, 76; residential
   growth in, 162; TAD options for, 146–47,
   161–62
Doyle Drive Replacement, 225n19
driveways, 90
drug use, 60–61
Duboce Triangle neighborhood, 58
Duboce Triangle Neighborhood Associa-
   tion, 103

Eastern Neighborhood Plan, 102, 167–68
E-Bay, 188
efficiency discourses, 171–74, 175, 177, 182–83

electric cars. *See* green cars

Emanuel, Rahm, 135

Embarcadero Freeway, 2, 54, 58–59, 70–71, 209n20, 211n1

environmental considerations, 6–9, 62, 198; in bicycle plan environmental reviews, 121–32; in Central Freeway environmental impact assessments, 68–70; climate change and, 24–25, 29; emissions reduction goals and, 6–10, 141–43, 156–58, 178, 221nn13–14; in freeway revolts, 43, 46; in MOBNP's environmental review, 95–98; in Muni expansion plans, 141, 173, 226n41; neoliberal views on, 24–25; in parking policies, 89–90; of private transit systems, 189, 190; progressives perspectives on, 19–20, 22

essentialism of automobility, 33–34, 37, 52–53, 99, 194, 195, 207n46; in the Central Freeway environmental impact assessment, 69; in the Central Subway plan, 169; in conservative ideology, 104–10, 125–26, 195–96, 200; in speed debates, 199–200

Excelsior neighborhood, 45, 81

Facebook, 188

family values, 35, 126; in bicycle politics, 133, 136–37; in parking policy politics, 99, 104–5, 109–10

fare evasion, 182–87, 228n74

Federal Highway Administration, 68–70

Federal Interstate Highway Act of 1956, 42

Federal Transit Administration (FTA), 181–82

Feinstein, Diane, 29, 168

Fell and Oak one-way couplet, 50, 55, 57, 67, 85; bicycling along, 126–27; Hayes-Fell-Oak *Z* configuration of, 57*f*, 58; traffic levels on, 59

Ferlinghetti, Lawrence, 1–3, 91

ferries, 142, 221n51

Ferry Building, 209n20

fifteen mph speed limits, 199

Fisher, Don, 107, 178

Fix Muni campaign, 179–80, 227n55

Franklin and Gough one-way couplet, 50, 55, 57, 85

freeway creation: first freeway revolt against, 40–46, 209n20; Interstate Highway Act funding for, 42; political consensus for, 42; proposals for, 20, 40–42, 209n13; in San Mateo County, 38; tax revenues for, 42

freeway removal, 2, 3, 20, 54–86, 224n5; of Central Freeway, 59, 64, 67–74, 84–86;

earthquake damage and, 15, 54, 58–59; of Embarcadero Freeway, 54, 58–59, 70–71, 211n1; politics of possibilities in, 84–86; transit-first policies and, 142

freeway revolts, 41–46, 58, 208n5, 209n20; against Central Freeway, 36, 54–86; class contexts of, 43–45, 57–58; property value considerations in, 44

Friends of 1800 Market Street, 83

Frum, David, 207n38

Fukushima Daiichi nuclear disaster of 2011, 7

gasoline sales tax revenues, 155

Geary Street/Boulevard proposals, 166–67, 169–70, 172–73, 226n28

Genentech, 189

General Motors, 62

gentrification, 15, 23; accumulation by dispossession in, 28; commodification of neighborhoods in, 60, 86, 100–102, 214nn64–65; dot-com boom and, 87–88; in Hayes Valley, 58, 60; livability movement and, 23, 28, 100–102, 160, 190–91; movement opposing, 84; parking policies and, 91, 100–102; revanchism in, 160–61, 224n3; super-gentrification and, 161, 224n3; of transit, 190–91

Ginsberg, Allen, 1

global greenhouse gas (GHG) emissions. *See* greenhouse gas emissions

global position systems, 171

Golden Gate Bridge, 38; bicycle access to, 115; connectors to, 164, 225n19

Golden Gate Park, 78, 115

Golden Gate Restaurant Association, 29, 147, 180

Golden Gate Transit, 221n5

Golden Gateway Center, 209n20

Golden Wheel Awards, 134

Gonzalez, Matt, 225n17

Google, 188, 190

Gordon, Deborah, 34

Gore, Al, 29, 95

grade-separated railways, 172

Gramsci, Antonio, 205n4

Great Recession of 2008–12: livability movement and, 8; public transportation and, 174–82

green cars, 20, 34, 95, 96, 111, 198

greenhouse gas emissions (GHG), 6–10, 141–43, 156–58, 178, 221nn13–14

Green Temple, 96–97

Growing Cooler: The Evidence on Urban Development and Climate Change, 24–25, 27–28

Gulf of Mexico, ix–x

Haight-Ashbury neighborhood, 46, 51, 76
Haight-Ashbury Neighborhood Council, 78
Hanna, Howard, 219n41
Harvey, David, 18
Harvey Milk Club, 63, 79, 83, 180
Hayes Valley, 55, 56–64, 70; development potential of, 72, 85; gentrification of, 58, 60, 87, 224n3; Market and Octavia Better Neighborhoods Plan in, 93–95; neighborhood activism in, 60–64, 71, 212n11; parking and livability debates in, 87–88, 93–95, 215n2; public safety work in, 60–61; response to Prop H in, 78; transformation of Hayes Street in, 59, 60. *See also* Central Freeway
Hayes Valley Neighborhood Association (HVNA), 83, 88, 98–100, 103, 215n2
Heritage Foundation, 33
Hestor, Sue, 220n46
The High Cost of Free Parking (Shoup), 89–90, 215n6
Highway 1, 38
historical geography of mobility in San Francisco, 38–53; essentialism of automobility in, 52–53; first freeway revolt in, 41–46; lack of alternative vision in, 49; 19th Avenue stalemate in, 38–41; traffic density of, 50–53; transit-first policy in, 52; transit revolts in, 46–49
homelessness, 186–87, 191
Housing Action Coalition, 93
Housing Element, 106–7, 122, 217n48
"Howl" (Ginsberg), 1
Hurricane Katrina, ix
hybrids. *See* green cars
hyperconsumption. *See* possessive individualism

I-280 (Southern Freeway), 45, 54, 56, 224n5
identity politics, 34–35
ideologies of mobility, 4–5, 15, 17–37, 193–97; automobility in, 17–18, 20, 24–28, 30, 31–33; conservative paradigms in, 4, 5, 18, 30–36, 195–96, 207n38; neoliberal paradigms in, 4–5, 18, 23–30, 194–96; new mobility paradigm in, 18; progressive-neoliberal hybrids in, 70–74, 85–86, 133–37,

194–95; progressive paradigms in, 4, 18–23, 35–36, 37, 196–202. *See also* politics of mobility
individual responsibility, 30–31, 36, 196
infill development, 25, 36, 72, 86, 90–91, 93, 196
infrastructure repair, 55–56
Ingleside, 81
International Longshoremen's Union, 46
intersection level of service (LOS), 116–17, 121–22, 199; in environmental reviews, 123–28, 220n46; multimodal metrics for, 129, 131–32, 217n15, 219n41; politics of, 124–26, 131–32; reform options for, 128–32, 220n54
Interstate Highway Act of 1956, 42
Issel, William, 43, 44

Jacobs, Allan, 74, 214n47
Japan's Fukushima Daiichi nuclear disaster of 2011, 7
Jones, David, 34
Jordan, Frank, 59–60, 65, 83, 147

Katz, Leslie, 83
Kerouac, Jack, 1
Keynesianism, 41–42, 47, 49, 71
Kittleson, Wayne, 219n41

labor. *See* organized labor
Lake Merced neighborhood, 81
Lakoff, George, 19
Laurel Heights, 81
League of American Cyclists, 114
League of Women Voters, 83
Lee, Ed, 134–35, 220n56
Lefebvre, Henri, 18
Leno, Mark, 83
level of service (LOS). *See* intersection level of service
livability movement, 5, 8, 21, 62, 192–93, 195; class aspects of, 100–102; compact development and, 85, 92; complete streets movement and, 129, 132, 220n51, 222n21; conservative views on, 33; in freeway debates, 55, 65, 74; freeway revolts of, 20, 41–46; gentrification and, 23, 28, 100–102, 160, 190–91; MOBNP's promotion of, 93–95; neoliberal views on, 27–30, 100–102; in parking policy debates, 88–93; progressive views on, 22; reduction of VMT in, 125; San Francisco as model for, 9–15, 204n20

Livable City, 21, 103, 158–59, 216n26, 219n23, 220n58; on Muni fare increases, 151–53; rail projects endorsed by, 165; transit-first Stockton Street corridor, 165; on the transportation sales taxes, 164–65

local transportation sales taxes, 162–71, 225nn12–14

Loma Prieta earthquake of 1989, 15, 54, 64

LOS. *See* intersection level of service

Los Angeles: conservative shaping of, 18; Northridge earthquake in, 64, 75; physical geography of, 13, 205n32

Lower Haight neighborhood, 76, 81

MacDonald, Elizabeth, 74, 214n47

Maher, Bill, 121

Map of Progressive Mobility, 16, 197

maps: of the geography of the Central Freeway revolt, 77*f*; of the proposed Central Subway, 166*f*; of proposed freeways (1959–66), 40*f*; of San Francisco neighborhoods, 12*f*

Marina District neighborhood, 58, 81

Market and Octavia Better Neighborhoods Plan (MOBNP), 11–12, 57*f*, 85, 93–95, 214n63; challenge to automobility in, 93–104, 109–10; conditional use permits in, 102–4, 109–10; conservative views on, 109–10; environmental review of, 95, 102; *Green Temple* installation and, 96–97; housing units in, 94, 98, 216n23, 216nn29–30; 55 Laguna redevelopment in, 98–100, 216n31; neoliberal views on, 95–100; Planning Commission review of, 102–3

Market Street, 50–51; BART access to, 53, 210n33; bike lanes on, 123; as public transportation hub, 167; traffic reduction projects for, 137

mass transit. *See* public transportation

mental illness, 191

Metro *M* light-rail line, 38

Migden, Carole, 83

Mission Agenda, 22, 153

Mission Anti-Displacement Organization, 22, 103

Mission Bay, 167–68, 190

Mission District, 76; anti-gentrification movement in, 84; bicycle space in, 120, 121; on Central Freeway removal, 81; gentrification in, 87, 224n3; parking policies in, 51, 102, 103; Sunday Street event in, 136

Mitchell, Don, 26–27

Moscone Convention Center, 167–68

multimodal LOS metrics, 129, 131–32

Municipal Railway (Muni) system, 10, 16, 39, 193; advocacy organizations for, 68; bus system of, 3, 127, 165–66, 173–75; class and race contexts of, 160–61, 180, 183–90, 222n40, 225nn13–14; connections to regional systems by, 142, 166–67; efficiency reforms of, 171–77, 182–83; emissions reduction goals of, 141–43, 158; expanding capacity of, 143–45, 171–74; fare evasion in, 182–87, 228n74; fares and budgets of, 22, 28, 142, 144, 149–54, 157–58, 172; financial crisis of 2010 of, 174–82; fleet of, 141, 176; funding mechanisms for, 111, 145–59, 161–71; goals of, 141–45; light-rail lines of, 38, 39, 165, 166–67; low-ridership routes of, 172, 173–74; meltdowns of, 147–48; neoliberal and conservative views of, 25, 28, 145, 148–50, 165–72, 175–78, 183–84, 187–90; on 19th Avenue, 38–39; oversight of, 213n36; premium transit proposals for, 187; progressive views on labor politics of, 180–81; progressive views on pricing automobility for, 150–59, 174; progressive views on sales taxes for, 164–71, 225nn12–14; Proposition A on, 109, 141, 152, 154, 221n12; Rescue Muni program of, 68, 83, 148–50, 180; revanchist discourses on, 160–91; ridership rates on, 139–45, 222n40; safety rating of, 167, 186–87; service and reliability of, 39, 51–53, 150–54, 175, 222n41; state funding of, 154–55, 168, 223n59; subway proposals for, 48, 143, 165–71, 181–82, 191, 210n38; transit revolt against, 46–49; unionized labor of, 28–29, 109, 160–61, 174–82, 226n42. *See also* transit-first policies

National Complete Streets Coalition, 220n51

National Trust for Historic Preservation, 83

neighborhood activism: on Central Freeway removal, 60–64, 69–71, 73–74, 79, 83, 212n11; in freeway revolts, 43–46, 49, 67

neoliberal ideology of mobility, 4–5, 23–30, 194–96; on automobility and unfettered access, 24–28, 31, 71–72; on bike space, 133–37; class considerations in, 28–30; commodification of neighborhoods in, 60, 86, 87–88, 100–102, 195; cornucopian discourse in, 27; efficiency discourses in, 171–75, 177; in freeway removal debates, 55, 70–74, 85; gentrification and, 28, 60, 86,

214nn64–65; laissez-faire capitalism of, 19, 24, 25–26, 125; livability in, 27–28, 195; on LOS policies, 131–32; on parking policies, 95–104, 108–9; possessive individualism in, 26–27; on premium mobility networks, 26, 28, 187–90; on private transit, 187–90; in progressive-neoliberal hybrids, 70–74, 85–86, 133–37, 194–95; on Prop K and the Central Subway plan, 165–69; in public transportation debates, 25, 145, 148–50, 171–72, 175–78, 190–91; revanchist views on, 160; on VMT reduction and compact development, 125. *See also* real estate development

new mobility paradigm, 18

New Orleans, ix–x

Newsom, Gavin, 96–97, 134, 137, 168, 175–76, 220n56, 225n17

New Urbanism, 196

New York City, 14

19th Avenue, 38–41, 53, 68, 208n2

Noe Valley, 224n3

North Beach neighborhood, 91, 169

Northridge earthquake, 64

Obama, Barack, 8, 144

Octavia Boulevard, 93, 96

One Bay Area Plan, 200. *See also* SB 375

One Bay Area Vision, 219n42. *See also* SB 375

one-way couplets, 50–51, 53, 55, 57, 93

On the Road (Kerouac), 1

organized labor: class contexts of, 175; in freeway revolts, 46, 78; of Muni transit workers, 28–29, 109, 160–61, 174–82, 201, 226n42; neoliberal perspectives on, 28–30; on Proposition A of 2007, 178; on Proposition E of 1999, 149; Proposition G of 2010 on, 177–82; on Proposition H of 2007, 178; two-tiered salary systems for, 182

Outer Mission neighborhood, 45

Pacific Heights neighborhood, 58, 81

Panhandle Freeway, 45–46, 58

Parking for Neighborhoods Initiative, 3, 107–9

parking policies, 15–16, 87–111; bicycling and, 126–27; car-free development and, 94, 99–102; class contexts of, 100–102, 110–11, 153; commercial and small business views of, 105–9; conditional use permits in, 102–4, 217n41; conservative views on, 30, 31, 35, 104–10, 153; in downtown, 101–2, 216n38;

family values in, 99, 104–5, 109–10; fees and costs of, 23, 91, 151–54, 216n12; gentrification and, 91, 100–102; Golden Gate Park garage proposal and, 78; in Hayes Valley, 87–88; livability debates on, 88–93; Market and Octavia Better Neighborhoods Plan and, 11–13, 93–95; neoliberal views on, 27–28, 72, 95–104, 108–9; number of parking places and, 92, 215n15; on off-street parking, 3, 51, 90, 91; Parking for Neighborhoods Initiative (Prop H) on, 107–9, 157; parking maximums in, 92–94, 96–98, 103–4; parking meters in, 111; privatization of street space in, 90; progressive views on, 92–98, 101–2, 102–4, 108–9, 111, 153; Prop A of 2007 on, 152, 154; 1:1 ratio minimums in, 91, 92–94, 216n14, 216n24; on residential parking permits, 154; in SFPD's *Housing Element*, 107, 122, 217n48

Park Presidio Boulevard, 38

Partnership for Sustainable Communities, 8, 204n17

Patton, Jason, 205n2

peak oil, 6–7

pedestrians, 38–39. *See also* walkability

Pelosi, Nancy, 29, 78, 168

People Organized to Win Employment Rights, 185

People Organizing to Win Environmental and Economic Rights (POWER), 22

petroleum production, 6–7, 8

physical geography, 13

Plan C, 180

politics of mobility, ix–xi, 3–6, 14, 15, 193–202; freeway revolts in, 40–46; ideology of streets and urban spaces in, 4–5, 193–202; in possibilities for transportation futures, 84–86, 192–202; revanchist discourses in, 160–91. *See also* ideologies of mobility

politics of parking. *See* parking policies

Polk Street, 121

POP fare-collection system, 183, 186–87

population density, 11–12. *See also* densification strategies

Portland, 14

Portola neighborhood, 45

possessive individualism, 26–27, 31–32, 105, 133

Potrero Hill, 102

Powell street, 134

premium mobility networks, 26, 28, 172, 187–90, 195

Presidio Heights, 81

Presidio Parkway, 225n19

priority development areas, 9

private transit, 187–90

progressive ideology of mobility, 4, 18–23, 35–36, 37, 196–202, 205n13; on bicycle space, 133–37, 200; car-free mobility in, 99–104, 192–93, 198–202; in Central Freeway activism, 60–64, 69–71, 82–84; class considerations in, 21, 22; détente with neoliberalism of, 26, 70–74, 85–86, 133–37, 194–95; empathy-based values of, 19; environmental movement in, 19–20, 22; in freeway and transit revolts, 43–46, 49, 60; on gentrification, 23, 84, 101; on growth control, 35, 208n50; on Muni and public transportation, 36, 146–59, 164–72, 180–81, 191, 201, 223n59, 225nn12–14; organizations working in, 21, 29; on parking policies, 92–98, 101–4, 108–9, 111, 153; politics of possibilities in, 84–86, 197–202; revanchist views on, 160; on role of government, 19; social responsibility in, 20–21, 196–97; on transit workers, 180–81; on VMT reduction and compact development, 125

progressive motoring, 199–200

Progressivism, 41–42, 209n6

proof of payment (POP) systems, 171

property values, 44, 71. *See also* real estate development

Proposition A of 2007, 109, 141, 152, 154, 178, 221n12

Proposition E of 1999, 148–50

Proposition G of 2010, 177–82

Proposition H of 1997, 75–79, 221n12

Proposition H of 2007, 107–9, 157, 178

Proposition K of 1989 and 2003, 162–71, 225n19, 226n28

Proposition M of 1986, 35

Proposition O of 1994, 146–47

Proposition 13 of 1978, 71, 145–46, 158, 197

prostitution, 60–61

Public Broadcasting Service (PBS), 62

public employee unions, 175

public transportation, 10, 14, 139–59, 192, 221n5; advocacy organizations for, 68; BART regional system of, 47–49, 52, 53, 167, 188, 210n33, 221n5; Better Neighborhoods project and, 11–13; bicycling and, 113; class contexts of, 16, 183–90, 225nn13–14; efficiency discourses on, 171–75, 182–83; emissions from, 10, 141–43; federal subsidies of, 145, 146, 157, 168, 181–82, 225n24; funding options for, 150–59, 164–71, 174, 201, 223n59, 225nn12–14; gentrification of, 190–91; neoliberal and conservative views on, 25, 145, 148–50, 165–72, 175–78, 183–84, 187–91; off-peak idle time in, 176–77; progressive views on, 36, 150–59, 164–71, 174, 191, 201, 223n59, 225nn12–14; proof of payment (POP) systems for, 171; ridership rates for, 20, 139–41, 144–45, 194; state funding of, 168; transit-first goals for, 52, 69, 92–93, 115, 116, 140–45, 148–50, 157–59, 171–72. *See also* Municipal Railway (Muni) system

quality of life. *See* livability movement

racial contexts: of fare evasion stings, 185–86; of the transit workers' union, 180

Radulovich, Tom, 83

rapid corridors, 171–72

rapid transit. *See* public transportation

Reagan, Ronald, 146

real estate development: of affordable housing, 30, 84, 91, 106–7, 199; along rapid transit lines, 48; car-free development in, 94, 99–104; Central Subway project and, 167–68; consumption of livability in, 100–102; gentrification and commodification of neighborhoods in, 60, 86–88, 100–102, 196, 214nn64–65; growth control in, 34–35, 208n51; housing costs and, 214n65; housing shortage and, 92, 106–7, 122, 192–93, 217n48; impact of government policies on, 23; neoliberal and Keynesian goals of, 28–30, 42, 47, 49, 71; parking policies and, 51

Reed, Shelton, 207n39

Republican Party, 75, 78, 80, 147, 149

Rescue Muni program, 68, 83, 148–50, 180

research methods, x–xi

residential parking permits, 154

Return of the Scorcher, 117

reurbanization, 15

revanchist discourses of mobility, 160–91, 195, 201; in fare evasion policies, 182–87, 228n74; in Muni efficiency debates, 171–74, 175; premium transit in, 187–90; in Prop K and the Central Subway plan, 161–71, 225n19, 226n28; on transit workers' unions and rights, 174–82, 201

reverse commuting, 187–90

revolts: antidensity movement and, 34, 48; against freeways, 41–46, 54–86, 209n20; lack of alternative vision in, 49; against transit, 46–49

Richmond neighborhood, 81

road building, 31

Rose, Mark, 219n40

San Franciscans for a Better Freeway, 78–79

San Francisco, 9–15; Better Neighborhoods project in, 11–13; conservatism in, 34–35, 207n39; environmental movement in, 19–20; high-technology industry in, 23; housing shortage of, 92, 106–7, 122, 192–93, 217n48; livability movement of, 9–15, 204n20; Map of Progressive Mobility of, 16, 197; neighborhoods of, 11, 12, 21; neoliberalism in, 28–30; outbound commuting from, 188–90; parking spaces in, 92, 215n15; physical geography of, 13; population density in, 11–13; progressive politics of, 19, 22–23, 205n13; school system lottery in, 35; sustainability goals of, 10–11; vehicle density of, 14–15; VMT in, 9, 11; voter turnout in, 76

San Francisco Association of Realtors, 180

San Francisco Bay Guardian, 21, 135, 164, 180

San Francisco Beautiful, 83

San Francisco Bicycle Coalition (SFBC), 21, 63, 78, 83; Connecting the City plan of, 135–38, 193; membership of, 112, 119, 120, 133, 138; opposition to, 121–28; on parking policies, 88, 103; political advocacy by, 114–20, 219n30; progressive-neoliberal hybridization of, 133–37, 138; Sunday Streets program and, 136–37, 177, 219n23, 220n58; on transit-first policies, 148–49; on the transportation sales taxes, 164

San Francisco Bike Plan Policy Framework, 123

San Francisco Chamber of Commerce, 41, 75–76, 78, 82; on congestion pricing, 156; on parking policies, 101, 102; on Prop G of 2010, 180; on Prop K and the Central Subway proposal, 168–69; on public transportation, 147, 148–49; on the transportation sales tax, 164–65

San Francisco Convention and Visitors Bureau, 29

San Francisco County Transportation Authority (SFCTA), 69–70, 80, 213n36, 225n11

San Francisco Democratic Central Committee, 180–81

San Francisco Environmental Organizing Committee, 82

San Francisco Green Party, 82

San Francisco Heritage Foundation, 83

San Francisco Jazz, 103

San Francisco Labor Council, 80, 180

San Francisco League of Conservation Voters, 78, 82

San Francisco Municipal Transportation Agency (SFMTA), 11, 141–42; creation of, 148–50; parking fee collection by, 151–52; Prop K and Central Subway plans of, 161–71, 225n19, 226n28; transit-first policies of, 157–59. *See also* Municipal Railway (Muni) system

San Francisco Neighbors Association, 66, 74–75

San Francisco Organization for Women, 83

San Francisco Planning and Urban Research Association (SPUR), 29, 93; on environmental review requirements, 131–32; Fix Muni Now campaign of, 179–80, 227n55; freeway plans of, 41; in freeway revolts, 46, 75, 78; on labor reform at Muni, 176; on LOS, 131; on Parking for Neighborhoods Initiative (Prop H), 108, 157; on parking policies, 88, 153; on POP fare collection systems, 183; on premium transit, 187; on Prop K and the Central Subway proposal, 168–69; on public transit, 146, 147, 148; Rescue Muni program of, 148–50; on TADs, 222n39; on the transportation sales tax, 164–65

San Francisco Planning Department (SFPD), 59, 72; affordable housing plans of, 106–7, 122, 217n48; Market and Octavia Better Neighborhoods Plan of, 85, 93, 214n63; on parking policies, 90–91

San Francisco State University (SFSU), 38–39

San Francisco Tenants' Network, 83

San Francisco Tenants' Union, 79, 83

San Francisco Tomorrow, 63, 78, 82

San Francisco Transit Riders Union (SFTRU), 157–59

San Mateo County, 13, 38, 62–63, 156

Save Muni, 165–66, 226n35

SB 375 (Sustainable Communities and Climate Protection Act), 8–9, 25, 27–28, 125, 132, 200, 219n42

Schwarzenegger, Arnold, 95, 155, 223n59

Sea Cliff neighborhood, 81

second freeway revolt. *See* Central Freeway

Senior Action Network, 22
Service Employees International Union
    (SEIU), 22, 109
SF Park, 154, 223n57
Shorenstein, Walter, 146
Shorenstein Company, 147
Shoup, Donald, 89–90, 92, 215n6
sidewalk cycling, 39
Sierra Club, 63, 79, 82, 103, 165
Single Resident Occupant (SRO) Families
    Unite, 22, 153
Smartcode planning guidelines, 92–93
smart growth, 8, 24, 62. *See also* livability
    movement
Snyder, David, 217n14
social responsibility, 20–21, 196–97
Southern Freeway (I-280), 45, 54, 56, 224n5
southern urbanism, 196
South of Market neighborhood, 19, 84, 87;
    parking policies in, 102; super-gentrifica-
    tion in, 224n3; Yerba Buena Gardens, 168
speed limit restrictions, 199
Sperling, Daniel, 34
Starr, Kevin, 209n20
Stockton Street corridor, 165, 169, 226n35
StreetsblogSF, 21, 173
subway proposals, 48, 143, 165–71, 181–82, 191,
    210n38
Sunday Streets, 136–37, 177, 219n23, 220n58
Sunset neighborhood, 81
super-gentrification, 161, 224n3
Sustainable Communities and Climate Pro-
    tection Act (SB 375), 8–9, 25, 27–28, 125,
    132, 200, 219n42
sustainable transportation, 10–11, 34, 192–202
Sustainable Transportation Award, 223n57
SUV model of citizenship, 26, 32, 105, 109

Taken for a Ride documentary, 62
taxes: for freeway creation, 42; on gasoline
    sales, 155; on parking, 151–53; Proposi-
    tion 13 of 1978 on, 71, 145–46, 158, 197;
    transportation sales taxes and, 162–71,
    225nn12–14
Tea Party, 219n42
Tenderloin district, 61, 172–73
Tenderloin Neighborhood Development
    Corporation, 172–73
TEP Enhanced plan, 143, 226n41
TEP Implementation Plan, 143, 159, 165, 168,
    171–72, 173

Third Street Light Rail line, 165
Transbay Terminal, 167
Transform, 21
transit assessment districts (TAD), 146–47,
    150, 154, 157, 158, 161–62, 196, 197, 222n39
Transit Effectiveness Project (TEP), 142–43
transit-first policies, 2–3, 52, 69, 140, 148–50,
    157–59; bicycling in, 115, 116, 148–49;
    expanding capacity in, 143–45; funding
    for, 140, 143–44; goals of, 141–45; parking
    caps in, 92–93; rapid corridors in, 171–72;
    Stockton Street corridor, 165–66
transit impact development fees (TIDF), 146,
    157, 158, 162, 224n7
Transit-Not Traffic coalition, 157
transit-only lanes, 172
transit utility fees, 158
transportation. *See* automobility; bicycling;
    public transportation; walkability
transportation sales taxes, 162–71, 225nn12–
    14
Transportation Sustainability Program,
    131–32, 158, 220n54, 224n9
Transport Workers Union (TWU)-250A, 176,
    178, 180–82, 201
Twitter, 187
Two Billion Cars (Sperling and Gordon), 34

unions. *See* organized labor
Union Square Business Association, 106, 134
Union Square neighborhood, 168
United Nations Environment Program, 95
United States: aging infrastructure in, 55–56;
    car ownership and consumption in, 7; liv-
    ability movement in, 8
UNITE HERE!, 22
Upper Market neighborhood, 81, 106
Urban Ecology, 83
urban spaces: congestion in, 62; environmen-
    tal planning for, 95; infill and densification
    strategies for, 11–13, 25, 36, 72, 86, 196; low-
    density sprawl in, 8, 13, 62, 90; physical
    geography of, 13; priority development ar-
    eas of, 9; public funding for renewal of, 71;
    sustainable transportation for, 10–11, 34,
    192–202. *See also* compact development;
    livability movement; politics of mobility
U.S. Highway 101, 42, 56, 58

Valencia Street, 120, 121
Van Ness Avenue, 56–57

vehicle license fees (VLF), 154–55, 223n59
vehicle miles traveled (VMT), 13; compact growth and, 125, 131–32; goals for reduction of, 8–9, 125, 131–32; impact of bicycling on, 113; impact of parking policy on, 89–90; by reverse commuters, 189; in San Francisco, 9, 11; in San Mateo County, 13
Veolioa, 190
Victorian Belt neighborhoods, 11, 12*f*, 21; bicycle advocacy movement in, 60; freeway removal advocacy in, 63–64, 76, 81; parking policies and, 78, 91; private shuttles from, 190; super-gentrification in, 224n3. *See also* Hayes Valley
Vistacion Valley, 81

Wachs, Martin, 119
walkability, 5, 20, 192; automobile density challenges to, 50–51; Better Neighborhoods project on, 11–13; neoliberal views on, 25, 27–28, 195; pedestrianization projects for, 134; in the 19th Avenue neighborhood, 38–39
Walker, Richard, 19, 145

Walk San Francisco, 21, 83, 164
Walkup, Patricia, 212n11
Webcor Construction, 107
Western Addition neighborhood, 45–46, 51, 76, 81
Western Addition Political Action Coalition, 83
Western Freeway, 43–44, 209n13
West of Twin Peaks neighborhood, 81
west side neighborhoods: automobility in, 45, 49, 52; freeway opposition in, 43–44; transit revolt in, 48–49
White, Ted, 219n25
the Wiggle, 126–27
The Wild One, 1
Wilson, Pete, 155
Wilson, Woodrow, 209n6
World Environment Day (WED), 95–96, 123, 216n27

Yahoo, 188
Yee, Leland, 76
Yerba Buena Gardens, 168

JASON HENDERSON was born in New Orleans and earned a PhD in geography from the University of Georgia in 2002. He is an associate professor in the Department of Geography and Human Environmental Studies at San Francisco State University, where he teaches courses on transportation, land use, and the environment. He has published articles on the politics of mobility in Atlanta and on parking and bicycle politics in San Francisco. He lives in San Francisco.